In 1860, the Comstock Lode was discovered in Virginia City, Nevada. By 1864, maritime San Francisco had become a mining city, her citizens obsessed by the lure of silver. William Chapman Ralston, the financial wizard of his time, wrested control of the fabulously rich bullion of Sun Mountain, and with his shrewd band of associates—Ralston's Ring—created a financial empire whose tentacles spread out across this country and into the stock markets of Europe.

The crash was inevitable, and when it came, its tragic reverberations shook the world. The story of this empire built on ruthless enterprise and incredible daring, the fierce quest for metal underground, beautiful women in gilded ballrooms, fast horses, closed banks, bonanzas and suicides is one of the most stirring legends of the West.

MORE COMSTOCK EDITIONS YOU WILL ENJOY

THE BIG BONANZA, Dan De Quille $1.25
The exciting story of the discovery and development of Nevada's fabulous Comstock lode. "Dan De Quille is the Boswell of the silver miners. Readers can recapture the life and times of the extinct Old West."
R. G. Lillard, *New York Times*

THE SAGA OF THE COMSTOCK LODE: Boom Days in Virginia City, George D. Lyman $1.25
The wild adventure of thousands of reckless Californians who rushed to Sun Mountain, Nevada, to stake their claims in the richest vein of silver in the West. "George Lyman has simulated the breathless speed, the tempestuous life of the Mountain, and enclosed it once and for all between the covers of a book."
—*Saturday Review*

BONANZA INN: America's First Luxury Hotel, Oscar Lewis and Carroll D. Hall $1.25
A delightfully varied history of the Palace Hotel in San Francisco and the colorful people who inhabited her in the first thirty years of her existence. "A delightful story, well worth reading. A significant chip to the brightly colored mosaic of America's yesterday."
J. H. Jackson, *BOOKS*

SILVER KINGS: The Lives and Times of MacKay, Fair, Flood, and O'Brien, Lords of the Nevada Comstock Lode, Oscar Lewis $1.25
A magnificent account of fabulous men who led strangely fascinating lives. "Those who enjoy an unusual and dramatic story, as well as students of western Americana, will find this a richly rewarding volume."
R. A. Brown, *Christian Science Monitor*

For a complete list or to order by mail, write to Dept. CS, Ballantine Books, 36 West 20th Street, New York, N.Y. 10003

RALSTON'S RING

California Plunders the Comstock Lode

GEORGE D. LYMAN

BALLANTINE BOOKS • NEW YORK
An Intext Publisher

SBN 345-02263-7-125

This edition published by arrangement with
Charles Scribner's Sons.

First Printing: May, 1971

Cover Art by Joe Reboli

Printed in the United States of America

BALLANTINE BOOKS, INC.
101 Fifth Avenue, New York, N.Y. 10003

TO
Dorothy Quincy
AND
Elizabeth and David

CONTENTS

ACKNOWLEDGMENTS

Most of the characters in this book I have met, many times, either on the Comstock or in San Francisco. All of them were my father's friends or acquaintances. With some of these, for forty-odd years, he enjoyed the closest intimacy; while others were business associates, pure and simple. As such, the facts of their lives as they pertained to "the Lode" or "the city" were familiar to me from childhood.

What were they? Lilliputians or men of heroic mould?

To me they seemed made of the stuff which inspired the Norse sagas; of the fiber out of which the Lied of the Nibelungs was woven.

Theirs were the same problems: first the struggle with fire, water, earth, and air for bare existence. When those elements were subdued, the contest with man's greed, avarice, envy, hatred, and duplicity. For what? For gold, plaudits, or supremacy? The goals of most human ambitions.

In verifying my facts, I have had the archives of the State Library at Sacramento and the Bancroft Library at the University of California to draw upon. In that connection, I am endlessly indebted to Miss Mabel Gillis, State Librarian, Miss Caroline Wenzel of the California Department of the State Library, and Mrs. Edna Martin Parrott of the Bancroft. To them I gratefully acknowledge my tremendous obligation.

In the same connection I have to record the assistance afforded by Miss Stella Drum of the Jefferson Memorial, St. Louis, Missouri; the aid of the New York Public Library, the Chicago Historical Society, the Ohio Historical Society and of Miss Margery Huggins of the California Historical Society.

To Mr. Alfred Sutro of San Francisco I am greatly indebted for permission to use cherished family pictures; to Doctor W. R. P. Clark, whose parents were married at the Ralston residence and whose father was one of Ralston's paying tellers and an employee of the Bank of California for fifty years, I am grateful for family reminiscences and the use of two invaluable scrapbooks of the Ralston regime; to Mrs. W. C. Ralston, Jr., I am the debtor for data and pictures; to Mrs. J. R. Pringle, one of San Francisco's grande dames, I am grateful for lively reminiscences of Belmont in the time of W. C. Ralston. Often Mr. and Mrs. Pringle were guests of the Belmont Prince, both at his Fremont Street, San Francisco residence and his country villa, on coaching trips, beach picnics, and house parties; to Mrs. Covington Pringle thanks are due for the use of Belmont pictures. At one time the villa-estate was the property of Mrs. Alpheus Bull, mother of Mrs. Pringle. Mr. H. L. Slosson, Jr., mining engineer, San Francisco, has been a never-failing source of mining information.

Further acknowledgments are due to Miss Gladys Deal, for the use of her books; Mrs. Pio Morbio, Adolph Sutro's daughter; Mrs. W. E. Sharon, for pictures and books of reminiscence; Miss Hope Bliss of Dedham, Massachusetts, for use of her manuscripts; Mr. William S. Bliss of San Francisco; L. Hardaker of Stanford University, for photographic assistance; J. F. Bourke of San Francisco, once in Ralston's office employ; Mrs. Knox Johnson of Gardnerville, Nevada, and Doctor Harry J. Pruett of San Francisco, who helped to locate an extensive part of my Sutro material.

Doctor Cecil G. Tilton, Associate Professor of Economics, Connecticut State College and author of *William Chapman Ralston, Courageous Builder* (Christopher Publishing House, Boston, 1935) has been most helpful. Never has the "Ophir deal," the crux of events bearing on Aug. 27, 1875, been thoroughly understood. Doctor Tilton has been generous with his assistance in the interpretation of existing facts.

Mrs. Thomassine Meagher, my secretary, has typed the manuscript of this book in its entirety no less than four separate times, each time even more carefully and painstakingly than the time previous. I am grateful for her assistance, patience and stick-to-itiveness.

To the Wolves of Los Altos my gratitude for constructive criticism and continuous inspiration is unceasing, God speed them!

GEORGE D. LYMAN.

"There is tears for his love; joy for his fortune; honour for his valour; and death for his ambition."

Julius Caesar, Act III; Sc. II.

RALSTON'S RING

CHAPTER I

BONANZA DAYS

San Francisco Stock and Exchange Board

11 o'clock Session, 1864

Black-painted hacks bounded over the wet cobblestones of Montgomery Street toward the Metropolitan Theatre. Already a mob of people were milling about the doors and half-way up the stairs leading to the board room of the San Francisco Stock Exchange. So dense were the crowds that the carriages could scarcely thread their way through them.

One by one, before the imposing façade of the Metropolitan, the carriages stopped, wide flew their doors. Down from their cushioned interiors stepped ladies: beautiful ladies with well-turned ankles; tightly laced ladies in rustling black silk; mysterious women in flowing black veils; perfumed women with sparkling eyes, flashing teeth and diamond-studded ears.

The ladies were hurrying to the 11 o'clock session of the San Francisco Stock Exchange Board to gamble on Comstock stocks. These were exciting days on the market. "Uncle Sam" and "Overman" had become leading features. "Bears" had worked them up hundreds of dollars. For years both properties had been in litigation. "North America" claimed that "Uncle Sam" and "Overman" overlapped their holdings. Now, "North America" intended to get control of the stock of the other two mines and put an end to all lawsuits. The supposition was that "North America" was in bonanza.

The fact had thrown the street into turmoils of excitement. Stock had boomed out of all proportion, and the district had responded in fervid tempo. Fortunes would be made and the women curb-brokers wanted to share the spoils. These women were one of the peculiar features of the San Francisco stock market. Some were the wives of operators; others of plungers, but the vast majority were the victims of the Comstock. The prodigious wealth of the Lode and the excitement attending the selling of these mining stocks had weaned them from homes, schoolrooms and the city's bright lights. In all their fine black plumage they flitted about the Exchange, picking up "tips" on stocks and ready at a moment's notice to pounce upon some favorite with all the resources at their command. Their silks and satins, diamonds and furs all recorded recent lucky encounters with the market. For Comstocks had been booming. Now the agitation over "North America" promised to increase those gains. All excited, these women alighted from their carriages and rushed like so many carefully plumed Myna birds toward the door leading to the board room.

Silk-hatted, well-groomed curb-brokers milled excitedly about the entrance. With difficulty the women elbowed their way through the throng. Some of the brokers seemed to know those black-robed ladies, yet they did not bother to salute them as they rustled past on their way to the reserved section of the board room.

So intent were the veiled operators on getting into their places before the gong sounded that they did not care whether the brokers saluted or not. At that very moment Comstock stocks were far more important than Comstock curb-brokers and far more profitable.

By 1864, the Comstock comet was blazing full blast across the Western horizon. Unmindful of her maritime past, San Francisco had become a mining city and had plunged wholeheartedly into a gambling mania, the like of which had never before been known on the coast. With millions of dollars in bullion in sight on Sun Mountain, Californians had thoughts for nothing but the stock market.

As millions of dollars of San Francisco money were invested in Washoe hoisting machinery and reduction works, corporate organizations had been formed in San Francisco to which the mining claims were sold or exchanged for shares of stock. Large dividends were earned and paid.

Shares advanced with incredible speed and became favorite securities for investment of money and were daily bought and sold on the San Francisco Stock and Exchange Board.

Even Ralston, factotum of the Bank of California, had invested a goodly share of his bank's three million dollar capital in Comstock securities and had earned large dividends both for directors and stockholders. When a prospective investor came to Ralston for advice, invariably he would reply: "buy Comstocks." Acting on this counsel, tremendous fortunes had been made. This fact had been largely responsible for the reputation Ralston had gained in the money world as a financial wizard.

Not only with Ralston but with every other investment expert, the impression prevailed that the Comstock Lode was inexhaustible. The San Francisco press teemed with arguments in support of that belief. Hadn't the great silver lodes of Mexico and South America, from time immemorial, produced thousands of millions of dollars? Was not the Comstock Lode far richer than any other known mineral deposit?

The years from '61 to '64 had justified that belief in the Comstock. Incredible fortunes had been accumulated. Regular monthly incomes, measured by thousands of dollars, were received by many upon whom fortune had never before smiled. Overnight, chambermaids and courtesans had been converted into courted heiresses. In the twinkling of an eye, bartenders, hostlers, and watch-peddlers had become plutocrats, and had built incredible gingerbread houses on the ramparts of the city.

Seeing these results, the most conservative of investors had been infected by the Comstock allurement. San Francisco men, women and children dabbled wholeheartedly in Comstock stocks. Often every penny gleaned from any source went into the great maw of the Stock Exchange.

Transactions in the Lode's mining shares had become so enormous in California that on the 11th of September, 1862, the San Francisco Stock and Exchange Board had been organized. It consisted of fifty members, and included the names of the most substantial Californians. Here all the Comstock stocks were formally listed. Here stock orders from all over the coast, from all over the world, were received. Here shares were bought and sold. The facilities thus afforded for operation increased the speculative character of the business and gave opportunities for combinations and stock jobbing manipulations that resulted in great fluctuations of market value.

It was in answer to this game of chance that men as well as women flocked to the daily board. No wonder, when many entered poor and came forth rich as Croesus; no wonder, when ragamuffins became plutocrats; and derelicts princes of finance. It was exhilarating to watch that wild-eyed, anxious-eyed, shifty-eyed throng elbowing their way through the door during the last five minutes before the gong sounded.

Excitement over "Overman" and "Uncle Sam" was tremendous. Shares had been boomed up to $1000 each. And all because they overlapped and adjoined "North America." And "North America" was supposed to be in bonanza. The supposition was that whoever could get control of "North America" would get hold of the other two mines and be on the highway to great fortune.

Bill Sharon had made a study of these properties and had made up his mind to corner "North America." During the fourteen years since Bill had left Carrollton, Illinois, and had camped, in passing, at the mouth of Gold Cañon he had picked up a fortune of a hundred and fifty thousand dollars by conservative real-estate moves.

He had married the daughter of a sea captain, Miss Maria Mulloy of Quebec, had several children by her and lived on a handsome Stockton Street property. His integrity had earned him the esteem of his fellow citizens. Recently he had been elected by them a member of that City Council to which was intrusted the responsibility of organizing a municipal government for the growing city. The work required skill and judgment.

In convivial circles Sharon was known as an outstanding poker player who generally won, but when he didn't, paid his losses without quibble. When Sharon saw chambermaids, bartenders, hostlers, and ex-sheriffs soar to dizzy heights in the financial firmament with the help of the San Francisco Stock and Exchange Board he forsook slow-moving real estate for the new get-rich-quick scheme.

By 1864 he believed that "North America" offered him a chance to make a tremendous fortune. Having studied the situation carefully he concluded that whoever owned "North America" would likewise control "Overman" and "Uncle Sam." It stood to reason that the bonanza already known to exist in "Overman" would extend through to "North America." Throughout his speculative career, Sharon was often influenced by that circumstance: contiguity. Already he owned a thousand shares of the stock. If he could buy more and gain control, he would be made for life. So, along with the elbowing mob, he pushed his way into the board room and took a seat.

The hands of the clock reached the hour of 11.

Bang! went the gavel of the Chief Magician of the Board.

"Call the roll," boomed a loud voice from the curtained dais.

"Ophir!" shouted the caller in tones that could be heard to the farthest corner of the board room. "Ophir" was selling at $680. One of the highest-priced items on the board.

There was a rush of brokers to the pit in front of the dais. Almost instantly it filled with stamping, pushing, pulling, jabbering, roaring stock-fiends. Like wild men they waved their arms. Eyes glared, voices grew hoarse with bellowing. They pulled, tugged and jostled each other as if in anger. Buttons flew off, coats were torn, collars loosened.

"Sell 'em cash," yelled one.

"Sell 'em reg'lar," shouted another.

"Sell 'em seller, 30," called out a third.

Some wanted to sell, some wished to buy. Shouts, yells, gesticulations, pandemonium, but only for a moment. Then all was quiet again. The brokers resumed their seats. The calling of the list continued.

"North America!" rang out the caller's voice. Babel was let loose again.

Peckham, a broker from Montgomery Block, offered 100 shares at $290.

"Take it," said Sharon.

Peckham offered a hundred more.

"Take it," called Sharon excitedly. "Haven't you got any more? I'll take 500 shares if you have it."

"Here's 500," replied Peckham.

"I'll take 500 more if you have it," returned Sharon quickly.

"Here's 500 more," offered Peckham.

"Take it," shouted Sharon jubilantly.

By the time he left the board room, Sharon had bought 1700 shares at $290 a share.

Now there was no doubt. He had control of "North America." Into his purchases had gone the careful savings of his fourteen California years. He was a far wealthier man than he had ever dreamed of becoming when he graduated from Athens College. Now he must make preparation for paying for the stock. Before 2 o'clock that afternoon he must have the cash or else forfeit it. A colossal amount it seemed to the farm-bred Sharon. He must borrow. It would take more money than he had saved in the past fourteen years. But it was worth it. He would cash in on his property, his residence on Stockton Street included, and borrow the rest from Ralston. Good old Ralston, the friend of the borrower, the friend of the man with "margins" to cover, the friend of every man in need of help.

Before 2:30 of that day Peckham was in Sharon's office in the Plume Building (opposite the Montgomery Block on Montgomery Street). He wanted to make delivery of "North America" stock and get Sharon's check. Colonel J. C. Fry, a Carrollton fellow townsman with whom Sharon had crossed the plains, was in Sharon's office when Peckham entered. Sharon was looking worried. Peckham sensed that something had gone wrong.

"Peck," said Sharon, "I have an idea that there has been

a job put up to rob me in this stock sale. I don't believe you had anything to do with it, of course. Let us look at those certificates. If there is a red mark in red ink in the letter O in North America, it is my stock that I put into the pool."

Peckham and Sharon looked at the certificates. Sure enough, 1000 out of the 1700 shares had the red-ink mark in the letter O. Sharon had bought his own stock a second time at a big advance. He was the victim of a stock-jobber. There was no redress. Utterly ruined, he would be left with less than nothing. The $150,000 he had accumulated so laboriously in the past fourteen years would be wiped out. He was bankrupt. In less than an hour he had lost what it had taken more than a decade to accumulate. He was poorer than when he and Colonel Fry had camped in Gold Cañon in August, 1849. Poorer, older, and with less opportunity ahead —but wiser.

In spite of all his shrewdness and grasp of detail, Sharon had allowed himself to be gulled by a stock shark. Every one knew that such things went on in the San Francisco Stock and Exchange Board. But what could be done about it? The market was not a playroom for children. Often stocks were worked behind the scenes. The stock buyer, in the board room, was apt to be in total ignorance of what had gone on in the wings. It took a sixth sense to appreciate those facts. With all his cleverness Sharon had not developed that talent.

Sharon was disgusted. He had been gulled—fooled like a backwoodsman on his first trip to the city. That fact put iron in his soul—destroyed his faith in men and markets. Yesterday he had been a man of affairs, respected by his fellow citizens and elected by them a member of the City Council. Today he was a joke on California Street. Speculators were laughing up their sleeves at him. He was ruined and in debt. But at least he had his integrity. He would not go through bankruptcy. He must pay what he owed. He made up his mind to learn how to play that stock market game as it was played in San Francisco and beat it.

The more he considered his ills, the more he found himself thinking of Ralston, cashier of the Bank of California. Fry was Ralston's foster-father-in-law. He would take Fry and go and see Ralston.

Ralston was a man with a heart. The friend of every down-and-outer. The man who always stood ready to offer a helping hand. Ralston would help him now. Perhaps buy what was left of his real estate or advance him money on it.

Putting on his hat and urging Colonel Fry to accompany him, Sharon departed for Ralston's office at the Bank of California.

CHAPTER II

AT RALSTON'S OFFICE

1864

Ralston's office looked like the waiting room of a successful physician. From morning until night it was thronged with men, women, and children waiting to confer with the great cashier of the Bank of California.

Every man with anything to promote would be found there. In coast circles it was acknowledged that nothing could be accomplished socially, politically or financially in California without the official sanction of William Chapman Ralston. In ten years he had become the fountainhead of enterprise: the leader of the city. Within that time he had realized a position which he had long ago set out to achieve—a position which would permit him to do for San Francisco all the things which he felt the city and the State required. Industries and manufacturies were the backbone of progress. Every one would be an added spoke in the wheels of prosperity. Therefore, Ralston had encouraged every enterprise that would develope his scheme.

Ralston's plan was to make San Francisco the great financial center of the West. He wanted to give it metropolitan proportions. It must own its own opera house, theatre and stock companies. He wanted it to have public parks; broad, shaded boulevards; national monuments; free libraries, beautiful public buildings and first-class hotels. He wanted California to become a self-supporting, independent empire. Her isolation from "the States" required such a status. He meant to promote that idea; manufacturies and industries of all sorts. At the same time he would encourage shipping and commerce and make San Francisco Bay the greatest maritime entrepôt on the West Coast.

These were the days before the Civil War and transcontinental railroads. San Francisco's and California's isolation lent promise to this imperialistic dream. Ardent American and intense Unionist that he was, Ralston pictured himself as the titular head of this isolated Pacific empire that he was creating. Once he had the reins in hand he would brook no interference that might undermine his supremacy.

Ralston had ideal material upon which to work. California was hardly four years old when he had conceived his plan, and San Francisco was still a wild, red-blooded, unconstituted village. Both were unhampered by traditions. Nothing had been organized gradually, thus giving the builders valuable lessons in progression. Experience had had no chance to chasten or chastise them.

Their's had been a mushroom growth. Yesterday California had been Spanish pastoral in trend. Then had come the gold cry. Suddenly the young, hot-blooded Argonauts had found themselves inhabiting a commonwealth possessed of incredible riches. From the beginning there had been chaos. The village had developed into a city without plan or pattern. The inhabitants, volatile and mercurial in temperament, had fallen into all kinds of excesses. On this scene Ralston had appeared and, almost immediately, assumed leadership.

The Argonauts were all alike: boyish, joyous, debonair,

American to the backbone but Latin in tendency. Ralston was unlike them in that he nursed the germ of a great idea. They were all prone to melodrama; pageantry, prodigality, fiesta, music, and fights. They liked to earn large sums of money and spend it riotously: wining, dining, and dancing. Times and circumstances had made them gamblers. They were accustomed to taking great chances and accepted the fluctuations of fortune with equanimity.

Such was the clay out of which Ralston intended to mould a vigorous maritime community upon whose tides should ride the ships of every flag.

Having no family, one thought was always uppermost in Ralston's mind: San Francisco; the upbuilding of a great city; the development of a world-wide commerce and assistance to every honest enterprise that would promote these dreams.

Nothing in the project line was too small or too great to engage Ralston's attention. He had a marvellous grasp of affairs. He welcomed every man with ideas that would promote the prestige of his dream city. Such a one basking in the genial atmosphere of Ralston's smile felt himself moved to eloquence.

One time the caller proved to be the captain of a youthful baseball nine. His team needed new suits. With a reminiscent smile on his jovial, ruddy-complexioned face, Ralston wrote out a check, not for one, but for nine new baseball suits. The San Francisco contingent must be appropriately garbed when they faced their San José rivals across the diamond.

Once it was Leland Stanford. He wanted to borrow a hundred thousand dollars on a personal note. If he could get his railroad over the first sections of the line, Stanford explained, he would be entitled to government aid. If he couldn't he would have to give up the idea of a transcontinental railroad. Therefore he must have a hundred thousand dollars. Immediately, Ralston's sympathies went out to the Central Pacific Railroad. The completed road would be a tremendous spur to San Francisco. With the greater part of his bank capital tied up in the Comstock Lode, Ralston realized that he could not accommodate Stanford, but he knew where he could borrow those thousands: from the Pacific Insurance Company, of which he was a director. Without waste of time, Ralston took up the matter with the company, but those gentlemen were not so sure of the Central Pacific Railroad. Stanford's security was not of the best. The Central Pacific was a swindle. The Dutch Flat route was an outrage. The road should be constructed by way of Placerville. The enterprise was doomed to certain defeat. Influenced by such public criticisms, the directors were determined to lend no money. Ralston found himself standing alone in advocating the loan. The Dutch Flat route was the nearest to the Comstock Lode. It would be of incalculable assistance to the development of the mines. But the sentiment of the directors was adamant.

"Make the loan," Ralston finally advised them. "If at any time the directors become dissatisfied, the Bank of California will take it up."

The directors were satisfied as long as Ralston guaranteed the company against loss. The loan was made. Without Ralston's aid, the railroad quartet could not have extended their road over the difficult Sierra sections. With it, government aid was assured.

In advocating the loan, many of Ralston's friends felt that he was assuming too great a responsibility. It involved too much risk. But Ralston knew what it would mean to California.

One day it was Ashbury Harpending, a tall, slender, dark-haired Kentuckian, whose tremendous real-estate operations had made San Francisco gasp. Fascinated by his speculations, Ralston had written Harpending: At his convenience would he drop into his office at the Bank of California.

Harpending was greatly flattered to find that he had attracted the attention of the great central figure in California. He admired Ralston's dash, energy and success. In response to that letter, he found himself in Ralston's presence. In his swift, offhand manner Ralston said many pleasant things that put Harpending in a good humor with himself. He wanted to keep abreast with the active young men of the city, Ralston confided. He wanted to help, and co-operate with them. For that reason he had sent for Harpending.

Ralston's manner entirely won Harpending's confidence. Without hesitation he put his cards on the table, face up and told Ralston what he had in mind.

It was his purpose to solve the great traffic problem of the day: "Montgomery Street Straight South."

Ralston's heart was won.

Montgomery Street was the great artery of the growing city. To be a doctor, lawyer, broker or banker and not have offices on that great thoroughfare was to be beyond the pale. Montgomery Street began at Telegraph Hill and ended in obliquity on Market Street. It should be made to reach the Bay and the wharves of the Pacific Mail Steamship Company, claimed Harpending. Rincon Hill, then the residential district of the city, must make way for it. The millions of yards of excavated earth could be used to fill in "water lots." In this way 150 acres of land, between the Pacific Mail docks and Islais Creek, could be reclaimed. China Basin, too, could be filled in and added to the city. Two hundred blocks, now under water, could be retrieved from the sea and sold to the city at a profit of $5,000,000.

It was a matter of vast importance to San Francisco. Certainly, it would bring fame and fortune to the promoters.

Drive back the sea! Fill in tule lands, sell the reclaimed land to the city for millions of profit! A bold plan that had never occurred to the Ralston mind!

All the time Harpending had been speaking, Ralston, as was his custom, had been tearing papers into shreds and letting the fragments slip between his fingers. But all the time he had been listening with deep attention punctuated with an occasional word or nod of approval.

When Harpending finished he leaned back in his chair in a meditative way and thought a minute—drive back the sea!

"It looks like a noble game," he said at length. "Now, how would you like me for a partner?"

Harpending was astonished at the suggestion, but gratified

that the financial autocrat of the Pacific Coast was impressed by his proposition.

Arrangements were swiftly made. Harpending made a complete statement of his investments. Ralston accepted them and made an offer, based on cost plus a handsome profit, for a quarter interest. Harpending accepted the offer in an offhand way. Deeds were drawn up and signed.

From then on, it was understood that Ralston and Harpending would stand together to push Montgomery Street through to the Bay and reclaim 200 blocks of tide land in the process. Likewise, it was understood, that in this undertaking, Harpending should have the unlimited support of the Bank of California. The Ralston-Harpending combination was to be known as the Montgomery Street Real Estate Company.

The caller was George D. Nagle. He had come to Ralston's office to interest him in Alaska, her rich fur-trade, her timber and minerals. At that time Alaska belonged to Russia and was being exploited profitably by the Hudson's Bay Company. Nagle believed that it was possible to wrest the charter from the English company and transfer the rights to the management of an American organization, if a responsible one could be created. On that account he had sought out an interview with Ralston. Would he be interested in Alaska? Nagle needed his advice and assistance.

Ralston listened to Alaska's possibilities and jumped at the idea of her rich fur-trade and a contract with the Russian Fur Company. Just the sort of thing that did interest him. Alaska could be operated from a San Francisco entrepôt. Ralston suggested that a close corporation be formed, the membership confined to one Goldstone, Nagle, himself and two other gentlemen whom he named.

Nagle, for sundry reasons, objected. However, in the autumn of 1865, a differently constituted company, which included Ralston, was organized. The new company's first step was to send an agent and surveyor to Alaska to spy out the land. These surveys, maps of the northwest coast, and the collecting of information with regard to the interior had cost

Ralston's company between fifty thousand and one hundred thousand dollars. When completed, Ralston's company were ready to apply to the Russian Government for a franchise. Many letters were exchanged. The Russian ambassador at Washington was interviewed. Even the Czar was approached. While negotiations were pending, the maps and statistics collected by Ralston's company had fallen into the hands of the United States Government. Through Secretary of State Seward, Alaska was acquired by the United States.

"You," ran an official Washington letter to Ralston's company, "are responsible for the acquisition of the Territory, for to your correspondence is due the fact that it is now in the possession of the United States."

Often the caller was Joshua Norton—Emperor of the United States and Defender of Mexico—in blue uniform with huge gold epaulettes, a plumed hat and a shining sword dangling at his side. Norton had been a Forty-Niner. Unlike the vast majority of those adventurers, he had brought thousands of dollars to California. By judicious investment he had increased his fortune to a quarter million. In the great bank failures of 1854–55, Norton's fortune had been swept away. As a result his reason had been dethroned. Two years later, poor as a church mouse, Norton had emerged from a protracted illness. In his disordered state of mind, he believed he was Emperor of California and Defender of Mexico. Thereafter, he dressed the part, in gold epaulettes, sword and cockade. San Franciscans helped Norton to keep up the illusion, treating him like an anointed king. Often he appeared at Ralston's desk with a check in hand signed with a royal flourish and stamped with imperial seal. Ralston, his heart wrung over the misfortune of his old friend, always received "the Emperor" as his station demanded, and never failed to honor his checks although the gold for every one came eventually out of his own pocket. Too, the Emperor's splendor was maintained by Ralston's bounty.

Again it was a committee of women: Mrs. Cyrus Palmer, Mrs. John Hooker, Mrs. A. L. Stone, Mrs. C. L. Taylor,

Mrs. Thomas Flint. They were founding the "Pacific Dispensary for Women and Children." San Francisco was filled with women needing medical attention. Was Mr. Ralston interested in their cause? Interested? Why of course he was interested! Ralston took a life membership—the first one on the list. This gift and future munificent ones were contingent upon only one condition. His name must not be used. No publicity. Not until long years afterward did recipients of that charity know who had been the institution's most generous benefactor.

Often it was a committee of men interested in founding woollen mills, or sugar refineries, or a shot tower or lead works, or in planting tobacco or cotton, or wheat, or in reclaiming tule lands. To all these propositions, Ralston lent a ready ear. His time, his money, his inclinations were with those who were trying to promote the welfare of California and helping to establish a Pacific Empire. California must become self supporting—a unity unto itself. "The States" were far away by water. In spite of Stanford, the journey overland was unthinkable.

Now it was Mrs. Bugbee, Mrs. Morrow, Mrs. Orr, Mrs. Conkling, and other founders of "The San Francisco Female Hospital." San Francisco needed more than a clinic to help ailing women. Never did they call upon Ralston but that he contributed to the hospital's efficiency and existence. Always his gifts were handed over with but one condition: they must be anonymous. His purse was a treasury upon which they could draw again and again providing they did not mention the Ralston name.

Once it was an eager-eyed street urchin—ragged, unkempt. He must see Mr. Ralston. His father was lost, or had died at the mines. The lad wanted a job. He had heard the bank needed an errand boy. He had a mother to support. All sympathy, Ralston took him by the hand and visited the different department heads. Did any of them need a messenger or errand boy?

"No."

So Ralston put on his hat and visited the near-by brokerage offices of his friends until he found one that needed an eager-eyed lad who was trying to support his mother.

No one was ever turned away from Ralston's office who had something to contribute to California welfare or who needed help or a word of encouragement.

Once a black-robed woman with five hungry youngsters tugging at her weeds was ushered into Ralston's office. Her man had been killed in the mines and had left not a dollar. She was penniless. Would the great banker help her to get a start in business? In the fervor of her supplication, tears streaming down her face, the woman slipped to her knees at Ralston's feet.

"Don't weep, my good woman," said Ralston, lifting her up, "every one needs a friend and if you will tell me how I can help you, I will try." A few words followed.

Wheeling in his chair, Ralston wrote out a check. "Here is enough to take care of your babies and start you in business. The only thing I ask is that you will not tell any one who befriended you. If you don't succeed, come again."

Ralston's office had become a social-service bureau as well as a promotion center. Rushed as he was, Ralston was never too busy to see any one whom he could help, who was ill or down on his luck. For such, there was always a coin, a cheery word, and a warm clasp of the hand: he intended that his city should be fed on the milk of human kindness.

Once the callers were the presidents of the "Six Chinese Companies of California," in pigtails and rich brocade. There was a visiting celebrity in San Francisco: the Vice-President of the United States. The Chinese wanted to honor him with a dinner. Would Ralston be their guest? Make a speech perhaps? Ralston would, and the Chinese departed. No social function was complete without W. C. Ralston of the Bank of California to grace the occasion.

One day along came Billy Sharon. The loss of his money

in Comstock stocks had left a canker in his bosom. With him was Ralston's foster-father-in-law, Colonel J. D. Fry.

"What can I do for you?" Ralston said in his warm friendly manner, as he held out his hand to the small, gray-headed, wiry, black-eyed individual before him.

Sharon told Ralston about "North America" and the dastardly way he had been handled on the stock market.

Immediately Ralston was all sympathy. He hated anything of an underhanded nature. Clear as a sunny day himself, he liked everything open and aboveboard. Most of all, Ralston wanted to help the thin, drooping-shouldered, drooping-moustached, undersized man before him. He was sorry for him. Too, he wanted to help him because Sharon was an old friend of Colonel J. D. Fry, and Colonel Fry was Ralston's father-in-law. It was only a few years since that Ralston had married Lizzie Red of Carrollton, Illinois. And Miss Red had been Colonel Fry's niece and ward. So inclination and friendship urged Ralston to do his utmost for William Sharon of Carrollton, Illinois.

A few days later the directors of the Bank of California, at Ralston's suggestion, took over Sharon's real estate and loaned him enough money to pay for his mining stock. But it left Sharon without a cent in the world. And Sharon had a wife and several children to support. Ralston could not turn any man away in that condition. Out of his own pocket he advanced Sharon $500. Sharon was satisfied enough but not Colonel Fry. Money was only temporary assistance. He wanted a permanent position for Sharon. Ralston hesitated. It was not easy to find a job for a man who had just proven himself an utter failure.

At this very time, Stateler and Arrington, bankers of Virginia City, and the correspondents of the Bank of California there, had failed—failed, owing the Bank of California thousands and thousands of dollars. Besides owing all this money, they had overdrawn their account. Ralston was not only disappointed, but worried. The Bank of California was embarrassed.

CHAPTER III

WILLIAM CHAPMAN RALSTON

1864

Ralston had recently founded the Bank of California. So far as his previous partners Eugene Kelly and Joseph A. Donohoe had been concerned, it had been a secret founding—following precipitately on the heels of the dissolution of the firm of Donohoe, Ralston & Co.

Immediately the new-founded Bank of California had become the outstanding financial organization of San Francisco, of California, of the Pacific West. On its directorate appeared the names of prominent financial leaders. Every one of them was a business headliner, president of this or that organization: of the Oregon Steamship Company, which controlled all the steamers plying between San Francisco and the north and on the Columbia River; of the Pacific Mail, whose ships ran between California and the Orient; of the California Steam Navigation Company, which controlled the entire business of California inland waters. Ralston intended to monopolize California's sea-lanes. San Francisco, like New Orleans, must become a great maritime city. He recognized that the future greatness of his empire depended upon control of her commerce. Aside from the water, although every line of endeavor was represented, Ralston's other chief interest lay in the fabulously rich mines of the Comstock Lode. Thus his interests in the sea often came in conflict with his interests in the land.

Ralston had purposely rounded up these leaders. From the first he had intended that the pulses of economic California,

Oregon, Washington, and Nevada should throb synchronously under his thumb. Particularly Nevada, for the mines on the Comstock were largely the bank's debtors.

No doctor ever followed his patient's pulse with more intense ardor than Ralston did that of the Bank of California and of the Comstock Lode. Well he knew that what ailed one would affect the other. For Ralston's dreams of empire were entirely based on the mines of Nevada.

When Ralston felt that Pacific Mail or California Steam Navigation Co. or Oregon Steamship Co. or Comstock Lode needed financial bolstering, he knew it long before the directorate of those organizations even surmised it. His financial acumen was no ordinary faculty. It amounted to genius. "Genius, financial genius," those were the words which D. O. Mills, conservative president of the Bank of California, had often applied to his cashier.

When he founded the Bank of California, Ralston could have made himself president, but he was modest and didn't care about the title. He wanted his bank to have presitge—high-sounding prestige. Even more prestige than the name Ralston could bestow. At that time the fame of Mills could add more luster to a bank than any other in California.

Mills himself had not had any desire to head the list of officers in Ralston's bank. When approached, he had begged off. He had no ambition to be president of a San Francisco concern. Already he was the head of Sacramento's big bank: D. O. Mills & Co. Already he had amassed a fortune in California nuggets, gold dust and paper. He intended to go back to "the States," to New York from whence he had hailed. Although California gold dust had satisfied Mills' wandering lust—Ralston was not satisfied to see him go. He needed Mills' prestige in San Francisco. He promised Mills that he would double, treble his present holdings if he would consent.

"Look here," Ralston had urged. And no man could be more persuasive than Ralston. "You need be president only in name. I will do all the managing." And because Mills believed implicitly in Ralston's "genius" and the star of his ascendancy, he had agreed to this anomaly: he would be the president but Ralston would be the power. Thus the Bank of California had been launched on California's turbulent financial seas with Ralston on the bridge as the captain of industry.

At thirty-eight years of age Ralston found himself with something to say about every worth-while industry in California; about every mine on the Comstock Lode; about every boat on inland waters; and about every steamer bound to the northwest or westward to the Orient. His influence was paramount as far north as Alaska; as far east as the Rockies, and as far west as Hawaii, Japan, and China. So far so good. But Ralston had greater ambitions for his Pacific economic empire. His would be the breath to bring order out of reigning chaos. No other State, nor other country would have a capital such as he planned to make of San Francisco. Perhaps Lorenzo il Magnifico had dreamed such a dream of Florence. Perhaps Sforza of Milan or Ludwig the Second of Munich, but none had more opulently colored dreams for a great city than those formulated in the fertile brain of W. C. Ralston. San Francisco had become an eager passion which he intended to translate into deeds.

Ralston had not always been a banker nor an industrial organizer. Nor unfortunately, had he come up by slow gradations in a monied establishment to his lofty position as cashier of the Bank of California. If he had only had such experience! Such traditional background! If he had only been an errand or a messenger boy, in some big banking institution, he would have become one of the greatest financial organizers that had ever lived. But Ralston's had been a stellar rise. One so rapid and precipitate that it would have dizzied a man of lesser caliber.

In the early '50's Ralston had been one of 75,000 colorful, robust, young gold-seekers who had adventured California-wards. Among them had not been one outstanding personality. Shortly after his arrival, with the suddenness of a sky-rocket exploding in mid-air, a great flashing star had been seen blazing in the financial firmament of the Western horizon. That star had been Ralston's.

What had given Ralston the impetus to outstrip his fellow-men so rapidly? Family? Tradition? Wealth? Environment? Training? Lady Luck?

No! None of these; something far more elemental.

Water: clear, colorless, odorless, innocuous water. Fickle, vacillating water. Water that drives the paddles of boats; that turns the wheels of mills; that grinds the kernel of wheat; that pounds the lump of ore. Water that can purl in a rippling brook or roar in a plunging Niagara. Water it was that supplied the motive power that whirled the wheels of Ralston's destiny. Slowly at first. Then faster and faster until they revolved with fearful velocity.

Before he had come to San Francisco in 1854, Ralston's whole existence had been gauged by water. Born at Plymouth, Richland County, Ohio, his father, Robert Ralston, had "followed the river" as a source of existence. His maternal grandfather, William Chapman, for whom he had been named, operated a river ferry at Chapman's Landing on the Ohio. While Ralston had been yet a lad the family had taken up residence at Wellsville, a small town on the Ohio, and embarked in the lottery of river trade.

From the banks of this Ohio hamlet, Billy Ralston had watched packets sailing down the river, puffing, blowing and sending forth a Vesuvius of sparks. Whither were those monsters bound? was the question that filled his boyish mind. While he had been speculating on the answer he had launched in their wake a flotilla of paper boats. What Ohio or Mississippi mart would they reach? St. Louis? Vicksburg? Louisville? New Orleans? or the Gulf? Soon, imagination and incentive had been adrift with his paper argosies. Billy was longing for the unseen ports, the uncharted seas toward which they floated.

Thus the river became the breast from which Billy Ralston suckled his knoweldge of the outside world. Capable mentor that it was, the river fed his imagination and fertilized his creative power. When his mother died, as she did following the birth of her fourth son, the river became solace and refuge. To it, he took his troubles.

For decades, the Ohio had been a life-giving stream to

the Ralston clan. Bounteously it had given. As swiftly it had swept away. Thus the river had early accustomed Billy to wide fluctuations of fortune. Yesterday the Ralstons had been affluent. There had been horses and carriages. And such horses! Then, one day, his father's keel-boat, loaded down with potential wealth, had struck a river-snag and had sunk. The sinking had plunged the Ralstons into abject penury. Everything had been swept away. But blithely young Billy had turned to lathe and plane and mastered the ship-carpentering trade. Before long he had helped his father to fashion the hull of a river boat that soon went puffing, blowing, and snorting up and down the Ohio.

The Ohio had been Billy's training school. Like a lathe it had fashioned his lithe young body into that of an athlete. On it he had learned to swim and to dive, to tread and to float. Under water he was as skillful as he was on the surface. He could dive from perilous heights. He could pick up coins from the river bottom. Before long, Billy was as familiar with the topography of the river-bed as he was with the familiar streets about Wellsville.

The river taught Billy to be philosophic, to accept whatever life had to offer without cringing or bitterness. Never could the river discourage him. Boilers might explode, snags rip open the hulls of his father's boats, fire destroy them, but never could the majestic Ohio implant dismay in his soul, nor dampen his ardor nor douse his ambitions. Great teacher—that river. It gave him confidence, taught him the meaning of power. It prepared Billy for a manly existence, to be sanguine and constant. Even in the face of overwhelming disaster, to be magnificent.

Once his father built a boat, the *Dominion*. Sam Tyler was captain and Billy became clerk. Proud and happy had been the lad to become part and parcel of the great river traffic.

One night at Keokuk when the *Dominion* had been overloaded, adverse tides had seized her, whirled her about and smashed her midships across a submerged rock. Her hull had split wide open, and she had sunk. Down with her, in the best traditions of the river, had gone Billy Ralston. But not until he had helped to salvage the greater part of her cargo did he think of himself. Even in catastrophe the river taught Billy to consider others before he thought of himself.

Once the sailors on one of his boats had mutinied; but Billy had armed himself with a gun and had driven them below before they could take possession of the boat.

From the wreck of the *Dominion* Billy had become clerk on the *Constitution,* a Mississippi floating palace. Soon he was being introduced to a wider life: Natchez and Memphis, Vicksburg, Nashville, and Louisville. Billy was sixteen now—tall, vigorous, brown-eyed, with high color, handsome physique, and engaging manner. What can I do for you? his manner seemed to say. Gladly will I be of help. And he would bend his back to any task to prove it. Liked by men and admired by women, Billy was welcomed wherever he landed up or down on either side of the river.

Oft ill-luck pursued Billy down the river. One day the *Constitution* caught fire at Memphis and was destroyed, and he became clerk on the *Convoy,* another floating palace, which plied between St. Louis, Memphis, and New Orleans. Cornelius K. Garrison was captain. There was a river man to Billy's liking! Bold, aggressive, courageous. Equal to any emergency. Not for a moment did he fear river bandits, nor the bullies or pirates that lurked in the cane brake.

Always acquitting himself honorably and courageously, Billy had soon earned the admiration of Captain Garrison. Through him he had met many other river men—men like J. C. Ainsworth and Ralph S. Fretz, captain of the *Memphis.* Every one, river man or land broker, was attracted by the handsome, athletic, genial-mannered Billy Ralston. He had a positive genius for making friends, and for leadership.

Every one liked to do things for Billy—to take him to the horseraces at Louisville, to a levee at Memphis, the theatre, the opera or a dance in the Orleans ballroom at New Orleans. Hospitable doors opened on a fabulous life for him, a *dolce far niente* existence of gracious living, doing and receiving. Here were handsome pillared houses, set well back in gorgeously laid-out gardens, luxurious carriages, blooded horses, homes presided over by beautiful women and gallant men. Here were glass, crystal, silver, French tapestries and heavy silk hangings: all things which Billy learned to admire.

In the '40's New Orleans was a "city of sin," the very air had a volatile, mercurial quality. In it the word "honor" hung "like the refrain of a popular melody." It was a community that enjoyed its opera, its theatre, its music, its balls, its coffee-houses, its frappéd drinks, its gambling-tables, its bull-fights, its bagnios, its circus. It was a city of men who had inherited the Latin traits of French and Spanish mothers; fiery men, highstrung Creoles, who loved pomp, pleasure, drama, and pageant; who enjoyed any game that stirred the senses; who lived for excitement; who danced with abandon and who protected their honor with an ardent sword and bled and died under the duelling oaks rather than brook the most trivial of insults.

It was a city after his own heart. It fascinated Ralston, stirred him to the core of his being. It became the dream-city of his imagination. Here, Billy learned to dress with the rest of the river dandies, to hold himself erect, to wear his beaver at a rakish angle, to flourish his cane with the swagger of a Boulevardier. At the same time he developed a pair of mean fists that offenders feared to see descending upon them. It was a many-colored, many-sounding, magical life to which the river-boats introduced him. Every port was fantastic: whisking cotton bales, slaves, slave markets, horse-racing, cock-fighting, opera, quadroon balls, dancing, laughter, song, sorrow, and duelling.

As soon as the cry: "gold in California" rang among the canebrakes, Captain Garrison and Colonel Fretz sailed away. Ralston missed their companionship. Soon he, too, decided to strike out boldly for California's golden shore, but he was short of cash.

On his way down river to the sea Billy hunted up his old friend Adam Sproule of Louisville.

"I'm going to quit steamboating and go to California," Ralston announced when they met.

Knowing what was coming, Sproule anticipated his young friend.

"And how much do you want?"

"I want to go like a white man," Ralston had retorted. "And I think it will take about $300."

Sproule handed over the money. While Ralston was writing out a note, his benefactor interrupted:

"The obligation is just as good without the note as with it," he interjected. Sproule never had cause to regret that remark. Back came the money and with it a handsome souvenir of California: a watch-chain strung with golden nuggets.

One day, aboard the *Madonna,* Billy had sailed down the river that had borne, bred and nurtured him. To the sea, he came, and across the Caribbean to Panama. It was the year 1849. He was twenty-three years old: bronzed, brave, smiling, courteous, eager-eyed, ready to put in practice what the river had taught him.

Panama was in a hubbub. Luckily, at Aspinwall, Billy ran into his old river friends Garrison and Fretz. They had never been able to get away from the Isthmus. Panama had offered traffic problems not to be despised. Capitalizing on them, they had gone into the banking and shipping business and were literally coining money. It so happened that just at the time Ralston landed they were in trouble. They needed an agent to assist them in the sharp competition then going on between themselves and the Nicaragua Transit Company. They had goods on the Atlantic side which must be transported to the Pacific. Not an honest man could they find to superintend the work. They persuaded Ralston to help them. Because he liked to oblige a friend in need, Ralston had tarried. The goods were transferred across the Isthmus to the entire satisfaction of his exacting employers. Other opportunities offered. The firm of Garrison and Fretz prospered more than ever.

Forty-nine passed. Still Ralston lingered on the Isthmus. His friends needed him. That was enough. He would not desert them. Fifty ended and Fifty-one began. There was no let-up in Panama congestion. No lessening in the numbers seeking California's golden shores; nor cessation of those returning, bound for "the States" loaded down with golden loot. The Isthmus became a mad place. There were not boats enough, nor steamer berths enough, nor graves enough to accommodate the gold seekers.

One day in August of 1851 the 1100-ton steamer *New Orleans* limped into port from San Francisco. She had engine trouble; besides, the captain was too ill to take his boat back to the golden-gated California city. The *New Orleans* had a full passenger list of 200 people scheduled. Garrison and Fretz were in a predicament. There was not a sea captain on the Isthmus whom they could press into service.

Garrison appealed to Ralston. Would he take the *New Orleans* back to San Francisco?

Captain of an ocean-going steamer and clerk on a riverboat were two different occupations. But Ralston felt equal to the emergency. Nothing ever pleased him more than taking desperate chances, and achieving magnificent results. Besides, he had studied the sea and understood its moods. He was not afraid of it. It challenged him. Being a born pilot, he could read the floor of the ocean by the shadows thrown on the surface. Well he knew that submerged rocks revealed their presence by darkening colors. So he accepted the dare.

To see him guiding the *New Orleans* up the treacherous, fog-wrapped Lower California Coast by Point Conception, by Point Arguello, that graveyard of California argosies, one would have supposed that Ralston carried a chart of that dangerous coastline in his head.

Rarely during that passage did Captain Ralston leave the bridge. Hardly did his vigilance relax. Never did he forget till his dying hour the phosphorescent track the *New Orleans* left in her wake, the warning note of her foghorn, or the wind in the rigging, as the steamer crept slowly but safely up the coast. On September 20, 1851, eighteen days after leaving Panama, Captain Ralston came in sight of California's rolling upland, as barren as a treeless desert. Then he sighted the Golden Gate. Straight as an arrow the *New Orleans's* prow clove a passage down the narrow opening connecting the Pacific Ocean with San Francisco Bay. Cannon boomed on Telegraph Hill as the *New Orleans* rounded the Point.

Ah! What a vision met Ralston's eye.

San Francisco was built on the tip end of a rocky peninsula, on the mailed fist of a long arm of California mainland, that thrust itself menacingly into the sea. Around its three sides swept swift tides, seething with passion. Around and around they swung, dashing angrily at cliff and shore.

Seen through curtains of mist, San Francisco presented a chaotic vision: a white, canvas-covered city tossed hit-or-miss up and down seven hazy hills. Seven bare, brown hills that rose precipitately from dark blue water. Through the mists Ralston could hear the roar with which those vast currents carried on their incessant warfare against their ancient enemy. The air throbbed with the vigor of the assault. Like the hoof-beats of a troop of cavalry dashing into a fray. "Neptune's horses," Ralston always called that pounding sound.

At the Golden Gate Ralston could gauge the strength of the sea's enmity. What other power than water could have torn that breach through the low Marin hills to the sea.

Even then, Ralston was stirred by the mist-veiled city, as stirred as an Oriental at the approach of a veiled houri. He longed to sweep those veils aside, to breathe upon her confusion, to bring order out of chaos.

After discharging cargo and passengers, Captain Ralston embarked for the Isthmus. So delighted were Garrison and Fretz with the exploit that they reorganized their company. Henceforth the firm became known as Garrison, Fretz & Co. Ralston had become "the Company."

So well was the shipping-banking firm of Garrison, Fretz & Co. doing at Panama that they determined to reach out not only toward California but toward New Orleans and New York steamship lines. An opposition to the Pacific Mail Steamship Company was organized. At different times business connections were made with Howard & Sons, Shipping and Commission Merchants; Davis, Brooks and Company; E. Mills, Importer and Commission Merchant; Commodore Cornelius Vanderbilt, and finally with Morgan & Sons, steamship owners and operators of New York. All of these firms represented the flower of New York commercially.

With these men Ralston came in constant contact—rubbing elbows with them not only on the Isthmus but also in New York. The doors of their homes were open to him. Among others, that of the Thornes. On one of these trips Ralston became engaged to Miss Louisa Thorne, the granddaughter of Commodore Vanderbilt. Suddenly, before they were married, the young lady had sickened and died. A memento of that tragedy was the miniature that always stood on Ralston's desk.

Back at Panama cutthroat tactics reigned. Conditions were changing. A railroad crept across the Isthmus. The supremacy of Garrison, Fretz & Co. was threatened. Joining forces with Commodore Vanderbilt, the Independent Opposition Line, afterward the Nicaragua Transit Company, was organized. Headquarters were established at San Francisco. Vanderbilt offered Garrison a salary of $60,000 to take charge of the California office. Garrison accepted.

With the departure of his chief, Ralston was drawn like a filing toward its magnet. The Panama business was closed up. What little was left was put into the hands of a younger brother of Captain Fretz. Embarking on the *Uncle Sam*, Ralston arrived in San Francisco March 20, 1854, and was put in charge of Garrison, Fretz & Co.'s San Francisco office with headquarters on Sacramento Street adjoining the Chinese Salesroom. As agent of the Independent Opposition Line for New York, via Panama, Ralston had a fleet of magnificent ships under his charge, notably, the *Uncle Sam* and the *Yankee Blade*. Of these the *Yankee Blade*, launched June 1, was the pride of the Coast. Built for speed, it was believed nothing on the Pacific could pass her.

On the 30th of September, when the *Yankee Blade* made ready to sail for Panama, Ralston was at the Jackson Street wharf to give final sailing directions to Captain Henry Randall. Competition demanded a speed-record. On board were 800 passengers. In her hold was $153,000 in California nuggets. Ralston impressed the captain with what the company expected of him.

Several boats sailed out of the Golden Gate at the same

misty hour that the *Yankee Blade* weighed anchor. Bets were freely laid, fog or no fog, the *Yankee Blade* would be the first into Panama. Almost immediately she outstripped her competitors and took the lead. As she disappeared through the Gate, some gambler made a $5000 bet that she would be the first ship into Panama. Ralston was delighted at the splendid way the *Yankee Blade* had gotten under sail.

In the dawn of a few days later a mounted expressman was pounding on the door of Ralston's Stockton Street home. Encompassed by dense fogs, the *Yankee Blade* had piled up on the hidden reefs of Point Arguello and had sunk in fathoms of water. Three hundred men, women and children and $153,000 in California nuggets and gold dust had been lost forever.

In the wake of the messenger, the survivors, aboard the *Brother Jonathan,* arrived in San Francisco and held an indignation meeting in Portsmouth Square. Ralston was roundly censured for sheer negligence in directing the *Yankee Blade's* course. Speed had been the main issue. The mob marched on Ralston's office demanding passage to New York. Police had to be called to quell the disturbance. Forever after, that sea tragedy palled upon Ralston.

Shortly thereafter, Ralston's firm went out of the shipping business. On January 1, 1856, Ralston organized the banking firm of Garrison, Morgan, Fretz and Ralston with a paid-up capital of $700,000 and New York connections. As Garrison and Morgan were more or less figureheads and Fretz was waxing old, Ralston was left largely in charge. Ralston made it a point to make the acquaintance of the leading business men in the city, catered to their whims, and fancies, and soon had all the big accounts in his bank.

By July, 1857, Morgan and Garrison had definitely withdrawn from the firm and Ralston took in as partners Joseph Donohoe and Eugene Kelly, under the firm name of Donohoe, Ralston & Co., in San Francisco and Eugene Kelly & Co., in New York.

From the beginning the enterprise was wonderfully successful. The rise in gold succeeding the outbreak of the

Rebellion had been a fortunate fluctuation for them and they reaped a splendid fortune.

In the midst of these financial successes, Ralston married Miss Elizabeth Red, formerly of Carrollton, Illinois. The wedding was a social event at Calvary Church. The bride, "a mass of crinoline, gauze, orange blossoms and tulle," walked up the aisle on the arm of her uncle, Colonel J. D. Fry.

Following the ceremony, the bridegroom made a typical Ralston gesture: the whole wedding party, numbering some fourteen persons, were invited to participate in the Yosemite Valley honeymoon. They accepted. As the wedding party, aboard the *New World,* headed up the Bay, they passed the steamships *Orizaba* and *Sierra Nevada.* In honor of the occasion, both vessels had been decked out with flags and fired continuous salutes as Ralston and his bride sailed away.

On a moonlight night, several days later, the bridal party arrived in the Valley of the Yosemite and pitched their lodge, "Still Water Camp," in a dense copse of evergreen and flowering dogwood on the banks of Merced River. Within sight and sound were Bridal Veil Falls. About them the dogwood was a riot of bloom. Seen through the heavy evergreen foliage, the white-flowering trees looked like so many pale-robed acolytes attending a nuptial altar.

All that evening the bride was entranced with the silvery, film-like texture of the Bridal Veil cataract and by the continuous sounds of falling waters about her.

Noting her absorption, one of the party proposed that she should slip behind the falls so that the rest might see how a watery veil became her.

But the bride was equal to the occasion. "Married women," she retorted, "were not permitted to take the veil . . . her husband had not yet made her dissatisfied with the world."

CHAPTER IV

TIBBEY OR SHARON

1864

Back in San Francisco, Ralston plunged immediately into making his bank the center of San Francisco and California development.

From the first, Donohoe, Ralston & Co. took the lead in financial circles. Immense bullion shipments from the mines of the Comstock Lode passed through their hands. In no time at all, with the magic of California, the firm made a great deal of money, and Ralston became a prince of fortune. Now he lived on Rincon Hill surrounded by gardens and attended by horses, carriages, and servants galore. One night, shortly after his marriage, he gave a magnificent ball there in honor of his bride. For the occasion, a beautiful ivory-tinted, temporary ballroom was constructed adjoining his house. Its interior was lined with mirrors and finished in the Empire style. Out of compliment to their princely host the women guests came garbed in gowns that would have done credit to the court of Napoleon III and Eugenie.

From the first the Comstock Lode had fascinated Ralston. He had been the first to appreciate the possibility of harnessing its wealth to the business development of San Francisco. On the strength of those mines he intended to develop San Francisco into a greater city than New Orleans. He looked upon those mines as an excellent investment. He felt they would go on producing forever and paying big returns on any investment. To all who came to his office seeking advice regarding investments, he always recommended

Comstock holdings. To show his faith in them he had already loaned a large percentage of his bank's principal to Comstock enterprises or establishments of different kinds, like Donohoe's foundry or the Vulcan Iron Works of San Francisco, which were constantly engaged in turning out machinery, cages, engines, etc., for the mines. Thus San Francisco and the Comstock Lode became one and indissoluble: a vicious circle. Californians invested their wealth in the Lode. In return Comstock bullion, in a steady stream, poured into the development of San Francisco.

But the lure of the Comstock did not entirely wean Ralston from his love of the sea. Once in a while he made loans to promote water-ways. When Captain J. C. Ainsworth, his old Mississippi River friend, wanted to develop a steamship line on the Columbia River, Ralston accommodated him with a large sum of money.

Kelly, Ralston's New York partner, looked with ill favor on such loans.

"If you're going to lend money outside of California in that way," he complained testily, "we had better dissolve partnership."

In the past Ralston had often been provoked over these remarks. The relationship had become strained. When Kelly wanted to move their banking concern to New York, Ralston would not listen. By that time he had become too deeply involved in California. The firm had made its money in San Francisco, he retorted. Its profits should promote the city's welfare. Continually now Donohoe found one thing or another to criticize in the character of Ralston's loans: his security was inadequate; such loans were not good banking, or he was taking too many chances.

Kelly was too conservative for a new country, Ralston contended. While the controversy waxed increasingly bitter, Ralston made up his mind to break away from his partners and found a new company in which his own policies would be paramount. Secretly he went about his plans. Before either Kelly or Donohoe knew what had happened, the Bank of California had been organized, and Ralston had taken with him some of the best accounts, notably all of those connected with the Comstock Lode.

As quickly as subscriptions to the new bank stock poured in, Ralston invested them in choice paper, discounts, bonds, etc., but mostly in Comstock Lode properties. So that when the new bank opened its doors, it started out with a goodly amount of business on its books. So quietly had Ralston planned these maneuvers, that never once had Donohoe and Kelly suspected what was happening beneath the surface.

When they discovered what had occurred, they were both amazed and not a little nettled. They would make Ralston regret his secrecy. He had not been frank with them.

So had the Bank of California come into existence. More and more, as Ralston's faith in the Comstock had increased, the capital funds of the organization had been re-invested in or loaned to mills, foundries or mines directly dependent on the continued production of the Comstock Lode.

Thus Ralston had been greatly alarmed for the safety of his institution when, one day, a terrific crash occurred on the San Francisco stock market and Comstock holdings began to crumble in value. The Lode was finished, ran street gossip.

"Gould and Curry," which had been paying a dividend of $125 a share or a foot, cracked at $6300 and ran rapidly down to $2400, and then to $900. "Ophir" fell from $1580 to $300. "Savage" went down from $2600 to $750. "North America" to $105. "North Potosi" to $68. It was frightful.

So rapidly did shares rain on the market from all directions that hundreds of prominent men were ruined. Was it a panic? Ralston asked himself. Never had there been such a tumble in Comstock stocks. Worst of all, alarming reports were circulating: the underground workings of the greatest producers like "Gould and Curry" and "Ophir" were flooded with water. An inexhaustible flow, from where, no man knew, was rushing pell-mell through drift and winze, drowning out ledges and clogging up stopes. Old miners said it was the end of the Comstock. No pump could handle such floods. They began to fold up their tents, buy prairie schooners and strike out for Austin, Belmont, and other desert camps to the East.

It was at this very time when the mines were being drowned out, and the San Francisco stock market was crashing, that word had reached Ralston that the Bank of California's trusted correspondents on the Comstock Lode, Stateler and Arrington, had failed. What alarmed Ralston most of all was that Stateler and Arrington owed the Bank of California a large sum of money.

For several years Stateler and Arrington had handled the large account of the rich "Gould and Curry Gold and Silver Mining Company," of which Ralston was treasurer. Because Ralston had trusted the firm as honorable men he had given them the privilege of overdrawing their account. On the first of every month "Gould and Curry," "Ophir," "Mexican," and other mining companies with which Ralston was connected, needed large amounts of gold coin to pay off their miners, teamsters, and oremen. To facilitate matters, Stateler and Arrington had been granted the right to supply this money. But they had imposed upon the privilege. Without Ralston's knowledge they had become gamblers and carousers, and had overdrawn their account and failed when really solvent. It had been a shameful proceeding. More than anything else Ralston hated to be disappointed in those in whom he had placed trust.

Not only had the Comstock firm overdrawn their account, but they had left the Bank of California greatly embarrassed. As a large percentage of the Bank's capital had been involved, Ralston feared that its security had been jeopardized.

Besides, it was imperative to continue the business relationship with the Comstock Lode. Not only did the safety of the bank depend upon the continued productivity of the mines, but also on salvaging as much as possible from the defunct Stateler and Arrington account.

On account of the seriousness of the situation, Ralston resolved to send Edney S. Tibbey, his receiving teller, one of the most reliable men in his employ, to Virginia City. Tibbey was thoroughly familiar with the bank and its mining loans.

He understood Ralston, and Ralston understood him. For such an important post, Tibbey was the logical choice. He could be trusted. One day Ralston sent for Tibbey to come to his office. He explained to him about the Stateler and Arrington failure, their account and the importance of the Lode investments.

Would Tibbey "go up there?"

Tibbey replied that he would.

Ralston took up the appointment with the directors. Finally, it was agreed that Tibbey should be shifted to Virginia City.

Tibbey made ready to depart. He even had the place of residence on his life insurance policy changed from San Francisco to Virginia City.

When Colonel Fry and Wakelee heard of this Comstock opening, they came to Ralston: he must consider Sharon for the position.

Ralston, though favorably impressed, hesitated. Sharon was hardly the man for the emergency. He knew nothing about the mining game. Besides, Ralston had made final arrangements.

When Fry and Wakelee found out about Tibbey, they offered to pay Sharon's $15,000 bond which the bank demanded. Still Ralston did not like the idea. Virginia City would require a man familiar with the home bank and its investments, he explained. Sharon knew nothing about banking.

Fry and Wakelee were insistent. Always liking to please his friends, Ralston allowed himself to be persuaded. Sharon was slated for the appointment. One day he came to Ralston's office for final instructions. Ralston outlined the importance of the Comstock to the Bank of California and to San Francisco's development. Did Sharon think he could handle the situation?

But Sharon was hardly listening to what Ralston was proposing. Past events still lay too heavily upon his mind.

"I'll get even," he swore, as he left Ralston's office to take up his duties in Virginia City. "I'll get even with the Comstock yet."

CHAPTER V

A PERILOUS POSITION

1864

At the last moment Ralston weakened. He dispatched his brother, James Alpheus Ralston, to Virginia City. He was far from confident that Sharon could straighten out the Bank of California's tangled affairs on the Comstock. In the meantime Brother James would be a check upon his movements.

On the heels of his stock-market fiasco, Bill Sharon arrived in Virginia City and put up at the International Hotel on "C" Street. Not only was he bent on getting even with the Comstock Lode, but he was determined to justify Ralston's faith in him. Not every banker would have entrusted matters of such colossal import to one who had so lately lost his money. And Sharon intended to prove to the directors that Ralston's choice had not been misplaced.

By the time of his arrival, Wells Fargo & Co. had carefully sifted the Stateler and Arrington securities and appropriated the cream to satisfy their own account. From the remainder, Sharon chose so wisely that the Bank of California recovered nearly the full amount of Ralston's advancements.

Sharon's able execution of this matter pleased Ralston, but did not lessen his worries. Unfortunately, aside from the Stateler and Arrington account, the greater part of the Bank's capital was tied up in Comstock mines and mills. And mine security meant ore: potential and actual. Failure of those deposits would mean the failure of the whole woof and warp of the Pacific Coast's financial fabric. So closely had the business life of San Francisco, affairs of the Bank of California, and production on the Comstock Lode become interwoven. When Ralston had made those investments, he believed with all speculative San Francisco that the Comstock Lode was as inexhaustible as the mines of Peru. Like the Bank of England or the Rock of Gibraltar, he had felt that the mines would endure forever and would withstand any amount of financial shock. Convinced of that opinion, he had poured the Bank's capital into Washoe mines and mills, without stint.

When he had finished the Stateler and Arrington matter, Sharon began examining the general Virginia City situation. The financial outlook was dismal. Sharon could see that Ralston was in an embarrassing position. Where could he get enough ore to feed those mills, to which the bank had made big commitments? One by one, Sharon visited the mines: the "Ophir," the "Gould and Curry," the "Chollar," the "Belcher," the "Yellow Jacket," and a score of other hitherto promising properties in which Ralston had tied up his capital. Down he went into their dripping shafts: in every one, to be stopped by water. Try as he would in any one of them he could not go below the 500-foot level, not even if he had donned a diving-suit, for the water in the sumps was dark, offensive, and scalding hot. Poisonous gases pricked at his eyes, burned his lungs and made his head swim. The moist, ill-smelling air sickened him.

In every shaft pumps were groaning and grating. Every stroke proclaiming louder than words that the task of lifting those underground floods to the surface was too great for machinery. Every sense convinced Sharon that the great Lode was drowned out. Where could Ralston find the means to relieve the Lode of water?

Sharon rounded up all the mining experts on the Comstock, and confronted them with the problem. He talked to foremen, to superintendents, to the miners themselves. The outlook was the gloomiest old Comstockers had yet faced.

Every one was dismayed by the unprecedented underground floods. Their conviction was fixed! The Comstock was not so much a played-out camp as a drowned-out one.

From the water question, Sharon turned to the Lode itself. He made himself as familiar as a geologist with its formation, its ore-bodies and their relationship to the barren portions as well as their relative positions one to the other. He studied the cost of lumber, of teaming, of ore reduction, of operating hoists, of pumping and furnaces. The struggle of horse, ox, and mule to carry on the Comstock's gigantic lumbering and wood program was galling to him. Work on the Comstock was not systematized. Too many men had a finger in the pie.

Besides, he had assays made of the ore in every mine in which Ralston was interested—not one assay but many assays. Not trusting local assayers, he had one of his own nephews trained in the art. "We must have an ore expert in the family," he had explained. Together they had tested and retested. Checked and re-checked. Down to the very water-level in the mines tests ran high. In many cases the higher the assay the closer to the water-level, thus substantiating Sharon's belief that there was richer ore under the water than had as yet been uncovered. Deep mining was Ralston's salvation. They must get below the water-level.

Thus Sharon became somewhat of a mining expert: one of the best informed and most skillful then on the Comstock. No man on the Coast, not even Ralston, had so clear an understanding of the exotic conditions under which the Lode thrived, of the difficulties under which it was provisioned, mined, milled, supplied with water to drink and wood to burn.

After his examination was complete, Sharon came to a shrewd conclusion: he had reached the place where all the money on the Pacific Coast was coming from. But it was being mined and milled in an extravagant manner. Perhaps the Comstock was exhausted to the depth of 500 feet—but only perhaps? Below the ill-smelling sumps, Sharon felt assured, the Lode was alive with probabilities.

Below the water it would continue foot after foot, bonanza

beyond bonanza. All Ralston had to do was solve that problem. Sharon had absolute faith in Dame Nature. She was not given to eccentricities. One line of mineral gave promise of another. She might exhibit faults, even dance upon a tangent; but eventually she would get down to business. The Comstock was a fissure vein—a true fissure vein. Upon that, all geologists had agreed. Many times that fact had been decided beyond a scintilla of a doubt, in spite of the millions squandered to prove the opposite before packed juries and profligate judges.

Beyond the water, Sharon was confident, nature would continue to lay down her bonanzas, row after row of them, tier upon tier, like eggs in a crate. A future brighter than any past awaited the Comstock. The drowned could be resuscitated and made to live again. Ralston had no worries provided he would listen to him.

Sharon made two recommendations to his chief, first:

The Bank of California must monopolize the Comstock both above ground and below the earth's surface. It must control the water which the miners drank, the food they ate, the timber in the Sierra, all hauling and draying. Most of all the Bank must control every mine and mill on the Comstock Lode. Everything on the bald old mountain must be under Ralston's thumb, and he, William Sharon, must be his representative on the Lode.

Second: The water must be drained off the Lode. How? Sharon didn't know. But before anything could be accomplished they must get rid of that problem.

To accomplish these ends, Sharon suggested that Ralston should establish a branch of the Bank of California at Virginia City, which would carry on a general banking business of deposit, discount, and exchange, and should put him in charge as manager. In that way, Sharon pointed out, Ralston would at all times know the exact status of local mining operations, of all collateral, industries, and enterprises. The financial pulse of the Comstock, as it were, would throb under his thumb and he could administer to the Lode's plethora or debility as the case might be.

Sharon insisted that Ralston, having risked great financial

outlays on mining enterprises, should know every detail of their operations and have the power to control them. This could be accomplished only through founding a branch bank at Virginia City and appointing a manger. If Ralston would agree to this plan, Sharon promised to move to Virginia City, to devote the next five years of his life to the Comstock Lode and to salvaging the capital funds of the Bank of California.

Daring operator that he was, the future of the Comstock Lode filled Ralston with qualms. If the mines should fail, if there was nothing beyond the sumps but porphyry, how could he extricate himself? What would become of the large sums already advanced upon milling and mining property? The capital of the Bank of California would be lost. His dream of a greater San Francisco would be more fallacious than a desert mirage. Mills, machinery, all the towns of Washoe would be worthless if the fissure continued barren below the water-level. Collapse of the mines would mean collapse of the Bank of California and all its subsidiaries. It was a sickening thought. He was inextricably involved.

Ralston clung to Sharon's recommendations as the drowning to a straw. He had not failed to mark Sharon's shrewd intelligence, his boldness of enterprise, his strength of will and perseverance. In the end, in spite of initial doubts, he was convinced. If any one could salvage the Comstock, Sharon would; and he determined that a branch bank must be established in Virginia City and that Sharon must be put in charge. But the Bank's directorate was not so confident. They favored the project of a Bank branch, but they did not second the appointment of Sharon as manager. They were technical in their regard of men. They had amassed their possessions by care. They held them by watchfulness. Sharon was a plunger. With one misstep, he had lost his wealth. No, Sharon was not the man for this emergency. A far saner individual, not a gambler, was required.

"A man who has lost his own fortune," announced one director, "is not the most suitable person to administer the affairs and fortunes of others."

But Ralston was determined. He knew the stock market, he knew the treacherous manner in which Sharon had lost his estate. He also knew all the care, forethought, and knowledge that had gone into the making of that fortune. Failure had added to Sharon's stature. Ralston made up his mind quickly: Sharon was the only man for the Comstock job. The directors must yield.

But the directors were not convinced. One day it was brought out in meeting that Sharon was a confirmed poker player.

Ralston listened with amusement to this random gossip. He was only interested in one thing.

"Does he play poker well?" he queried.

"No one on the Coast can play better," came the reply.

"There," affirmed Ralston. "Sharon is the very man we want."

Ralston pressed his advantage. As usual the directors yielded to Ralston. After all, they had perfect confidence in his masterly methods. Had he not raised the Bank of California to foremost rank among financial institutions on the Pacific Coast? Did he not give them a one per cent dividend every month? Never had they seen any one make money as Ralston did.

On the 6th of September, 1864, in the quarters lately occupied by Arnold and Blauvelt, on the corner of C and Taylor Street, a branch of the Bank of California was founded. The wily William Sharon was put in charge.

With no illusions left, Sharon's one idea was to get even with the thing that had almost destroyed him.

CHAPTER VI

WATER

1864–1865

"Water, water, everywhere!"

Nothing in sight but water.

Interminable floods of subterranean water. Dry as the Lode was on the surface, underground it was as wet as the bottom of the sea. Mine after mine was afflicted by the influx. Water that neither man, ingenuity, pump, nor engine could handle. All of Sharon's reports began and ended with the scuttling of the mines.

While Sharon was probing and inspecting old ground in the "Chollar" and "Yellow Jacket," Ralston began to have misgivings. Every report from Virginia City bore but one import—water. Apparently there was to be no end to the fight against it.

Perhaps Sharon was right—perhaps there were undiscovered bonanzas in the "Ophir," "Gould and Curry," "Best and Belcher," "Chollar," or "Yellow Jacket." Bonanzas richer than any yet disclosed. But what good would they be if they were submerged in water and vaporous heat? Who could tap them or even reach them? It was not a question of pick or shovel or crowbar, but of hoisting-tanks and some bailing-out method. Such were the problems that crowded Ralston.

Nor could Ralston get the most out of his underground workmen. They were fear-ridden. Every second, dread of hidden reservoirs of pent-up water in unseen chambers assailed them. Their blasts would liberate a flood. They would be drowned like rats in a tunnel. With every stroke of the pick against the header, they would look for a trickle or spout of water. Before swinging it again they would listen for the throb of the pumps. It was horrible to work in darkness consumed always by fear of pent-up water.

Once an unwary "Ophir" miner, working in the semi-darkness of the 400-foot level, had plunged his pick through a clay-seam. To his surprise a stream of hot water had shot out of the opening, almost knocking the workmen over. One miner had been badly scalded. Another had been caught and killed. Others had run, barely escaping with their lives.

Fifty hours later, candles in hand, the miners had returned to the drift to investigate. What did they find in that stygian darkness? A subterranean lake of hot, steaming, ill-smelling water, 100 feet long, 30 feet wide, and 21 feet deep. The glow from their candles burned feebly in the oxygen-impoverished atmosphere and threw a sickly track of light across its turgid surface.

Hardly had that lake been drained than another "water-pocket" was tapped and the miners set racing for ladders and safety. The day following had disclosed a well of water, 160 feet deep, at the bottom of the shaft. Although the "Ophir's" ore-body had not exhausted itself, work had to be abandoned until more powerful pumps and more engine power could be engendered.

Water gave the Comstock such a discouraging outlook that Ralston would have recalled, if he could, every cent invested in the Lode.

Everywhere the same story repeated itself. The water seemed to lie in wait for the miners and dispute the ground with them inch by inch. Insentient monster that it was, it seemed endowed with human cunning. Foiled at one point, it would appear at another. When the miners were off guard and working in fancied security, it would creep up on them and scare them half to death. If they lopped off one head, a hundred others, with inexhaustible vigor, would crop out elsewhere.

When the shaft of "Central No. 1" sank to a depth of 562 feet and ran into a flood of hot water, the Company became disheartened and gave up the attempt of making further progress. Had they only had the fortitude to penetrate a little further! For the "Central" and all adjoining territory then belonged to Ralston's Ring.

In their turn, "Overman" workers were drowned out and the Company forced to suspend underground operations. When "Yellow Jacket's" shaft reached a depth of 317 feet, an unsuspecting pick-prick liberated a stream of water 2½ inches in breadth. Swiftly the works had been flooded and another mine had to be surrendered to the hundred-headed hydra that was uprearing its head in practically every shaft on the Lode. It was as if those floods were trying to warn Ralston in time, and drive him away from Washoe forever.

But Ralston responded to these inundations with greater vigor. In the "Gould and Curry," which had become one of the wettest shafts on the Lode, he had installed a monster engine and pump, designed and built by the Vulcan Iron Works on Third Street, San Francisco. When finished, he had it set up in a rock-hewn chamber 42x22 feet, 200 feet below the earth's surface. To give this colossal engine proper support, a massive foundation of stone, 22 feet long, 8 feet wide, and 16 feet deep, had been laid. To this ponderous groundwork, the engine's bed-plates were securely clamped with iron bolts. With this Vulcan-constructed pump Ralston felt he had worsted the subterranean floods.

After the installation, the superintendent, the foreman, and a delegation of San Francisco officials, many of them in broadcloth and silk hats, were lowered into the shaft and took up their positions. When all was ready, a signal was given. Slowly the huge iron machine, like a great antediluvian sloth coming to life, began to move and hiss. Then the friction wheels of the hoisting gear, ten feet in diameter, began to revolve. Gradually the water in the sump was seen to recede. There was great rejoicing. So pleased was the superintendent with the result that chilled champagne and Russian caviar, previously provided, were served. Standing, all drank a toast to the Vulcan pump, which had worsted the Comstock's bitterest enemy: water.

One day, eight months later, the aqueous monster tore that

fifty-horsepower Vulcan engine from its foundations. Was there ever anything more discouraging?

The sinking of the shaft had to be discontinued. Ralston was disgusted but only for a moment. Comstock floods must be subdued. From a San Francisco foundry he ordered an engine of 120 horsepower, a bigger boiler and a new pump bob, capable of reverse motion. By then, the "Gould and Curry" had reached a depth of 725 feet, but 100 feet of water stood in the sump. Daily the evil-smelling monstrosity was rising higher in the shaft. Almost a year had elapsed before he could turn the power of those 120 horses against the sump.

In the meantime it began to look to Ralston as if the Comstock Lode had met the fate of the Real del Monte in Durango or the Quebradilla in Zacatecas, or that of the rich mines of Guanaxuato.

Not only the fate of the Comstock, but the fate of San Francisco was dependent on the war which iron and steel pump must wage against water.

Never had Ralston dreamed that he would be forced to resort to such drastic measures.

CHAPTER VII

THE KEY TO THE MOUNTAIN

1865–1866

It was Adolph Sutro.

Tall, dark-haired, massive physically, with the look of a dreamer, and the burning eyes of a seer. Resolution, determination, ambition exuded from every pore.

Like every one else in need of assistance, Sutro had come

to Ralston's office at the Bank of California. He needed financial help to drive a tunnel from the banks of the Carson River through Mt. Davidson to the Comstock Lode—a distance of four miles. He intended to drain the Comstock mines. Of one thing Sutro was absolutely convinced: its necessity. From the beginning the construction of such a tunnel had been self-evident. Such a bore would draw the water from every inch of the Lode. If Ralston would help him, morally as well as financially, the construction of the projected sewer would be a foregone conclusion. No longer would Ralston have to worry about underground floods.

As soon as he had seen the topography of the Comstock country, away back in the spring of 1860, the idea of a tunnel to mine the Lode had flashed, flame-like, through Sutro's mind. The intervening four or five years had added brands to the fire of that earlier enthusiasm. Nothing since had been able to dampen his ardor, neither five years of merciless ridicule nor a wilderness of indifference. He was not even discouraged when such mining engineers as the country afforded denounced his idea as Utopian or chimerical. When mine managers had refused to listen to his tunnel project as the ravings of a monomaniac, he had kept right on broaching the subject on every possible occasion. He was convinced a four-mile drainway was practicable.

Probably Ralston, too, would have failed to listen to a plan so fantastic were not the foundations of the Bank of California threatened by the floods of water which were undermining the Lode. Better than any one else Ralston realized that a cheap and effective means of ridding the Lode of water was the Bank's only salvation. In such a predicament it behooved him to listen even to a lunatic.

While Sutro outlined his project, Ralston was tearing papers into shreds and letting them fall between his fingers into the basket. He could listen more intently that way.

He intended to begin his tunnel on the banks of the Carson River and drive it straight toward the heart of the Comstock Lode, Sutro was saying. Somewhere between the "Ophir" and "Yellow Jacket," probably at the "Savage," the tunnel would bisect the Lode. At its deepest part it would be 1800 feet below familiar Virginia City streets. When finished it would be over four miles long.

It was a gigantic project, the like of which had never before been attempted in the West. It would be the most important piece of engineering in America. The eyes of Sutro burned like coals as he talked about his bore. Its very magnitude fascinated Ralston. Nothing he liked better than being connected with large conceptions. Such a tunnel, as Sutro proposed, would drain every mine on the Lode. In doing that, it would uncover many a "blind bonanza." At the same time the tunnel would ventilate the mines. No longer would there be danger from working in a deadly gas-ridden atmosphere nor in sweltering heat. There would be no more pneumonia, no more miner's consumption. No more back-breaking loading of ore-wagons. No more heartbreaking hauling for ox and mule. Ralston's river mills would be connected directly with his ledges. Down the shafts would drop his loaded ore-cars, out through the tunnel they would run to dump themselves automatically into his own ore-bins in the mills along the river banks. It was a superb conception.

With his quick perceptions Ralston grasped the full significance of the projected bore. Deeper mining would become practicable. It promised to salvage Bank of California investments. Once more the rich ledges of the "Ophir," "Gould and Curry," "Chollar," "Best and Belcher," "Yellow Jacket," would be freed of water; once more his mill-pans would clatter; once more the music of his stamps would arise like anthems to the heavens; once more there would be bullion galore in his bank. Once more there would be money to boost San Francisco industry. That was all that Ralston asked of the Comstock: to bring prosperity to California.

Neither did Sutro come to Ralston begging for help with only dreams and empty hands to offer. With indomitable courage he had gone a long way toward accomplishing his ends.

Already Sutro had had the projected tunnel-way surveyed. Already he had consulted world-renowned engineers regarding it. Baron Von Richthofen, the great Prussian mining expert, had come expressly from Germany, at the solicitation of Sutro, to pass judgment on his scheme.

The Comstock was a true fissure vein of extraordinary length and breadth, the Baron had reported. It extended downward much farther than any known mining machinery would permit man to operate. Therefore, a tunnel was the only economical way to mine the Comstock. The only mechanical way to reach levels below the water.

Already Sutro had organized a corporation, the Sutro Tunnel Company, to drive the underground passage. No less a dynamic personage than Bill Stewart, William M. Stewart, United States Senator from Nevada, was president. Louis Janin, Jr., the well-known Pacific mining engineer, D. E. Avery, and H. R. Mitchell were trustees.

In the fall of 1864, with commendable foresight, Sutro had appeared before the Nevada State Legislature and outlined his project. Although the majority of the legislators had ridiculed the idea and had told Sutro to his face that he was hopelessly insane to propose a tunnel of a kind he could never carry out, on February 4, 1865, they had laughingly but unanimously granted him a franchise and right of way through Mt. Davidson to the Lode. At the time it looked as probable of accomplishment as a trip to the moon.

Now the only thing that Sutro lacked to put his project into action was money. His fingers fairly itched for gold. And that was the reason he had come to Ralston. He could not proceed without the approbation and assistance of the great central figure in the Bank of California and the mining and milling companies directly under his supervision. Would Ralston come to his rescue? Would Ralston make him a loan?

No one was more anxious to help Sutro than Ralston. No one could appreciate better than he the great benefits which would accrue to the Bank to say nothing of the whole Pacific Coast, if Sutro succeeded in securing the permanent drainage of the Comstock Lode.

Ralston, thereupon, promised Sutro to do everything in his power to help him carry out his great scheme. Gladly would he endorse Sutro's proposition to all the mining companies under the Bank's jurisdiction as well as to all others operating in Virginia City.

Accordingly, on March 1, 1865, Ralston indited a personal appeal which was destined to reach every mining company then operating on the Comstock Lode. In it he thoroughly endorsed the Sutro Tunnel project and asked every company to give Sutro such assistance as lay in its power. On the heels of these entreaties, Sutro went to work.

Even with the help of these Ralston letters, and all his persuasive talent, it took Sutro eight months of persevering labor to finish these contracts. By March, 1866, he was back at Ralston's office in the Bank of California. During that time he had succeeded in signing up twenty-three of the principal mining companies. Those twenty-three represented the cream: 95 per cent of the market value of all the mines on the Comstock Lode.

By these contracts the twenty-three representatives of the Bank of California, who signed the articles of agreement, bound themselves to pay in perpetuity the sum of $2 for every ton of ore extracted from their respective mines, after the extension of the tunnel and its lateral drifts within their boundaries. At the same time they agreed to the payment of stipulated sums for the transport of men, rock, timber, and tools. On his part, to guarantee the completion of the drainway within a reasonable period, Sutro promised to secure subscriptions amounting to $3,000,000 before the 1st of August, 1867, and to devote $400,000 yearly to the completion of the enterprise.

All of this preamble was pleasing to Ralston. He regarded the $2 royalty as a mere bagatelle. If the tunnel drained the mines, $2 would not be adequate compensation for the manifold benefits conferred on him, the Bank, and all concerned. Under such conditions even a royalty of $6–$8 per ton would not be excessive.

As much as he favored the project, as much as he anticipated its completion, still Ralston realized that neither he nor the Bank of California syndicate had $3,000,000 to loan to Sutro. Nor if he had had it, would he have risked further funds in an adventure that could not pay interest for years to come. Already he had enough frozen mining assets.

Sutro must raise those $3,000,000 elsewhere—in New York perhaps or abroad, where rates of interest were cheaper. This decision did not dampen Sutro's ardor. For such a project, and with Ralston's backing, he could easily raise the money in New York and he made ready to depart.

On May 4, 1866, Sutro made a final visit to Ralston's office. At that time Ralston furnished him with letters of introduction to Leese and Waller, the Bank's correspondents in New York, and to other banks there and in London. In every one of these letters, Ralston stressed the fact that so far as the Comstock Lode was concerned, the Sutro Tunnel was practicable. Therefore it could not fail to be profitable.

One of these letters Ralston addressed to the Oriental Bank Corporation in London, with which his bank did a large business:

THE BANK OF CALIFORNIA

D. O. Mills, *President* — W. C. Ralston, *Cashier*

"San Francisco, May 4, 1866.

"To the Oriental Bank Corporation, London.

"Dear Sirs:

"This letter will be presented to you by Mr. A. Sutro, of this city, who visits England with the view of laying before capitalists there a very important enterprise, projected by himself, and known as the 'Sutro Tunnel,' in the State of Nevada. This tunnel is designed to cut the great Comstock Lode or ledge, upon which our richest silver mines are located, at a depth of two thousand feet from the surface, to drain it of water, render it easily accessible at that point, and thus increase the facilities and diminish the expenses of the progressive development of these mines.

"Too much cannot be said of the great importance of this work, if practicable upon any remunerative basis. We learn that the scheme has been very carefully examined by scientific men, and *that they unhesitatingly pronounced in*

its favor on all points—practicability, profit, and great public utility. Mr. Sutro, we presume, is furnished with the necessary documents to make this apparent; and our object in this letter is simply to gain for him, through your kindness, such an introduction as will enable him to present his enterprise to the public fairly and upon its merits.

"Commending Mr. Sutro to your courteous attention, we remain, dear sirs, your very truly,

W. C. Ralston,
Cashier."

Armed with Ralston's letters, Sutro left for the East. First he would go to Washington to get certain rights from the United States Government. He must have a fee to the public domain. Then he would go to New York and perhaps to Europe for the purpose of negotiating stock or obtaining pecuniary loans that would be required to carry out the work. With Sutro went Ralston's best wishes.

If Sutro could drain off the water from the Comstock Ledges, Ralston's worries would be at an end.

CHAPTER VIII

COMSTOCK AGENCY OF THE BANK OF CALIFORNIA

1865

Apprehension as to his investments drove Ralston into big business. He must get a strangle hold on the Comstock. He must force the small fry out. The Bank of California must be as omniscient in mining circles as it was in San Francisco. Everything on the Comstock must be controlled by him or quit. No interference could be tolerated. Accordingly, he mapped his program.

All other Virginia City banks, such as Wells Fargo & Co., with Homer S. King as cashier; Paxton and Thornburgh; Ruhling & Co.; and B. F. Hastings, with Joseph L. King as clerk, were making loans to mine and mill owners at the rate of 3 per cent to 5 per cent a month.

Ralston changed all this. To get business, he reduced the prevailing rate of interest to 1¼ per cent, even to 1 per cent when necessary. With commendable assurance he advertised he would take certificates of stock as well as property as security. As a consequence, mill and mine owners found it to their advantage to borrow from Ralston at the lower rate of interest and to change their accounts from the Wells Fargo and other banks to the new agency. Before long, Ralston's branch bank had made loans of varying degrees to all the biggest and most important mills and mines. He wasn't interested in the smaller ones. He would take care of them later. In his safes certificates of stock began to pile up. They could be used for voting purposes and hence for control of the San Francisco stock market.

As long as ore bodies had endured, the mills could easily pay interest and make money; but as soon as the ore product began to dwindle, the music of the stamps ceased and mill owners found themselves at the bank. They could not pay the interest on their loans. But Sharon would not listen to any tales of woe. "Business was business," he told the owners when they appealed for time. Mercilessly, down he clamped when interest failed to materialize promptly. Pay or surrender. That was the ultimatum. This was all part of Ralston's program. No exceptions were to be made. The Ring must control.

First the "Swansea," one of the finest mills on the Lode, in a twelvemonth seven other large equipped quartz mills, with all their water right contracts and privileges, came into the Bank's clutches. Before long, ten to thirteen others fell into the hands of the agency.

When a mill, to which Sharon had made a loan, did not capitulate as rapidly as he felt it should, that mill was starved into submission. The amount of ore supplied would be cut to a minimum. In a short time the owner would find that he could not pay his workmen, let alone his interest. Then that mill, too, would surrender. If mine owners objected to this high-handed policy, they were told they could expect no more loans. Thus, one after the other, all the big mills, that the Bank had had their eyes upon, fell into the Bank's possession. Neither did the California institution mind the ruthless reputation it was earning on "C" Street. With so much at stake, they could not afford to be squeamish. What matter what disgruntled mine and mill owners thought? The Bank must be protected at all hazards.

All this time while mill property was capitulating and stock certificates were piling up in Ralston's vaults, water was rising higher in the sumps of his mines, gases were increasing in drifts and fire-damp was racing through his winzes. But no new bonanzas were discovered. With dread foreboding, Ralston realized that the underground water had not been conquered. How could shafts sink deeper or another bonanza be found, under such conditions?

The atmosphere in Ralston's San Francisco office became increasingly gloomy. Disgruntled directors haunted his desk. They regretted the organization of the branch agency in Virginia City. What good had it done? It was a drain on the Bank's resources. It was costing money, not paying. What good were the twenty mills in the Bank's possession if they had failed to realize a tenth of their liabilities? What good were the mines? On account of the floods no one could get at their ore bodies. The directors became as despondent as the mine and mill owners in Virginia City. Some of the directors went to Ralston. They insisted that he close out this whole Virginia City business and stop the drain on their capital, abandon further effort there, realize what could be gotten out of the almost valueless assets and charge up the deficiency to profit and loss.

Ralston turned a deaf ear to such a proposition. The directors didn't realize what that would mean. It would be suicide. It would mean the failure of his San Francisco program. Nevertheless he was filled with apprehension. His quick perceptions grasped one fact after another. If the large sums he had loaned on the Comstock were lost the credit of the home institution would be impaired. That was an unbearable thought to his pride.

He summed up his strategy. It had been a failure. Mills had been bought for a song. But what good had that done? Unproductive mines and rusty ore crushers could not possibly relieve the heavy burden resting upon his shoulders.

For Ralston had become the Atlas of the Pacific. Upon his capable shoulders already rested the financial structure of the whole Pacific Coast. No one realized more bitterly than he that he could not sustain that position without the Comstock. His plans for a Pacific Empire, with San Francisco as the capital, had been founded on its continued support. Never had he dreamed that that great source of wealth could fail. He had counted on its continuance for centuries. With that idea in mind he had founded one manufactory after another in California.

By 1865, Ralston had taken over the defunct Mission Woolen Mills. He hated to see an industry that meant so much to California fail. Although, at the time, he was strapped for money, he had no intention of letting this occur.

For a long time wool had been a leading Pacific staple. Therefore wool was worth a gamble. With the Mission Woolen Factory out of existence it would mean that raw material would have to be shipped to remote countries to be woven into cloth before the goods would be ready for California consumption. Now Ralston corrected this economic absurdity by founding the Pacific and Mission Woolen Mills of San Francisco.

The factory buildings, partly built of stone, 793 feet long, 50 feet wide and two stories in height, occupied three blocks of land at 15th and Folsom Streets.

In his employ Ralston had 387 whites and 456 Chinese. The average payroll was $18,000 to $21,000 per month. The mills had a capacity of thirty-six sets of cards, 7000 spindles, and 87 broadlooms. In one year 2,300,000 pounds of California wool had been consumed.

Every year the department of hosiery, alone, turned out $200,000 worth of stockings. Their tweeds, shawls, flannels, and blankets were the equal of anything imported. Some of the cassimeres were things of remarkable beauty. Goods were dispatched everywhere; to Japan and China, and up and down the Pacific Coast. Sierra mining communities and California government presidios became absolutely dependent on Ralston's looms. The mills represented a land, building, and machinery investment of about $1,000,000. Behind that million-dollar investment had lain the potential wealth of the Comstock.

California's '49 civilization was not yet fifteen years old when her ranging sheep were harnessed to Ralston's mills and the product was reaching the Antipodes.

In addition to this, Ralston had founded the San Francisco and Pacific Sugar Refinery which occupied the largest buildings in the State, at the corner of Harrison and Eighth Streets. Here he employed 250 men. Every month the refinery turned out 35,000 gallons of golden syrup, 5000 barrels of white syrup, and 1000 tons of raw sugar. The products were shipped all over the West.

About the same time, Ralston had interested himself in the Buena Vista Vini-cultural Society. Italian grape-growers had been imported from the Mediterranean's sunny slopes. Vines of the Mission vintage had been crossed with newer imports. Six thousand acres of land in Sonoma and Los Angeles Counties had been acquired and 110,000 plants had been dispersed over a 400-acre vineyard. Soon red and white wines of surpassing flavor had made their appearance on the San Francisco market. In this venture, Ralston had associated himself with George W. Beaver, George H. Howard, F. L. Olmstead, and H. W. Carpenter.

With unfailing supplies of bullion in mind, silk-worms had been imported from China and Japan; mulberry trees from Russia; Shetland lambs from Scotland, and cattle from Hereford. There was no stint in developing California industry on a par with that of other countries.

When Peter Donohue had started building the San Francisco and San José Railroad it was Ralston who helped him to run his rails down the Santa Clara Valley. Again in 1869, when he wanted to extend his line to the tobacco fields of Gilroy, it had been the same Prince of Finance who had softened his worries. When Ralston saw carloads of fresh vegetables, fruit and sun-dried apples, prunes, and almonds being rushed daily to San Francisco markets, he had felt justified in the use of his funds. Besides, that railroad had inspired the beginning of his stables. Nothing Ralston relished more than fast horseflesh and racing his steeds against the San Francisco and San José time-table, and beating their schedule to Belmont. That rare sport begot some of the fastest racers in California.

Little by little the Comstock had exerted a profound influence in making Ralston land-minded. Less and less funds went into maritime development and more and more into mines, gravel beds, wheat-fields, vineyards, orchards, and railroad development. Twenty-five acres of tule land near Hunter's Point were being filled in and sold to the city. When it came to Sherman's Island, which had been the plaything of the Sacramento for ages, Ralston was determined to wrest it bodily from the river and give it over to wheat farming.

The weight of all these projects had grown heavier and heavier on the shoulders of Atlas Ralston, and he faced with dismay a future with no Comstock to bolster him. Something must be done.

In the midst of these worries, Sharon wrote for an advance of $750,000. He needed that sum to continue his explorations on the Comstock.

Was there ever a demand more absurd? Right then, Ralston needed $750,000 to support his flagging San Francisco industries. Not a penny more could he sink in Comstock sumps.

Greatly alarmed over the requisition, Ralston and Mills determined to visit the Comstock. Before leaving San Francisco, the Bank's directorate made it plain that they intended to demand Sharon's resignation at the next meeting. They were through sinking money in mining camps. From the beginning they had been correct. Sharon had not been the pilot to steer the Bank of California argosy into safer waters.

Meticulous and conservative Mills was determined on one point: they must write Comstock Lode affairs off Bank of California's books. Ruthlessly they must be slashed. Their Washoe experiment must be put down to bitter experience and forgotten. Ralston knew what that would mean to San Francisco.

On rode Mills and Ralston, as fast as stage and steed could travel, over the Sierra, down into the Valley of the Carson and up the Washoe range to the Comstock. By the time they arrived, Ralston could see that Mills was right. Never had he known a more depressing outlook.

The Comstock presented a picture as melancholy as Ralston's thoughts: the camp was in eclipse. Fast and furious the miners were emigrating to Austin, White Pine, Belmont, and other desert-rimmed mining districts. Cabins, hovels, hotels were being pulled down and packed on prairie schooners. Already the population had shrunk 50 per cent. Merchants had grown grim-faced. Bartenders had pawned their diamond studs. Long ago the denizens of the crib district had doused their red lamps and relighted them on the rim of the eastern desert.

Not a mine was in bonanza. Many were abandoned. Their dilapidated works had become the haunt of coyotes. Old dump piles were being reworked for scraps of pay ore. The prevailing feeling was one of discouragement. Ralston and Mills were alarmed. The leading financial institution of the Pacific Coast had allowed itself to become a mine-supply company to a mining camp. Now it was played out. Icy grew the feeling about Ralston's heart. Perhaps there were bonanzas beneath the water. But where was the pump to prove it? Where the engineer to purge prevailing dropsy?

When Ralston and Mills went into conference with Sharon they were of one mind: to close out the Comstock so far as the Bank was concerned; realize what could be obtained from almost valueless assets, and charge up the deficiency to profit and loss. Mills was determined to get the Bank of

California back into legitimate banking channels. What business had they dabbling in silver mines? That was not legitimate banking. He had said so all along. It was speculation. There must be an end of gambling.

When the conference opened, Sharon sensed it was the crucial moment of his career. But his cold black eyes were never bolder, his face never grayer, his expression never more inscrutable. What poker player could have foretold what trumps he held in his small shapely hand?

Sharon listened while Mills carefully outlined the firm determination of the Bank of California to abandon the Comstock and return to legitimate banking.

As soon as Mills had finished speaking, Sharon took the floor. Fortified with data and statistics, he exhibited in cold figures the enormous extravagance under which, in every department of administration and of operation, the affairs of the Comstock had been conducted while producing ore. After ore bodies had failed he pointed out that this extravagance had been continued at the expense of the Bank of California.

Sharon went on. Now all the mills, mortgaged up to the hilt, had fallen into the Bank's power. They could close them or keep them going as they saw fit. The most productive of the mines, due to loans made on stock certificates, had likewise fallen under the control of the Bank of California. It was the duty of the Ring to consolidate this control, to increase it, to elect mine directors whose management would be in accord with the wishes of the Bank. On he went, into the questions of timbering, teaming, provisioning, water rights. What fortunes had been made out of supplying the exotic Comstock! The Ring must control all these privileges. He envisioned the Bank with as many feelers as an octopus. Tentacles must extend into mine, mill, forest, toll roads, transport, stables, into the very body politic. Their suckers must drain every ounce of sustenance out of them into Bank coffers. Whoever heard of a bank running mills, mines, forests, stables? But that was what Sharon proposed.

Sharon laughed at the idea that the camp was played out. If the Comstock had produced 75 to 100 million dollars in its first 500 feet in depth, what would it disgorge in the next 500? The next 1000? It would be an anomaly in mining experience if it failed to disclose greater bonanzas at greater depth. True enough, the Lode was waterlogged. But a means could be found to drain it. Sutro was working on the problem. His tunnel would serve the purpose. The Bank must help him with a loan. Perhaps the Ring could dig the tunnel themselves. And he fortified his own beliefs by introducing into the conference the most capable experts and engineers on the Lode. All men were agreed on the benefits which would accrue to the Bank and the whole Pacific Coast when the Lode was drained and such bonanzas as were found were judiciously and economically worked.

Then he turned to the other side of the picture—the lugubrious side. Suppose, at this critical moment, the Bank should withdraw its support? What would happen? The Comstock would be abandoned. Miles of winzes would crumble. Years of development would be lost. Virginia City would be a ruin. The Bank would lose every dollar already in jeopardy. San Francisco could not escape financial catastrophe. With so much money invested, it would be a dark day for the Bank of California, a blacker one for the whole Pacific Coast. What of those bank-fostered industries—sugar refineries, woolen mills, railroads, foundries? They would go by the board. Without the mines, San Francisco would be crippled. Alone, she could not stand. The Comstock was her crutch. Take it away. Down she would topple. Her being was centered in Washoe. From there she drew her sustenance. Since California's gold crop had failed, silver and silver alone had maintained her. What would Mills and Ralston do? Destroy the city?

San Francisco had become Ralston's passion. Her future activated him. Her welfare was his last thought at night, his first in the morning. Their careers were one and indissoluble. San Francisco was his ambition. Her fall would be his ruin. Sharon knew those facts. He was gambling upon them now.

On he went rapidly. If the Bank of California would stand behind him they would levy assessments on the stockholders and explore. In the end it would cost the Bank nothing. Then they would take two of the most promising mines on the Lode, two at its southern end, where there was less water and hence less risk, and sink to a deeper level. On his way down he was bound to unearth a bonanza or two. During these explorations he would re-work, economically, such surface ore-bodies as had been neglected. These upper bodies would defray the cost of deeper exploration. As favorable points for such explorations, he suggested the "Chollar" shaft or the "Yellow Jacket" group in the Gold Hill district. All these properties were Bank controlled.

Mills had heard enough. "The Board of Directors of the Bank of California," he interrupted, "would not consent to take the risk."

Sharon turned toward Ralston. It was risk or ruin: which? Ralston wanted to take the chance. Sharon could tread where lesser men would fear to venture. With his help what might they not accomplish? Now that Sharon had pointed out the way, Ralston was ready to steer in that direction.

"I'll agree to be personally responsible," Ralston vouchsafed, "for any loss that may result to the Bank by its adoption of Sharon's plan."

The staid Mills was swayed by Ralston's guarantee. He knew of Ralston's great wealth. If Ralston would hold himself personally responsible for all losses, that was another matter. On those premises Sharon might proceed with his explorations.

As soon as they reached San Francisco, Ralston called a meeting of the Bank directors. Swept away by his enthusiasm and Mills' favorable opinion, those gentlemen, though unconvinced, passively yielded. Dividends alone interested them. Assessments were levied on the "Yellow Jacket" stockholders. Arrangements were made to open the mine.

So confident was Ralston of the gamble that he formed a partnership with Sharon: "On all transactions in San Francisco pertaining to real estate or stocks." Articles of partnership were drawn up and signed. By the irony of fate Tibbey had had to copy them. Ralston put his in an envelope, sealed it, and wrote upon the cover: "Contract of William Sharon to be delivered to W. C. Ralston only."

This agreement he locked up in the Bank's vault.

Away sailed the Bank argosy with Captain Ralston at the helm and Sharon as first mate.

CHAPTER IX

"KENTUCK'S" BONANZA

1865

While Sutro was seeking Eastern capital, Sharon was prospecting on the "Chollar" and "Yellow Jacket" properties. Those mines, at the southern end of the Lode, had been picked out as there was less water to impede explorations there than elsewhere.

Simultaneously, the shafts of the "Chollar" and the "Yellow Jacket" bit deeper into seams of yellow porphyry. Salaries were reduced and the work of salvaging Ralston's bank loans progressed as economically as possible. At the same time, all the mines over which Ralston had control were re-worked. Every cent of the profits was used to liquidate Bank liabilities. But the Virginia City miners had but little confidence in ultimate success. They regarded Ralston's explorations as the effort of a forlorn hope, giving only a spasmodic vitality to an exhausted lode. As for Sutro and his tunnel—they were the laughing stock of the Comstock.

Sharon felt keenly the responsibility of his position. He might be an old poker player, but never had he sat in on a game with stakes of such magnitude. Unless he discovered a new bonanza, and discovered it quickly, Ralston's Bank would founder on the difficulties which encompassed it.

sands would be ruined, and the friend who had helped him would be hopelessly involved. As for his own future, unless—the picture could not be blacker.

Heart and soul went into his work. Not only had he the affairs of the local bank to administer, but every detail of Ralston's mining and milling operations. But he employed his time well. If a promising body of ore in some mine was reported, Sharon would send for the shift-boss or foreman, and by hook or crook get the information wanted. Then the news would be wired to San Francisco. Stock of that mine would be "bulled" up and the market would be milked.

Every morning at dawn found Sharon going down some shaft. There with lantern and pick he would seek out the most promising places to dig, and the most talkative underground shift-bosses to pump.

Then there were the mills. If superintendents were sending ore to other than Bank-owned ones, they were threatened: no more loans from the Bank of California. Every night there were reports to be made out. The stockholders of this or that company must be assessed to keep the mines going. Ralston was kept in close touch with the work which meant financial life or death.

For more than a year there was nothing to report, no profits but small ones derived from re-working old ground. But Ralston was gratified. He could see that the work of exploration was being done systematically. Expenditures were diminishing. Every day Ralston wrote a letter spurring his emissary on, a bonanza must be found.

When "Crown Point" and "Yellow Jacket" disclosed little, Sharon sank a shaft in "Kentuck" to the depth of 100 feet. No ore was found. That was a disappointment to Ralston. Next Sharon ran a drift into "Kentuck" from the 230-foot level of the "Crown Point," which adjoined "Kentuck" on the south. "Yellow Jacket" lay next to and north of "Kentuck" from the level mentioned. In this drift he found a vein of promising ore. Feverishly he pursued it. With every inch the assays grew richer. Sharon was confident that he had gotten hold of something—just what he didn't know. He imparted his enthusiasm to Ralston. Ralston must purchase all outstanding "Kentuck" and "Yellow Jacket" stock. It was a gamble. The Bank was hopelessly involved. It was worth the chance.

While Ralston was in the market purchasing all outstanding stock, the vein slowly developed into a ledge of rich ore. Wider and wider it grew. The news reached California Street. Wild rumors were afloat. Stock soared. Shares sold on the San Francisco Stock Market for $500. Sharon had discovered a bonanza. Before the end of 1865 it had yielded two million dollars. Subsequently, $2,905,000 more.

The miners no longer looked on Sharon as visionary. The directors of the Bank of California grew more confident in his judgment. Ralston triumphed in Sharon's success and his own escape. The pressure on the Bank loosened its hold. More and more he believed in himeslf and the Comstock: his foresight; and the Ledge's future. The dread of a run was abated. The ore discovered was followed to a depth of several hundred feet, always profitably.

A controlling interest in the stock of "Yellow Jacket" and "Chollar" followed. Vigorously Sharon pushed explorations in those mines. In both he discovered large bodies of pay ore which produced many millions of dollars. Payment of dividends was resumed. Rich returns poured into the Bank directorate. The Bank refinery filled with bullion. Ralston was jubilant. His faith in Sharon had justified itself. His star was in its ascendancy. Why had he ever doubted? For several succeeding years the three mines fanned the flame of public faith in the Comstock and stimulated exploration by other companies at other points along the Lode.

Stock boomed in the San Francisco Stock Market. Daily the streets before the Exchange were crowded with excited men and women. Incredible fortunes were made and the veiled women in black with diamond-studded ears multiplied by the score.

Ralston, with millions flowing in from the Comstock Lode, rebounded like a rubber ball suddenly released from pressure. Now he would have money to do those things for San Francisco and California that he had always wanted to do.

CHAPTER X

SUCCESS

1866–1867

By August, 1866, Adolph Sutro was back in Ralston's office in the Bank of California, facing the smiling, ruddy-complexioned banker across the green expanse of his baize-covered desk.

Since spring, Sutro had travelled hundreds of miles in behalf of the tunnel that was to drain the mines in which Ralston was interested. He had been in Washington, D. C. He had been in New York City. He had appeared before Congress. He had interviewed the foremost statesmen of the United States. All of them had been acquainted with facts concerning his great work: the Sutro Tunnel. Washington had lent a favorable ear to his proposition. New Yorkers had promised to raise a working capital of $3,000,000 just as soon as Sutro could provide "home-indorsements." It was in behalf of those provisions that Sutro was back so swiftly in Ralston's office.

Ralston was in a better financial condition than he had been when Sutro had gone East to raise funds to drain the Lode. His mines had not been unusually bothered by water and his pumps were working well. Nevertheless he listened carefully to all Sutro had to say and Sutro had a-plenty to tell, and he told it eagerly with flushed cheeks and flashing eye. He had made a contract with the United States Government. Even the President of the United States had ratified his privileges. On the 25th of July a law of Congress had been approved granting him a right of way through the earth, from the foothills of the Carson River, direct to the Comstock Lode, a distance of 20,489 feet.

Besides, Congress had confirmed his title to 1280 acres of land at the mouth of the tunnel, which he already owned by location, and the right of claim to such veins of ore as he might cut in driving his tunnel towards its goal. Most important of all, the Government had confirmed the two-dollar royalty rate, to be paid by the mining companies, on every ton of ore transmitted through the finished tunnel. Further, it had made their title, the very patents of Ralston's mining companies, subject to the paying of that royalty.

That two-dollar compulsory tax was not pleasant news to Ralston, nor would it be to the members of his Ring. It was excessive. But without interrupting he allowed Sutro to go on with his story. It had been absolutely necessary to have those Government rights, Sutro concluded. When the bill had been presented in Congress, the representatives from California and Nevada had agreed and the bill, which he had so earnestly desired, had become a law.

Fortified with his Government sanctions and contracts, he had hurried to New York, no longer anticipating any trouble in raising $3,000,000 to complete the tunnel. The more clearly to demonstrate the tunnel's absolute necessity to Comstock mining and its possibilities as a money-making scheme, he had written a little booklet, and had had it published at his own expense. On arrival in New York he had distributed copies among the city's most intelligent and prominent investors.

Among others to whom he had sent copies were Commodore Cornelius Vanderbilt, William B. Astor, Peter Cooper, August Belmont, R. L. Cutting, M. Morgan's Sons, Eugene Kelly, J. C. Frémont, and Seligman & Co.

These men, although dumbfounded at the magnitude of the proposed bore and its almost impossible accomplishment, had taken a profound interest in the project.

But immediately a fatal objection had presented itself to them. Sutro had no "home-indorsement." If the proposed tunnel was of such prime importance to Bank of California mines as he said, why had Sutro not been able to raise at least a part of the construction funds in California? Ralston's integrity and financial standing were well known in New York's financial district. If the drainway was so important why had Ralston not subscribed to its building?

This same question was brought up by Commodore Vanderbilt. Vanderbilt could recall Ralston. His association with him on the Isthmus—his connection with him in New York. Besides, he was aware of Ralston's association with the Comstock mines. Why hadn't Ralston subscribed to this tunnel which would drain the very mines in which his bank was known to be heavily interested? Vanderbilt, as well as other New York tycoons, felt keenly that the lack of "home-indorsement" was a serious drawback to the proposed drainway—a lack which created a suspicion that something lay behind the scenes. What was it? Perhaps the tunnel was not such a great project as it appeared in blueprint. Before they would go any further they must have Ralston's indorsement to brush these suspicions away.

In the end these gentlemen had advised him not to waste any more time in New York nor in going to Europe trying to raise $3,000,000. The thing for him to do was to go right back to San Francisco and get the work started.

"Let some of the leading men on your coast," counselled others, "form a preliminary board of directors. . . ." If he would go back and raise four or five hundred thousand dollars in California and commence work on his tunnel they would promise to get $3,000,000 for him in the East.

Convinced that this was the course to follow, he had requested those New Yorkers to express their views in a communication which he might submit to Ralston and the mining companies under his jurisdiction.

As a consequence they had drawn up such a letter. With it he had set out for San Francisco. As he finished speaking, Sutro drew the letter out of his pocket. Ralston read it. He could see that it was signed by the foremost financiers in New York. Now Sutro put the question to him.

Would Ralston and his companies raise an initial fund —so that Eastern financiers would know of the Bank of

California's attitude and so that he could commence work? He must have a "home-indorsement."

Ralston needed time. He would take up the matter with his Ring. While this discussion was progressing, Sutro went up to the Comstock Lode.

By chance the Nevada legislature was in session when he arrived, and Sutro decided to appeal to them for an indorsement. So forcibly did Sutro impress the legislators with the necessity of the tunnel, its future value, not only to the State, but to the nation, that he prevailed upon them to pass a memorial asking Congress to make him a loan. This resolution was drawn up in handsome printed form. Among other things the book cited the tunnel's politico-economical significance to the nation: it would increase national revenues; but foremost, it would help to pay the national debt.

In the meantime, Ralston consulted Sharon and both of them put their heads together with other Comstock mine owners and capitalists. Subscriptions to the tunnel were fully discussed. After some delay it was decided to indorse Sutro's tunnel project. A number of Ralston's companies subscribed through their trustees sums aggregating together, with subscriptions from private persons, about $600,000. Sutro was overjoyed at this news—already over half-a-million dollars subscribed. In a few weeks there seemed every prospect of seeing this sum increased, in San Francisco alone to $1,000,000 or more.

Sutro had never been so aware of success. The great Bank of California, supreme in the Pacific West in politics, in social matters and in business, had nodded its corporate head in wholehearted approval of his tunnel. Sutro knew what that meant. All the lesser magnates would nod their heads in assent. To Sutro, to California, to the mining world, to financiers all over the country, Ralston's nod bore but one significance. The Ring approved of the Sutro Tunnel. Such a drainway would be a great thing for Nevada, for California, for stockholders' dividends. When the mines were in borrasca, there would be tunnel dividends to carry them over. On the line of the tunnel new bonanzas might be developed.

Now Sutro felt that his troubles were well-nigh over. The great tunnel would be an accomplished fact. New Yorkers would supply the $3,000,000 working capital. Perhaps, later, there would be a governmental loan. The tunnel would be pushed to rapid completion. Soon there would be a town about the mouth of his proposed bore, a town filled with river mills, machine-shops and bustling with activity. Its name would be Sutro. Its promoter was supremely elated.

Then, one night, there was a secret conclave in San Francisco. Ralston, Sharon and all the Bank Ring were present. That Nevada legislators' memorial to Congress and the likelihood of a national loan had not pleased the Ring. Nor were they over-delighted with that two-dollar royalty. It would be a continual tax—an exorbitant levy for service rendered. Loans and taxes would make Sutro the richest man on the Coast. That would not be good. His wealth would be a threat to Ralston's supremacy. Besides, the question of water was not as baffling an obstacle as it had been to earlier explorations of the Lode. Apparently the water belt had been passed. They were working in a dry zone. Sharon had taken out three successive bonanzas with hardly any difficulties at all. Moreover, in the last few years Ralston had discovered many things about underground water. He had learned to measure its power. His San Franciso-made pumps were powerful enough to cope with any flood. Ralston knew that they were holding their own in the contest. For all practical purposes water on the Lode was conquered.

If water was vanquished, why should the Ring pay Sutro an exorbitant tax to drain it off? Why should they make Sutro a money power on the Coast—a potential rival of the Ring? Sutro was not one of them—and never would be. He must be crushed, he was a menace to their power.

Now the Bank of California nodded its corporate head in disapproval. Everybody knew what Ralston's displeasure could accomplish. Immediately, all financial heads on the

Pacific Coast were set wagging: Ralston did not want Sutro to build his tunnel. The Ring was against him. Sharon was working in a dry belt. Further, they did not want Sutro to get his hands on a Government subsidy. No—nor did they want New Yorkers mixed up with the Comstock monopoly. Together, business men in Virginia City and San Franicsco frowned in unison. The Comstock did not want Sutro's Tunnel, nor need his meddling. No! Nor Sutro! He must be outlawed financially—banished. He was nothing but a carpetbagger—trying to get a slice of the Comstock!

Quickly the Bank of California's edict went forth. The tunnel would never be constructed by Sutro, nor by any of his friends. He was far too independent to suit Ralston's Ring. He was beyond the pale of the controlling forces on the Lode. The Ring must prevail. On the Comstock, in San Francisco, the Ring must remain supreme. Ralston must be omnipotent in the West now and forevermore.

If the Bank of California had had a medieval crier, a muezzin, at this juncture and had he appeared upon the Bank's bronze balcony on California Street and proclaimed in stentorian tones to assembled San Franciscans: "There is no power on the Pacific but the Bank of California," he would have fully expressed the prevailing sentiment. There was only one acknowledged force in California, on the Comstock, in the West; and that was Ralston. Nothing must interfere with his vigor. Therefore Sutro's Tunnel could never be. It would be a potential threat to the Bank's omnipotence.

At once a telegram signed by Sharon and other Bank henchmen flashed across country to both of Nevada's United States Senators: Nye and Stewart at Washington. "We are opposed to the Sutro Tunnel project and desire it defeated," ran those messages. Instantly Senator Stewart wired to Sutro his resignation as president of his Tunnel Company. He had no intention of antagonizing the Bank of California. Washoe bad men, he could face; but not for an instant the displeasure of the great Bank of California. Well he knew that one frown from the august presence there and his Nevada political career, like a house of cards, would topple in ruins.

Suddenly Virginia City merchants and citizens discovered that they did not want the tunnel and began to fight Sutro and his scheme. Inside one hour Sutro's prospects of obtaining a million dollars on the Pacific Coast went a-glimmering. And telegrams expressing the Bank's attitude reached Lees and Waller their correspondents in New York, the Oriental Bank of London their British representatives, and other European connections. Everywhere on the Comstock, down Gold Cañon, in San Francisco, this opposition to the tunnel scheme was voiced and felt. Practically every person who had previously stood by Sutro deserted him. They shunned him on the street. They avoided him as if he had been a leper. Even to be seen talking with him was contamination. When one of Ralston's satellites spied Sutro walking towards him, he would cross over the street rather than risk a chance encounter. Every miserable bank hireling turned a cold shoulder on him. Actually afraid to let his masters see him in Sutro's company.

Sutro understood. He was a financial outlaw. For the first time he realized the immense, the overwhelming, the widely ramified power which the Bank of California exerted. Men knew, as if by magic, that Ralston and his Ring had proscribed him. To Sutro it seemed as if everybody had been informed of the fact at once and through some invisible power had received instructions as to how they were to behave. Sutro must be crushed physically and mentally. He must be used up financially. He must be driven out of the Comstock. He must be expelled from San Francisco and the West. He was a pariah.

Then and there a man of lesser fiber would have given up the fight and have died of a broken heart in the cold waters of the Bay. But not Sutro. At that time he was made of more tenacious, sterner stuff. He was not so easily disposed of. He was a born fighter. Openly he proclaimed that the Bank of California's opposition arose because they were alive to the tunnel's importance, to its financial possibilities.

They were robbers. They would steal his plan. They would build the tunnel themselves. They would try to secure help from Nevada. They would appropriate subsidies to themselves. They were traitors. They had beguiled him when they needed him. They had betrayed him when they didn't. They were rascals. They were liars. They were thieves.

Clearly Sutro saw the position into which the Bank of California had forced him. He would have to fight for a proposition which the very persons to be benefited declared against their interests. He would have to prove that Ralston and his Ring did not know what they were talking about. He would have to fight Ralston's whole machine, his subsidized newspapers, his publicized bosses, his political, financial and social power. It would be like fighting an octopus. What had he, one lone man, to fight them with? Neither wealth, nor backing, nor friends. Nothing but his bare fists, his wits, his determination; his resolute soul; his forcible pen and a logical tongue. He was unafraid. He would write: books, pamphlets. He would talk. He would shout: he began by calling names.

Ralston's Ring were "Traitors." "That was what they were: traitors." A pack of rascals. They had signed contracts with him. They had urged him and helped him to spend his and his friends' money. They had induced him to labor day and night for years. And how he had worked! With what zeal! With what enthusiasm!

After having known all that, Ralston was now determined to rob him of his idea, of his labors, to take the tunnel out of his hands, and defeat him in the hour of success. Ah! No! that Ralston would never accomplish. Never would the Bank succeed in its dastardly efforts. Never would he allow such abuse; never permit such an unscrupulous and mercenary combination as the Ring to carry out its purposes and drive him ignominiously to the wall.

He would fight them on their own ground, where their authority was supreme, their word law, their acts unquestioned, their insolence—their arrogance unbounded. He would fight them to a finish.

He made a sacred vow: in spite of Ralston's opposition

he would drive the Sutro Tunnel through the earth, through Mt. Davidson to the Lode. If he had to devote the balance of his life to it, if it took the last breath in his body, he would succeed.

CHAPTER XI

THE SILVER ERA

June, 1867

It was evident to Sutro that his tunnel project did not have an iota of a chance on the Pacific Coast. By throwing cold water over it and calling it visionary and impracticable, Ralston had discouraged all prospective stock buyers. Eagerly the empty-headed and envious took up the Bank's slogan: "Away with Sutro! Down with his tunnel!"

Sutro felt sorry for these detractors. He recognized in them that class which has opposed every great work from time immemorial. Whether it was cotton-gin, railroad or tunnel, they were the people who were afraid of progress. But in spite of a philosophic frame of mind, Sutro saw his obstacles multiply. At times they grew insurmountable. He could see only one cause for the failure of his plans: the unscrupulous avarice of Ralston's Ring. In his eyes it became a gigantic monopoly, grinding the faces of the poor, crushing every enterprise that interfered with its scheme of aggrandizement.

How was he to convince prospective investors when Ralston's Ring, the most successful men on the Coast, told them not to touch the tunnel? Neither would the Ring hesitate at anything. They would play upon prejudice. Finally, they threatened reprisal: if any business man in San Francisco assisted Sutro that one could never expect any financial help from the Bank of California.

Not satisfied with their hold upon financial San Francisco, the Ring switched their attention to Virginia City. By this time the gas, the water, the lumber companies had fallen under Bank control. The Ring had their agents go among the people and warn them: if the Sutro Tunnel were built the town would be ruined. Mines and mills would have to move to the mouth of the tunnel. Real estate would become a drug upon the market. Gas-works and water company would be useless. Jobs would be gone. Would Sutro find them new ones? Certainly not. Sutro was only interested in making an underground raid on the Comstock Lode, the Bank of California was interested in the man and his job.

Sutro did his utmost to combat the Ring's insidious propaganda. In vain he countered with the problems of underground water, lack of ventilation and poisoned gases. Unless the floods were drained off, the Comstock Lode would have to be abandoned. Ruin would desolate Mt. Davidson. Virginia City would be deserted. But neither Ralston's Ring nor the Comstock's population paid the least heed. The throbbing of the pumps reassured them: drifts were dry. Miners were working below the water-level. All was well on the Comstock. Witness "Kentuck's," "Chollar-Potosi's" and "Yellow Jacket's" bonanzas! Millions of dollars in bullion were answer enough to Sutro's claims. And the Bank was paying their wages.

Keenly Sutro felt the Ring's antagonism. He brooded over the servile attitude of its followers. It hurt him when erstwhile friends shunned him. When they passed him, pretending not to see him. It was mortifying to engage a chance acquaintance in conversation and to note his nervous hurry to be off before some bank henchman took note of the meeting. Every miserable hireling feared Ralston's Ring and kowtowed to it.

Then Sutro developed a profound contempt for these men. In his own heart he knew that he was working for an ideal: to help his fellow men. He knew his finished bore would bring the blessings of fresh air, light, safety, and a dry place to work to thousands of laboring men now compelled by the Ring to toil in the dark, damp bowels of the earth. Most of all he wanted to prove to the world how the Comstock should be mined. Upborne by his ideals, he continued his efforts, refusing to surrender to Ralston. Truth was mighty. It must prevail. Something would happen to give him his opening. In the end his enemies would come to grief. Victory must follow the right.

Sustained by these thoughts, Sutro decided for the time being to give up the California-Comstock field to Ralston's Ring. He would return to New York. There something would occur to enable him to commence the Sutro Tunnel and bring help to the down-trodden working man of Washoe. Gradually, no matter how selfish had been the initial idea of the bore, his struggles with Ralston's Ring were turning Sutro into a champion of the people.

On the 27th of June, 1867, while Sutro was journeying eastward in search of tunnel funds, and Sharon was plundering the Lode of bonanza after bonanza for his patron, Ralston moved his bank into a palatial new structure on the corner of California and Sansome streets. That an institution only four years old could house itself so magnificently was the wonder of California's Silver Age. Proud San Franciscans pointed out the bank to strangers as an evidence of the city's prosperity and Ralston's liberality. "Had there been no 'Kentuck' to gut," Sutro countered, "there would have been no palatial Bank of California to admire."

Only a few years since the site of Ralston's bank had been the playground of the Bay. Waves had gently lapped its shores. Sandpipers had scurried across its sunny strand. And overhead the lone seagull had cried on slanting pinion.

Then all had been changed. A Gargantuan discovery had been made. The Argonauts had come. Gigantic shovels had contended with the surf for the mastery of the spot. In the end machines had won. Block by block the vanquished sea had been driven back to a deeper, angrier channel.

More and more as time went on, Ralston aligned himself with the land. He was always reclaiming, always driving the surf back; always making fills; always raping the sea of a well-earned victory. Always selling his spoils in the market.

Into this redeemed sand-pit Ralston drove row after row of piles. On them slowly arose the blue-stone walls—the light and airy walls of Ralston's financial stronghold. For their architectural inspiration Ralston had harked back to the spot where his mind forever dwelt, the edge of the Orient: the "Libreria Vecchia," the library of Saint Mark in the Piazza di San Marco in Venice.

Sansovino had never conceived anything half so sumptuous for his Grand Canal masterpiece as Ralston planned to construct with his Comstock plunder. As his interpretation unfolded itself, the same happy blending of Doric and Ionic, of double colonnades, arches and embedded columns as distinguished the library in the ancient maritime city on the Adriatic, disclosed themselves. Any Doge would have been proud of Ralston's adaptation. Ancient Rome would have yielded a palm on the purity of his architectural triumph.

For constructive materials Ralston had turned to California's storehouses. The blue-stone walls were quarried, block by block, out of rock-ribbed Angel Island right in the midst of the Bay. There they had been polished until they shone like polished mirrors. Out of the same marble quarry had been carved the forty-two columns which ornamented the façade. Each one represented single blocks of stone weighing 4–8 tons. From there, too, had come those exquisitely modelled medallions which adorned exterior walls. They, too, were Venetian in feeling, and brilliant in execution.

The cornice was crowned by a graceful stone balustrade, upon whose piers rested vases as intricately fretted as that Romanesque one at Warwick. In front of second-story windows hung balconies with bronze railings. The doors, the great bronze one on California Street, which would have amazed Ghiberti, and the Sansome Street one and the private one to Ralston's office, were of masterly conception. On the roof were spread sheets of burnished copper.

Surrounded as the structure was by buildings of a more commercial aspect such as the Merchant's Exchange, Ralston's bank looked not unlike a swan, a graceful Lido swan, preening himself in the midst of barnyard fowl.

Within, Ralston's bank was equally well appointed. The floors were fashioned of alternate blocks of black and white marble. The ceiling, even as those Titian- and Tintoretto-tinted ones in the library on the Piazza di San Marco, were frescoed by capable artists. The windows were wide panes of plate glass. Before them swung venetian blinds of light-colored California wood. Wainscotings were of bird's-eye maple. Desks, doors and chairs, fashioned in Ralston's furniture factory, were of heavily carved, highly polished San Domingo mahogany. The mantels of black marble quarried at Folsom were worthy of a Doge's palace.

At the rear of receiving and paying counters, patrons of the Bank could see the large coin table piled high with even rows of the Comstock's gold coin. Directly opposite was the bullion department, where large quantities of Lode metal, at least $1,000,000 or $2,000,000 worth in value, were held in reserve. Over this department as of the whole bank, Ralston had sole control. He alone kept the key.

The safes were marvels of strength, security and beauty. Walls, sides and roof were constructed of plates of chilled iron, each three inches thick. Impenetrable, it was said, to burglars, but alas, not to the well-intentioned! The vaults on the main floor were of bronze. From recessed openings, over each door, protruded the bas-relief heads of wary watch-dogs, keeping bold and silent vigil over the treasure within. If only they had been less silent how admirable those vigils might have been!

To the rear of bank officials' offices was the directors' room—a lofty marble-panelled apartment with frescoed walls depicting scenes dear to the Ralston heart: Bridal Veil Falls and the vernal floor of Yosemite Valley. In the four corners bronze Caryatides held aloft clusters of light.

About the many desks forty clerks stood to their duty—

forty immaculately dressed clerks, each with a white carnation stuck in the lapel of his coat. Among the forty was a grave bespectacled Chinaman garbed in dark silk brocade, carefully poring over Hongkong remittances. For Ralston's bank prided itself on its aplomb as well as Oriental connections.

Over this vast room running as smoothly as a mill stream, presided, as could be seen through the glass screen separating his office from the bank proper, a fine-looking young man of robust appearance, dark, all-seeing eyes, ruddy complexion, and black cameo-studded shirt-bosom: Ralston, the cashier.

His office furniture was oak. Chairs were upholstered in green leather. Over his flat-topped desk was stretched a length of green baize. Opposite his desk was a Morocco-covered one where clients might sit. In the office adjoining Ralston's sat a mild-faced, carefully dressed, dignified man, more amiable than commercial in aspect—Mills the president. The third office beyond was occupied by the stately, stock-collared correspondent, Stephen J. Franklin, whom Ralston had first met during those fabulous New Orleans days.

In the opinion of San Francisco, Ralston was the Bank of California: the magician of the city. Over his counters on the first of every month went a 1 per cent dividend to all his stockholders. Over his counters, by 3 o'clock every day and by 1 o'clock on Saturday, moved three millions of dollars in coin—moved with the certainty, the alacrity, the inevitability of the Falls of Niagara. Nothing could interfere with that gold and silver cataract. Of that every Californian was convinced. On that Ralston was resolved.

By 1867 Ralston's bank had become the heart and soul of San Francisco: a heart that kept Comstock bullion circulating throughout California; that pumped a never-failing golden stream into the corporate bodies of those infant industries which Ralston had sired; and a soul that would have been a credit to any generous, vigorous-hearted promoter.

By 1867 Ralston's economic empire had become absolutely dependent on the Comstock Lode. No one realized that better than its creator. No longer could the fruits of legitimate banking sustain it. Long since, California's gold placers had "petered-out." Her industries were still in the nursery. Let anything happen to Virginia City bonanzas and Ralston's half-grown fledglings would starve as ignominiously as deserted foundlings. It was that fact that worried Ralston, that drove him to desperate lengths when the need required. It was to sustain his industrial progeny through their years of adolescence that Ralston lived, breathed and toiled. Toward each one he developed a prideful parental feeling. Because of them he fought Sutro and prodded Sharon. For them he would make any self-sacrifice: beg, borrow or confiscate. Such was Ralston's devotion to the city he had created.

Engrossed as he was in the Comstock's development, Ralston could not entirely ignore the sea. Its vast pulsation, like the currents of life, flowed around and about and through him. Nor could walls of stone, nor vaults of steel, nor clink of gold shut out its throb. Its presence, like a memory, brooded over the spot where once it had held full sway. Its rhythms were as much an integral part of the blue-stone walls as the hollow reverberations in the conch of a shell.

Two or three afternoons of every week Ralston hearkened to those sounds. Just as soon as 4 o'clock came around, down he would lay his pen, pick up his hat and slip out the Sansome Street entrance. At the curb he would find a beautiful black steed saddled and bridled and a colored groom awaiting. Mounting, Ralston would clatter rapidly away, up Montgomery Street, to Telegraph Hill. From there he could look back on the picturesque city he was building: on its rising spires and pinnacles. To every one Comstock silver had contributed altitude. At last, the city was taking on the reality of his dream. From there he could see the Golden Gate, the tide plunging through and hear "Neptune's horses" racing on the beach. The sound thrilled him. It spelled freedom.

Arriving at the bathhouse at the foot of Larkin Street,

Ralston would divest himself of clothes and plunge into the Bay. With great powerful strokes his long, lean, lithe, sun-tanned body would cut through the blue waters of the surf, like a swordfish. When he was half way out to Alcatraz Island, beyond the middle of the Bay, he would turn about, dive, and swim to shore under water.

Ralston delighted in this violent exercise. It kept his muscles taut. It invigorated him. "My body is my temple," he was wont to say. "I'm going to keep it fit."

CHAPTER XII

UNION MILL AND MINING COMPANY

June, 1867

Only a small part of his recently acquired Comstock plunder had been consumed in erecting the marble walls in which Ralston carried on his vast network of business. By far the greater part was going to sustain those myriad infant industries that were his pride and joy.

Not yet had the railroad spanned the continent, nor weaned California from her legitimate dependence upon the sea. Although there was a limited consuming public and wages were high, Ralston went merrily ahead with the development of his industrial empire where capital would create capital. An empire that would be self-supporting, that would grow its own cotton, spin its own calicoes, weave its blankets, build its carriages, fashion its furniture, make its own clocks, brew its own beer, distill its own grapes, and cure its own tobacco leaf. His was a wonderful dream: to make California independent of "the States." Nobody realized better than Ralston how constantly he would need the Comstock to translate it into reality. That was why interlopers, like Sutro, could not be tolerated on Mt. Davidson.

Ralston had already invested $967,900 of his Comstock wealth in the Pacific Woollen Mills Company; into the New Montgomery Real Estate Company had gone $1,971,696; and to the Kimball Manufacturing Company on the northwest corner of Bryant and Fourth Streets he had loaned $578,580. In this latter factory Ralston employed more than 100 men. Monthly they turned out 100 vehicles. In one year they did a $3,000,000 business and supplied the Los Angeles and San Pedro Railroad, the Virginia and Truckee Railroad, and the San Francisco Trolley Company with rolling stock and railroad equipment.

Besides, Ralston had a great idea of manufacturing furniture. Already he was having the West Coast surveyed for suitable wood. But alas, California women were not proof against "round the Horn" exports and what was being used in "the States." Ralston might regiment their husbands in the business world but they refused to let Ralston dictate the cut of their clothes, the style of their carriages, or the furniture that lined their parlor walls.

Out in Visitacion Valley, beyond South San Francisco, Ralston was organizing the Union Pacific Silk Manufacturing Company, with a capital of $250,000. Every week it turned out about $6000 worth of ribbons.

Counting on the women, Ralston expected great things of the California silk industry not only on account of the climate but because of the 60 per cent duty demanded by Uncle Sam. But alas, women, like the sea, were continually undergoing changes.

On the reclamation of Sherman's Island, a peat formation in the Sacramento River, Ralston expended a large amount of money. Levees were built and two wharves pushed out into the stream. By 1873 the island was entirely reclaimed and the price of real estate shot upward. Ralston congratulated himself on the luscious fruit and the bountiful wheat crops that found their way into the San Francisco market.

Because there was no adequate place to repair damaged

sea-going vessels about San Francisco, Ralston was tremendously embarrassed. Immediately he set about building a gigantic dry dock at Hunter's Point near the city. One so enormous that it would be able to accommodate any hull then afloat on the Pacific.

On September 1, 1866, he commenced work on this project by giving employment to a hundred men who had been growing poor grubbing for gold. By the labor of these workers, an enormous graving dock was excavated out of solid rock. So large that the British ironclad *Zealous* could be handled without effort. But not large enough to handle some of the hulls that were coming through the Gate.

Ralston used the earth from this enormous excavation to reclaim the land adjacent to the dock. These lots he proposed selling to the workmen.

Another Comstock fortune went to foster the Culp Consolidated Tobacco Company at Gilroy. Seed was imported from Havana. Acre after acre of the broad flat leaves ripened in the warm sun of Santa Clara Valley.

In 1873 the company made over a million cigars and a large quantity of plug, fine-cut, long-cut and granulated tobaccos, all of which found a ready market. In one factory, 785 men were employed. The manufactured product was worth $600,000. About one-half found a ready California market. The rest was easily disposed of elsewhere. Ralston, with excessive confidence, was encouraged to organize a $1,000,000 company.

Still another fortune transported the Cornell Watch Factory from Cornell, Illinois, and set it up first in San Francisco and later in Berkeley.

Also, with the Comstock at his beck and call, Ralston had been a good friend to the "Big Four," Stanford, Hopkins, Crocker, and Huntington, in the trying construction days. In return the "Pacific Quartette" had promised Ralston all sorts of concessions. They would let him build all their cars. On the strength of that promise, Comstock wealth had fostered the building of an immense works where palace cars and freighters were to be fashioned.

Comstock wealth, actual and prospective, fostered the San Francisco, Oakland and Alameda Railroad.

Whatever else it was accompilshing, Comstock wealth had taken California industry out of its swaddling clothes and put San Francisco commercially on its feet. Its steady pulse kept time with that of his own heart.

These Ralston-fostered establishments gave employment to vast numbers of laborers, artisans, factory men and tillers of the soil. The Comstock assured them of high wages. All looked to Ralston as their great benefactor.

Ralston was gifted with the trait of remembering the names of many of his workmen. They came to him with their problems and he was never too busy to give a helping hand. Let a man fall from one of his building-scaffolds or get mangled in a factory wheel and Ralston would be among the first to the rescue; to rush the injured one in his own carriage to the hospital; to ease up pain on the jolting way; to engage doctors and nurses and to provide for the injured man's family during his incapacity.

All these acts endeared Ralston to a constantly widening circle of admirers: San Franciscans and Californians. Had Ralston wanted any political gift within labor's granting it would have been his for the asking. He could have been mayor of the city or governor of the State had he chosen. Since he didn't want it, these men gave him something that Comstock bullion could not buy: admiration, affection, adulation, the loyalty of a people for a well-loved sovereign. Right or wrong, he was their leader. They followed his every movement with devotion.

Sometimes when the men saw Ralston riding over Telegraph Hill on his way to his North Beach swim, they would uncover while he was passing. When his coach and four whizzed by them on the highway, covering them with clouds of dust and showering them with pebbles, they made no complaints. Never were these hard workers envious of Ralston. They were proud of him, proud of what he was accomplishing for California, proud to labor for him.

But those clouds of dust gave Sutro an idea. He had a cartoonist draw a picture of a prideful Ralston, his four horses and tallyho, going pell-mell down the King's Highway covering everybody and everything with his dust. The time would come when he could use that cartoon effectively.

Now Ralston decided to consolidate his interest on the Comstock Lode. Mills was getting restive. For some time he had not been satisfied with the seventeen ore crushers that had fallen into the hands of the Bank of California. They were not good security, he had complained. The Bank must be relieved of such an incubus. Accordingly in June, 1867, the Union Mill and Mining Company had been incorporated, with a capital of $1,500,000 divided into 15,000 shares. For the charter members of the new company, Ralston chose a galaxy from his Ring: Mills, Alvinza Hayward, Thomas Sunderland, Charles Bonner, Thomas Bell, W. E. Barron and Sharon. Eventually all the stock fell into the hands of Ralston, Mills and Sharon.

To Ralston, it was a foolish thing to have those seventeen mills scattered all over Mt. Davidson. It was ridiculous to run them by steam, with wood selling at prohibitive figures. They should be driven by water. Word to that effect went out, and the Union Mill and Mining Company concentrated its stamps on the Carson.

By this time, Ralston's policy had brought most of the independent mill owners to their knees. In a short time the Union Mill and Mining Company were the owners of all the big mills on the Comstock. Then onlookers realized what had occurred. The whole Lode, like a lemon, had been caught between the jaws of the colossal combine, and every ounce of juice was being squeezed direct into the coffers of Ralston's Ring. That was the only way to manage it, with an expanding San Francisco program.

From then on, Sharon fed the mills belonging to the Ring to their utmost capacity, while the few remaining independent ones were utterly starved. Their owners offered to reduce ore at half the price charged by the combine; but to no avail. Not a mine on the Lode dared to help the independents. So inexorably was Ralston's policy followed out that within a short time two more mills fell into the clutches of the Ring. Superintendents of every mining company were notified that the interests of the Union Mill and Mining Company were paramount to their own. All their ore must go to Ring-owned mills. A few complained of the "piratical policy of gutting the mines," but it was useless. Ralston's program must be followed out to the last letter.

As the stamps must be kept going night and day, ore was taken out of the mines more rapidly than Ralston's mills could reduce it. In consequence ore bodies exhausted themselves so rapidly that there was no dividend to pay stockholders, only enough to pay the combine for milling.

Sometimes when a rich body of ore was discovered, the superintendent was notified to mix worthless rock with the pay ore. In that way the Ring's mills could be operated much longer than they could by just milling the pay dirt itself. By this method many a small bonanza exhausted itself without benefit to the stockholders but with vast profit to the Ring. If the rich ore body was insufficient for this "gutting process" the stockholders were assessed to make up the difference in the cost of milling. Sun Mountain was casting sinister shadows over California Street: women were being degraded; youth was being defiled; men made corrupt; the city debauched.

Sometimes a showing would be made in a Virginia City mine. San Francisco news-hawks would play it up in the columns of their mining reports. Up would shoot the prices of the stock on the San Francisco board. Investors would be tempted. Women operators would get the mania. By private entrances they would visit their brokers and give orders to buy. For a brief period there would be wild excitement: wild eyes, wild buying on the market. Incredible scenes would be enacted daily. Ministers, clerks, lawyers and school teachers would throw their savings, and other people's savings, into the insatiable maw of the Exchange. Then adverse Comstock reports would reach the papers: ore was "petering out" or they had struck a "horse." Down would go returns as disclosed in mining reports.

Purchasers would be caught in the trap, while insiders reaped the benefit.

Veiled figures would drop out of the black-robed procession that hovered about the Stock Exchange. Hope would die out of their eyes and brilliants increase in the pawn shops. A few days later the procession, headed toward Leidesdorff Street, the "Pauper Alley" of the district, would receive new recruits.

So seductive was the influence of the market when the excitement was upon them that those with fixed resolutions could not resist a venture. The merchant would reduce his capital stock to raise a sum for Comstock investment. The lawyer would draw on his clients' money; the banker appropriate his deposits; the bookkeeper tamper with his employer's cash-box: all honest in their motives; all assuring themselves that they could replace the funds at a moment's notice. One young broker's clerk in a few months' time used money and securities belonging to his employer amounting to more than fifty thousand dollars. Result? The best part of his life was spent behind San Quentin's bars.

A minister had been investing for himself and a brother divine. So long as dividends were coming in there was harmony and unity between them. A sudden drop in stocks swamped their mutual capital. Ill-feeling was created. The breach widened. Bitter animosity cropped out. A scandal developed. Before peace could be restored the holy cause in which they labored was dishonored. Everywhere human debris from the stock market was being blown over California Street.

The Insane Asylum at Stockton filled up with living witnesses to Washoe's wild excitement. Mental wrecks who had gone stock mad haunted the streets. California buried more suicides in proportion to population than any other State in the Union.

One quiet morning, when nature was all smiles and the world looked brighter than for many a day before, a sharp report was heard in one of San Francisco's Nob Hill mansions; the owner was found a corpse. He had sent a leaden messenger direct into his heart. Cause? As the evening paper sympathetically expressed it: "He had lost in Comstock stocks."

The Bay gives up its dead. In the ghastly remains washed ashore, the features of a well-known business man were recognized. The jury brought in a verdict: "Accidental drowning." Later developments proved that the victim had sought relief from financial ruin by hiding beneath the billows. Stocks? Yes, it was Comstock stocks.

Gradually Comstock gambling was undermining the fiber of Ralston's realm.

CHAPTER XIII

SUTRO GOES TO EUROPE

July, 1867–July, 1868

Everything and everybody on Mt. Davidson found themselves at the mercy of the Union Mill and Mining Company. Many looked on it as an "unscrupulous combine." So complete had become its hold upon the mountain that men despaired of ever escaping from its relentless grasp. But not Mackay nor Fair nor Sutro. The strength of the combine was a challenge to them. They intended to destroy the monster that was gradually squeezing the life out of them.

Before long, the Union Mill and Mining Company had netted Mills over two millions of dollars and Ralston and Sharon each over four millions.

From end to end the Comstock resounded with renewed activity. The population doubled, trebled. New industries sprang into being. Spurred on by the Union Mill and Mining Company, corporations were organized for supplying the mines with lumber, timbers, water and fuel, at reduced rates. Vast watersheds and timberlands fell into the clutches of the combine. Sawmills were erected at strategic points. Railroads and highways pushed their way through the dense Sierra pine forests. Great monarchs of the mountains, centuries old, fell before the woodman's axe. Steamers, laden with lumber, plowed their way across Lake Tahoe. Flumes, skirting perilous heights, cascaded a continuous stream of timber into the valley, thousands of feet below. All destined to be gobbled up by the silver mines.

Ralston was now not only the financial dictator and social arbiter in San Francisco but just as powerful in Nevada. Sharon basked in his reflected glory, eagerly stretching forth his arms toward the laurels which fell so easily about his patron.

Sharon was happy. He was getting even with the thing that had almost destroyed him. The organization of the Union Mill and Mining Company justified the interests of the Bank of California in the Virginia City branch and himself. He wondered if Sutro's Tunnel could do as much for California as the Union Mill and Mining Company had accomplished. If he had anything to do with it Sutro would never be given another chance.

Ralston rejoiced. In financial circles his reputation as a financial wizard grew into a legend. He had proved to Mills and his directorate that he had not invested the capital funds of his bank in vain. All of them: Mills, Frey, Alvinza Hayward, Bell, Bonner, and Sunderland had been immeasurably increased in fortune by his genius. Not one of these men but congratulated Ralston on his acumen.

Only a few years since, Mills had been a provincial banker with a few thousands to his credit. Now, thanks to Ralston, he could count not thousands but millions.

Ralston had also proved that his confidence in Sharon had not been misplaced. From now on, his directorate would be more ready than ever to support what their cashier guaranteed. Best of all, the Comstock had just begun to yield its bonanzas. Not even underground water had hampered their delivery. Like the silver mines of the Sierra Madre, the Lode would go on producing indefinitely.

Before he was through exploiting the Ledge, San Francisco would have reached metropolitan proportions. His ambitions would be satisfied. His city would be as fabulous as New Orleans. Theatres, art galleries, libraries, superb hotels, broad thoroughfares, mills, factories, reclamations would bespeak his financial genius. Ralston's heart swelled with pride when he beheld his works. In the meantime not even Sutro would be permitted to jeopardize that program. Forthwith, Ralston sat down at his desk and dictated a series of letters intended to block Sutro at every angle. The Bank could not permit the driving of a drain that would threaten the existence of San Francisco.

In the meantime, with a feeling that Ralston had betrayed him, Sutro journeyed Eastward. In July, 1867, he arrived in New York. Almost the first thing he did was to visit the banking house of Leese and Waller, New York agents of the Bank of California. Just a few weeks before, he had been a welcome visitor there. Now he wanted to let those bankers know what had been happening in California. But he was unprepared to find that Ralston had anticipated him.

Placarded conspicuously on Leese and Waller's bulletin board was a telegram from Ralston's bank for every man to read. In large letters it proclaimed to the world of finance that "the stockholders of the Savage Company [a California Bank-controlled organization], at their annual meeting, had refused to ratify the subscriptions made by their trustees of $150,000 to the stock of the Sutro Tunnel Company. Therefore they were utterly null and void."

Sutro was astonished to find in a New York banking house a placard like that. Everybody who read it would think that he had committed some crime or been guilty of some rascality. But he saw what Ralston was up to. He intended to ruin his credit in New York. From the bank Sutro called on Vanderbilt, Morgan, Belmont and other capitalists who had promised to raise $3,000,000 providing he would get a "home-indorsement."

To these gentlemen Sutro showed the documents in which the Bank of California-controlled mines had subscribed $600,000. He told them briefly why those contracts had been abrogated. But he could not explain those facts away. No matter what he said they would not believe him. To those financiers, Ralston's telegram was a warning, such as those sent ahead of absconding bank-clerks or forgers or criminals. It spelt suspicion. It succeeded in ruining his chances in New York's financial centers. It was persecution.

Sutro did not know what to do, nor where to turn. He was not going to give up, to go away and hide his head in shame. He was going to fight, fight Ralston, fight his intangible, whispered words, his written ones; his innuendoes. He was going to pierce Sun Mountain with his bore. Then a thought occurred to him: an indorsement of the tunnel project from the Nevada State Legislature would be of help. He would take it to Washington. He would explain it to Congress. He would submit it to the House. At the same time he would let those representatives know how shabbily the Bank of California had handled him—what a set of scamps they were; in what bad faith they had acted; how they had perverted facts, betrayed him and done everything to break up his enterprise. Before Congress he could vindicate himself. Into those sacred halls of freedom, Ralston's long arm could not possibly reach. There his colossal power would be null, there his Ring dare not misrepresent facts. To them he would read the report of Nevada's Legislature. Before them he would bring out the importance, the magnitude of the proposed work and the great boon it would be to humanity. No matter what Ralston said, the Nevada report would be a conclusive argument in favor of Government aid.

Full of hope, Sutro took the train for Washington. It was the end of July when he arrived. Unfortunately for him Congress had adjourned. Not until December would it reconvene. Five months! It was useless to return to New York, to go to California or to the Comstock. In all those places

Ralston's word was supreme. In all those places Ralston had branded him with suspicion. Automatically, he had been exiled. On the other hand it was useless to remain in Washington. That would not bring help to suffering Comstock miners. If he would do that he must bestir himself. He would go to Europe. In foreign capitals he would find aid for Sun Mountain's exploited laborers.

At the same time he would increase his knowledge of mines, tunnels, methods, machinery and engineering. He would see what was being done in European mining circles. He would visit France, Belgium, Prussia, Austria, Poland, Saxony, Hungary, Bavaria, and Switzerland. He would meet their great mining engineers, he would go down in their shafts, he would study the continuance of mineral lodes in depth. He would go into their libraries. He would read their latest scientific writings. He would familiarize himself with what modern mining experts were doing. He would submit his project to them. He would see what they had to say.

All these things he would do in order the better to lay his Comstock tunnel before Congress. At the same time he would not neglect any opportunity which would enable him to raise capital with which to make a beginning.

Luckily Sutro was armed with letters of introduction. Among them was the one to the Oriental Banking Corporation of London which Ralston had signed and given to him. Sutro re-read it. In it Ralston had recommended his tunnel project to English financiers as an excellent investment. But after what had occurred Sutro could not present that letter. Instead he would use it to expose the Bank of California's perfidy.

Everywhere, that summer, Sutro came in contact with the leading scientific minds of the day. All of them were familiar with the famous Comstock mines, their water problem and Sutro's plan to drain them. Everywhere he was treated with consideration. He was taken down their deepest mines and into their longest tunnels. Methods were explained. Machinery demonstrated. More and more his investigations convinced Sutro of two things: first, the Comstock Lode was a fissure vein. As such it would descend into the earth indefinitely. Secondly, the only rational way to work the Comstock profitably was by the tunnel he was advocating.

During these investigations, Sutro contacted Von Cotta, the great geologist; Weissbach, the famous engineer; Baron Von Beust of Saxony; Chevalier, the French political economist; Sir Roderick Murchison, president of the London Geographical Society; John Stuart Mill; Baron Von Gengenau, chief of the mining department of Austria; Buekkhardt, Koch and many others. To all these men Sutro displayed maps showing Sun Mountain and the topography of the Comstock Lode. To them he submitted his plan for mining it by means of a great tunnel four miles long.

Unanimously these experts indorsed his projected drain. It was the only way to attack such a fissure vein. It was the greatest engineering project going on in America. It was the only possible means to drain off the water. Every one of them wrote a letter indorsing its practicability, feasibility, and magnificence. But even in Europe Ralston had sounded a warning against the stock of the tunnel. When Sutro would broach selling it or bring up the subject of a loan, the same old retort would be forthcoming: where were his "home-indorsements?" Why did not the Bank of California back him?

In Paris Sutro found one concern, the house of Erlanger Company, the great Parisian bankers, who took an especial interest in the proposed loan. They sent for their London partner to come to France and confer with them. Suddenly their attitude changed. War clouds were hovering over Prussia. American enterprises were out of the question. In the end the old specter arose: where were his "home-indorsements?" Sutro could not dispel those suspicions any more than he could dispel the clouds hovering over the Franco-Prussian frontiers.

Undismayed, Sutro left Liverpool. One December day of 1867 he arrived in Washington, shortly after the Fortieth Congress had convened. Here, if anywhere, the tunnel project must succeed or fail. He made it a point to make the acquaintance of all the members of both Houses of Congress and the leading men of the nation.

By this time Sutro's funds were exhausted, but he had a town lot in a little California village, which he arranged to sell for $200. Half starving, he managed to stay on that winter in Washington.

Finally the day came when he submitted the Memorial of the Nevada Legislature to Congress. Immediately it was referred to the Committee on Mines and Mining. They showed great interest in the tunnel. Twice a week they would meet with Sutro to discuss the problem and to question him regarding the Comstock Lode. After a lengthy examination of the subject they made an open report to the House: they recommended a loan of $5,000,000 with a mortgage to the Government on all Sutro's Nevada property.

Almost immediately Ralston's Ring had heard of the cordial reception Sutro was receiving in Washington. With concern they learned that his chances of obtaining a substantial Government loan were good. They accused Sutro of bribing Congress. Statements to that effect appeared in all Eastern papers.

With considerable show of humor, Sutro read those reports and retorted with a question: "Bribed—What with? Out of my $200?"

Weeks passed, but matters progressed in a promising manner, notwithstanding the secret machinations of the Bank of California to defeat them. Now the Ring had agents at Washington. Ralston had instructed them to do everything in their power to prevent Sutro from getting the loan. Congressmen were bombarded with letters and telegrams. One of these fell into Sutro's hands.

"Virginia, Nevada, Jan. 15, 1867.

"To Hon. Wm. M. Stewart and James W. Nye:

"We are opposed to the Sutro Tunnel project, and desire it defeated, if possible.

WILLIAM SHARON,

CHARLES BONNER, Supt. Savage Co.

JOHN P. JONES, Supt. Kentuck Co.
J. W. MACKAY, Supt. Bullion Co.
ISAAC L. REQUA, Supt. Chollar-Potosi Co."

In those names, Sutro recognized Ralston's hand. To him this move had only one meaning: the Bank was afraid. They feared a Government appropriation. They intended to defeat his plan so that they could step in themselves and get the appropriation. One day Sutro found substantial proof of this fact. A telegram intended for John Conness, United States Senator from California, fell inadvertently into his hands. Nor had Ralston stopped at telegrams. He carried on his fight against Sutro in newspaper columns and in pamphlets throughout the length and breadth of the land.

The gist of these articles was all alike: Sutro's Tunnel was not needed on the Comstock Lode; there was hardly any water; what there was was being handled satisfactorily by Ralston's pumps; and to prove it the Ring gave figures on the cost of extraction of several recent bonanzas. In every one of these articles the public was warned against Sutro. He was a bilk, persona non grata to the Bank of California. He was trying to worm himself into a proposition that was no concern of his and where he was not wanted. The Bank of California could run their mines and mills without his assistance. Every one of these thrusts Sutro answered with a parry and return.

To counteract this intrigue and bring his position more forcibly before Congress and Senate, Sutro again had recourse to his pen. All the letters addressed to him by the great authorities of Europe were collected, together with an account of his aims and ambitions. He had a book printed in Baltimore, handsomely bound and distributed among the members of both Houses. It cost him a lot of money, but he borrowed it. It was the only way he could reach the reading public.

Daily the bill recommending the loan became more popular in Washington. If anything, Ralston's persecution, as exemplified in telegrams and in press articles, increased the bill's popularity. Could the bill at this time have been put to a vote it would have passed with a three-quarter majority.

Unfortunately, at this crucial moment, just as the bill was coming up, the impeachment trial of President Andrew Johnson commenced and nothing was done in the House for months. But Thaddeus Stevens, the great political leader of the day, encouraged Sutro during this trying period. The old man took a particular interest in the question of getting down deeper into the bowels of the earth than had ever been reached before. He was ready to do anything to help Sutro. He became one of the chief advocates of the loan, making speeches on its advisability on every possible occasion. Even during Johnson's trial he kept the matter alive.

That spring, when Stevens was taken sick he would send for Sutro to hear how things were going. When Sutro would arrive at Stevens's home he would find the statesman propped up in bed reading his latest book and the account of Ralston's opposition to the project. Then Sutro would sit down beside him and dilate further on his project, and the persecution to which he had been subjected on account of it.

Just listening to that account would make Stevens madder and madder.

With men like Stevens interested in his tunnel, Sutro did not despair as much as formerly.

All that spring the impeachment trail lasted. All that time Stevens grew weaker and weaker. One day Congress adjourned. Never had the Sutro bill been reached. And the members had all been ready for it and would have passed it with a big majority. Was there ever such luck?

Sutro was almost despairing. He had exhausted all his powers. He had been under tremendous expense. He had spent all of his own money and all of his friends'. He was head over heels in debt.

All the time, Ralston was quietly and secretly undermining him. All the time, he was in continous telegraphic communication with his Washington agents and with the press throughout the country.

Before he left Washington, many Congressional representatives came to Sutro, shook him by the hand and bade him not to despair. That winter they promised to help him as they had never backed a measure before. They gave it as their personal opinion that during the next session the bill would pass overwhelmingly.

All of that talk heartened Sutro. Among other letters addressed to him on departure Sutro found one from Thaddeus Stevens. Good old Stevens, he was the best friend the measure had. He stated that at the next Congressional session he himself would again warmly support the tunnel bill. That meant a great deal to Sutro. There was no more powerful statesman in Washington than Thaddeus Stevens.

Try as he would to be otherwise, Sutro was downhearted. He felt that he had accomplished nothing. Nevertheless he promised his admirers that next fall before the Congressional session began he would be back in Washington.

Two weeks after his departure Sutro received a wire. Thaddeus Stevens had died.

The best friend the tunnel had in Washington was no more.

CHAPTER XIV

BELMONT

1867

While Sutro was moving heaven and earth to raise funds with which to start his tunnel, Ralston was squandering a million dollars upon the development of a summer villa at Belmont, twenty-two miles south of San Francisco.

Once the villa had belonged to a mysterious, exiled Corsican nobleman, Count Cipriani, one-time friend of Na-

poleon Bonaparte. When, for some unknown reason, th
Count had wished to avoid the haunts of man, he ha
found the desired seclusion in the wild, sequestered val
of the Cañada Diablo. He it was who had hedged the plac
about with a dense growth of trees, planted groves of lim
and ilex and laid out box-bordered parterres of heliotrope
phlox, and jasmine. But when the cause of Italian liberty ha
recalled the Count to his homeland, his estate passed swiftl
into the hands of Ralston.

From his first inspection Ralston had been carried awa
by the vale's rare beauty. At once he had coveted it a
a place where he might entertain the many distinguishe
travellers who were flocking to California; and so sprea
the fame of State and city abroad.

By 1867 Ralston was acknowledged as California's firs
citizen. Upon him had devolved the responsibility of entertaining all the distinguished travellers who found themselves within the Golden Gate. Thus Belmont became th
White House of the West. The ends of the earth sat dow
at his hospitable table in a wonderful social exchange o
the travelling world. Never did a statesman, ambassador,
diplomat, artist, or actor of note arrive in San Francisc
but that he was bidden to Belmont. For such a one, satirists
claimed, the ink would be hardly dry on his hotel registe
before Ralston's summoning invitations would arrive. Neve
was one of them refused. Not to have visited the Yosemite,
the big trees, Ralston and Belmont, was not to have seen
California.

For this very reason Ralston maintained his magnificent
hospitality: to draw the attention of strangers to the un-
rivalled resources of his city and State. How better could
this purpose be served than by entertaining regally at Belmont where California revealed herself in all her matchless splendor? Where climate, California fruits and flowers,
California horseflesh, California wine, California-made furniture, silks, satins, blankets, and broadcloth could be displayed to the best advantage. It was Ralston's intention to
make Belmont so alluring and instructive that travellers

would want to come to California to live and to invest their fortunes in the Bay counties' growing concerns.

Belmont was a small wooded amphitheatre, nestling between the lofty blue-rimmed, chemical-covered Coast Range Mountains and the lowly oak-clad foothills. On the further side thundered the mighty Pacific. From the nether came the incessant rumble of the surf beating upon the Bay-shore. Like the incessant throb of savage drums in the jungle Belmont was never free of the vibrations of the sea.

The vale was a little bit of paradise: the covert of bird, deer, and bee. Carpeted by many-colored grasses, shaded by century-old oaks and waxy-leaved magnolias, it was a spot to delight the senses of a connoisseur like Ralston. All day long one saw blue, red, yellow, and black-winged birds darting in and out of the green shrubbery; and heard the lazy drone of bees, the ecstatic call of larks and the brooding notes of doves. When darkness fell, the eerie hoot of owls, the poignant cry of deer fallen prey to prowling coyotes stabbed the stillness. In summer the breeze that blew over this favored spot was sweet with the citric scent of orange and lime and, in blustery weather, bitter with the tang of the sea.

With incredible dispatch and reckless disregard of money, the Count's villa was reconstructed in a typical Ralstonesque manner. The country-seat mentioned in "The Merchant of Venice" had inspired its architectural lines. Be that as it may, the new edifice hugged the northeasterly side of the basin as closely as one of Caligula's pleasure craft hugged the Liburnian shore at night. When Belmont was lighted from dome to corridor as it was at twilight, it looked not unlike one of that Roman Emperor's great white galleys with gem-studded stern and parti-colored awnings taking a night's mooring in a quiet, sequestered cove.

Owing to the placing of the house, there were no wide stretches of lawn. Instead, ascending terraces, planted with camellias, heliotrope, oleander, crape-myrtle, laurel and lilac, billowed about the foundations like an evergreen sea. On the brick coping of the stairs, leading from one terrace to another, were placed green vases of rare Chinese pottery bubbling over with brilliantly hued geraniums.

Everywhere about the reconstructed villa were gadgets reminiscent of Ralston's river years. The covers of ventilators were intricately carved; doors swung both in and out their glazed glass panels were as handsomely etched with conventionalized flower designs as any found on the Mississippi's floating palaces.

Surrounding ballroom, library, billard room, music, and banquet halls was another reminder: a glassed-in promenade, decorated with potted vines and flowering trees just like those found on elaborately equipped river steamers.

From second floor and third floor galleries, balustraded gangplanks with variegated awnings extended to corresponding richly planted terraces on the adjoining hillside.

The villa was full of surprises. Like Caligula, Ralston delighted in nothing so much as accomplishing the impossible and mystifying his guests.

Lift a trap-door under the hall's grand-staircase, concealed stone-steps, like those in the Villa Chillon, would be found leading down, down into murky darkness. The air which floated upward was dank and musty. Railings and walls were damp and chill. On the ear the sound of lapping waters gently smote. Descending, with candle torch in hand, a landing would be reached. With the light held overhead a subterranean lake stretching away into cavernous darkness would disclose itself. In the lurid pathway thrown across its inky surface, a small moored boat could be seen floating.

This was only a part of a colossal water system that had failed. Nearby was a deep shaft which Comstock diamond drills had dug. Branching off from it were twin tunnels that had run amuck in the flinty heart of the mountain. In the end, after all these tremendous excavations, water had failed to materialize and Ralston had been compelled to buy a nearby mountain meadow, throw a stone dam fifty feet high across a valley, and create an artificial lake. Like Caligula, Ralston intended to have floods of water to supply the porcelain tubs that adjoined his fifty odd guest-rooms.

Then there was "the room-of-only-one-night," an apartment built expressly to entertain a United States Vice-President. On the ground floor was a monstrous ballroom, panelled with huge plate-glass mirrors and lighted by chandeliers dripping with crystals—a chamber to vie with the one of mirrored fame at Versailles. Adjoining were a billiard room with a table inlaid with the rarest of California woods, and a music-room whose piano was incased in carved California laurel. At a moment's notice, walls would arise, all three of these rooms could be thrown into one grand apartment. On the library shelves were handsomely tooled sets of Scott, Byron, Milton, Plutarch, and Dante in scarlet, red, blue, and buff morocco. Here, there, and everywhere were urns filled with lilies, gardenias, and rare potted begonias from adjoining conservatories.

In the wine-cellars, Burgundies, clarets, sauternes, champagnes, and brandies, of California vintage, aged. Over them a fine dust sifted and spiders weaved a web. Whenever possible the products of California were magnified to the *n*th degree.

By no means were Belmont's furnishings or supplies confined to California production. For years every foreign bottom which sailed through the Golden Gate had consignments for Belmont: choice Aubusson carpets, Oriental rugs, Venetian and Bohemian glass, handsomely monogrammed Dresden and Sèvres china, paintings, bronze, marble, cloisonné, ebony, teak; harness with silver and ivory mountings; choice flowering shrubs from South America and the tropic isles of the Pacific; bulbs from Holland, lilies from Rome and peacocks and swans from Oriental lands.

Many of these choice works of art were gifts from guests whom Ralston had royally entertained.

Although the San Francisco and San José railroad passed near the entrance of his principality and daily trains connected with San Francisco, Ralston rarely availed himself of the service. Out into the Bay he ran a massive mole to accommodate his steamer the *Brisk,* which he used almost exclusively to handle freight and supplies.

For himself, disdaining tide and time-table, Ralston preferred a coach-and-four. Horseflesh was a Ralston passion.

In his ivy-covered stables were from sixty to a hundred horses and every conceivable kind of conveyance.

Ralston prided himself on his speed as a driver. Nothing pleased him so much as to take an even start with the San Francisco-San José train and beat, with horseflesh and coach, the scheduled time made from San Francisco to Belmont. Little by little this exhilarating race, from bank to villa, weaned Ralston from his evening swim at Black Point. All this ease and comfort was taking its toll, increasing his girth and dyeing his cheeks with a hectic flush.

On the nights he was going to Belmont, his coach-and-four and accompanying grooms would be waiting at the Sansome Street bank entrance. Always in a hurry, Ralston would dash out, climb into the box, pick up the reins, and the race would be on—horseflesh against engine and steam. Ralston didn't know what it was to lose a race. Daylight or black midnight, it was all one to Ralston, he never slackened his pace.

On one particular occasion the coach contained a party of ten, who had been invited by the grand Seigneur to spend the weekend at Belmont. Last of all they called at the bank to pick up Ralston.

Promptly at five o'clock Ralston rushed out, swung into his seat and picked up the reins. Immediately his four blacks pricked up their ears. They knew that touch. It required speed, speed sufficient to beat the train to Belmont. Barely had the grooms time to spring into the rear seat before the coach was off with a rush—out the Mission plank road to take an even start with the train as it left Valencia Street and beat it to Belmont, a good twenty-two miles away. To lose that race would spoil a weekend.

Wind blew and sand flew in the face of guest and driver. Ralston used both as an excuse to whip up his steeds. "We must get out of the bad weather," he would say, as he flicked the flanks of his leaders. Forward the tally-ho would lurch and the guests would brace themselves for the excitement ahead.

As Ralston's coach flew along, the old plank road would

rumble and sway beneath the weight. Flying sand would cut the faces of rear-seat guests, even those who were heavily veiled. Before Ralston could reach the end of the plank road, the train could be heard whistling to the rear. The guests would be tingling with excitement. Ralston would "whip up a little more" as he called it. For he must beat the train. As a matter of fact the horses needed no "whipping up." All they wanted was the chance and to feel that Ralston held the ribbons. They were willing to do the going. Go they went, over ridges and down dales. When they reached the top of the Colma hill, Ralston would salute the sea and increase his speed to a gallop.

"If the horses cannot trot fast enough, they can run," was his laconic rejoinder to the startled one in the seat beside him. As the rumbling sound of the train to his rear would fill his ears, the speed of his horses would automatically increase. And his guests would be clinging to one another and the arms of their seats for support.

At two prescribed places on this Belmont dash, Ralston would change horses: once at Uncle Tom's and again near San Mateo. Hostlers would have everything in readiness, horses champing at the bit, still Ralston would be impatient to be off. During these swift maneuvers he would lose a little on the train. But when the latter would slow up at the next station he would make up time, especially on the long San Mateo stretch which he had had resurfaced with pulverized rock, so that he could make maximum speed. Anxiously, all the way down, the guests would peer over their shoulders. Whenever the rumbling sound would increase to the rear they would brace themselves afresh.

It was always a close race. A gamble. As he approached Belmont, Ralston would swing his tally-ho out of the long straight white road into the tree-shaded lane which led to his villa. Never would he cross the tracks less than a hundred yards ahead of the train, which would be slowing down as it rolled into the village station. Over the rails, guests would relax. Satisfied, Ralston would sink back in his seat. Again he had won. No one in that part of California could boast of such horseflesh as Belmont.

In another minute Ralston would be clipping along under the tree branches that overhung his winding driveway. As he would enter his beautiful hazy mountain-rimmed domain, a burst of "Ohs" and "Ahs" would be forced from his astonished guests. On the left, just below the roadway, a heavy black smoke would be seen rolling out of several chimneys. "My private gas works," Ralston would announce. Ahead, the villa, light pouring from every door and window, would suddenly appear. Ralston always managed to arrive in the vale just at dusk when the immense white house against the back-drop of the cañon was a blaze of light.

On these Belmont dashes Ralston never allowed any horse or horses to outstrip his four. His must be the swiftest teams on the King's Highway. One day a stripling astride a gray mare outraced his blacks and won. So nettled was Ralston over the occurrence that he could not proceed until a deal had been consummated and he had paid the owner $300 for the little mare, about six times what the horse was worth.

Flushed and happy, Ralston would draw up under his porte-cochere. Liveried grooms would appear. Hastily guests would be hustled down from the coach. "Hurry, hurry," Ralston would admonish. His horses were shaking off great flaky masses of foam and lather and Ralston was anxious to get them into the stables to cool. A motherly housekeeper took care of luggage, and ushered the guests to their rooms, where they would find the porcelain tubs brimming over with clear mountain water.

Invariably before dinner Ralston would accompany his guests down an orangery and up a little rise to a hilltop where carved marble benches formed a semi-circle that commanded a wide sweep of the Bay—of white moth-like ferries, flitting across its dark surface, and lights twinkling at Berkeley, Oakland and on the Contra Costa shore. Such a sight became a never-to-be-forgotten memory.

If time allowed before dinner was announced, guests would be accompanied on a personally conducted tour of the art gallery where marbles, bronzes and oil paintings, collected from all over the world, were displayed.

Often a hundred guests would sit down to dinner. Yet so large was the room, so smoothly regulated the service, so pervading the powerful personality of the host, that all seemed to blend and concentrate into the smallest and coziest of family affairs.

During these Lucullan feasts, an orchestra, placed on the mezzanine, filled the house with music. After coffee, when billiard, dining room and reception hall were thrown into one huge room, dancing would begin.

Ralston rarely danced. During these occasions he would be found seated in a tribune with a few favored friends. This royal box, as it were, outfitted in satin, upholstered chairs, and surrounded with silver railings, jutted over the curve of the balcony. From this vantage point he could watch "a continuous stream of gorgeously costumed women and men in evening dress or uniforms, all dancing, whirling and unceasingly repeated a thousand times in mirrors on every side. The only figures in repose being here and there those marble statues on their pedestals, serenely contemplating the activity with which in their life-likeness they seemed ready to take part."

After breakfast next morning four-in-hands and prancing steeds would be at the door, Ralston in the box of one. He must take his guests over the rim of the distant blue mountains, and down on the other side to a beach picnic at Half-moon Bay. They must pay their respects to the sea: the great metallic-looking, restless, insentient sea whose waves pounding on the shore, like the hoofbeats of a thousand horses, could oft be heard above the tinkle of glass, or the prattle of voices at Belmont.

In June, 1866, Anson Burlingame, who was on his way to the Orient to conclude the treaty with China, which bears his name, was driven to Belmont at breakneck speed for the usual welcoming festival. There Burlingame found assembled to honor him a distinguished company from neighboring villas. Seemingly by chance, the guests had gathered in the library, their backs ranged against a glass-partitioned wall. Suddenly Ralston clapped his hands. Aladdin-like the "wall gave a sort of shiver." Slowly up it went, like the curtain of a theatre, and the surprised guests wheeled about to find themselves standing on the outskirts of a lofty banquet hall whose table was set for a goodly company, with splendid plate, glass, china, and a limitless variety of flowers and fruits. Behind each chair stood a motionless celestial in crisp white linen, a long, black, braided queue tied with cherry silk hanging down his back.

One morning as a finale to this visit, Ralston whirled his distinguished guest along the bay shore to San Mateo, where he was projecting a new San Francisco suburb. So delighted was Burlingame with the choiceness of the locality and its landscaping that he selected a villa site of 1100 acres for himself. He would retire there, he told Ralston, on his return from China. In honor of the occasion, Ralston christened the new townsite Burlingame and presented his guest with the princely holding he had selected.

On another house party a titled Englishman was among the guests. On arrival at Ralston's villa there were no Ohs! or Ahs! Instead the Britisher expressed great surprise that Belmont should be considered a palace or even a great country estate.

By chance Ralston overheard those remarks and was stung by them. Never had he referred to his villa as a palace, nor had he considered it other than a summer residence. Nevertheless the Englishman's tactless remark nettled him: Belmont did not measure up to great Continental country seats. California had failed in comparison. Ralston was visibly annoyed. Everything that he sponsored must be bigger and finer than could be found elsewhere.

"I'll build something," he confided to nearby friends, "that will be big enough to hold a dozen of their little palaces and show them that California is the place for human achievement." Then and there a new idea started germinating in the Ralston imagination. A palace that would fill a Doge with envy.

In such a scheme of things there could be no room for Sutro. Never would he be allowed to violate Ralston's source of supply. Even now it was barely adequate for San Francisco's needs.

Suddenly, on an early October morning of 1868, Belmont and San Francisco began to quake. The Bank of California on its pile foundations rocked like a ship on a stormy sea. There were those there, at the time, who said they could hear the gurgle of the sea underneath. A crack slithered down the wall of Ralston's private office, a part of the stone cornice crashed to the ground, and blocks of reclaimed land, nearby, slid gently into the sea.

By the time Ralston arrived at his bank his forty clerks were in a panic. Every few minutes, as one trembler succeeded another, the whole edifice would rock back and forth and his clerks would pale in an anguish of fright. Ralston was disgusted at this exhibition of fear.

Noting their agitated state of mind through his glass screen, Ralston sent out word:

"Whoever does not stand up to business with strictness and cheerfulness today can never put foot here again."

Among broken and fallen cornices, the day's routine was continued; confidence returned to the startled clients on witnessing Ralston's example. Of $650,000 overdue the Bank, not one cent was demanded from any person engaged in genuine commerce or productiveness, but the street operators and speculators were allowed no grace. The conduct of Ralston and his bank in this emergency did more to gain the institution respect and business than all the coin in its coffers.

That very day Ralston exemplified his faith in San Francisco's future by paying Selim Woodworth $150,000 for a lot on Market Street. For a long time he had coveted that piece of property.

It was part and parcel of a superb idea developing in his mind.

CHAPTER XV

THE CROOKEDEST ROAD IN THE WORLD

December, 1868

Before the Fortieth Congress reconvened, late in the fall of 1868, Sutro journeyed back to Washington. There would be no Thaddeus Stevens to help him but he would have to make the best of the circumstances.

More than ever time had convinced him that in Congress lay his only hope of driving his tunnel through to the Comstock Lode. That fall his many friends in Congress had promised to rally around him, and Sutro expected great things.

It was November! General U.S. Grant had just been elected President of the United States. A misunderstanding had arisen between the General and Andrew Johnson, who was still the titular head of the administration. Under the circumstances neither the incumbent nor his colleagues intended to undertake any legislation which would embarrass the incoming Grant. To his chagrin, Sutro saw his bill continually shoved aside and Congress occupy the whole of that short session in passing appropriation bills necessary for the support of the Government. But not until he heard the expiring gasps of the Fortieth Congress did Sutro give up hope that Congress would at last act upon his bill.

When the new Congress convened on the 4th of March, 1869, Sutro was still hopeful that, by hook or crook, it would get around to the Tunnel bill. Especially was he encouraged when President Grant in his inaugural address, in referring to the payment of the national debt, alluded to the importance of developing "our vast mineral resources" buried in the Western Mountains. When the President spoke of forging a key to unlock those treasure chests with which Providence had provided the country, Sutro took the key allusion as a personal one referring to the driving of his tunnel. In spite of that encouragement, he saw week after week elapse without Congress ever considering the bill so dear to his heart. Suddenly, after a brief session, Congress adjourned until the following December. Again Sutro had recourse to his fountain of hope. Perhaps, then, for the first time, he would get a fair chance to bring up his bill and have it thoroughly discussed, he said courageously. In the meantime he would take up his project with the working men of the Comstock. He would ask them for a "home-endorsement."

Back in California, Sutro found that the opposition to his tunnel had grown stronger and more bitter. While most moneyed San Franciscans looked upon the tunnel as a failure, not knowing anything of its history, nor of his fight against the California Bank Ring, Sutro had more confidence in its success now than ever before. Still, the outlook was discouraging. Old friends snubbed him more openly than ever. Children jeered at him. Sneeringly, the papers alluded to him: Sutro had just returned from boring Congress with his bore. Sharon referred to him as an "Assyrian Carpetbagger." Often he was disheartened. But never for an instant did he flinch from the matter in hand. If a man would accomplish great things, he told himself, he must suffer for them—even die for them. And Sutro intended to die or drive his tunnel to the Comstock Lode. Such was his ultimatum to fate.

Before Sutro could reach the ear of the working man, Ralston decided to spike his guns. He would make the bore-project unnecessary. He would connect his mills on the Carson River with the Comstock Lode by a railroad. Word to that effect was dispatched to Sharon.

Accordingly, one day in December, 1868, Sharon sent for I. E. James, the leading mining surveyor in Washoe.

"Can you run a road from Virginia City to the Carson River?" Sharon demanded of the amazed engineer, when he reached his office.

"Yes," came the laconic reply.

"Do it, then," commanded Sharon, "at once."

The next day there were twelve surveyors with tripods and twelve pairs of keen eyes directed against the steep slopes of Mt. Davidson. Could it be done? Could an engine and a train of cars run down that steep mountain from a point 6205 feet above sea-level to an objective spot on the river 1600 feet lower? If it could be accomplished it would be an amazing achievement in mining, to say nothing of railroad engineering. The road demanded a descent of 1600 feet in 13½ miles. Such a problem would stagger almost any engineer. But James was equal to it.

A railroad on Sun Mountain from Virginia City to the river valley was not a novel idea. For four years the idea, like a shuttlecock, had bounded about the Comstock. But no one had ever had the consummate nerve to proceed until the threat of Sutro's Tunnel and the lean years of '65 to '69 had all but driven the Bank of California to the wall. From that perilous position during those dark days, Ralston had made a mental survey. The Comstock's importance to California required continued monopoly. The mines must be wedded to the river. Sutro must be kept from tunnelling the mountain. The whole Comstock must still be dominated by the Ring. Ore reduction, freight, transportation, Sierra timber, the water the people drank, the fuel they burned, the gas they consumed—all these commodities the Ring must monopolize. On the Comstock the Bank of California must remain omnipotent: the source and giver of light, life, warmth, and water.

So Ralston struck out boldly. Bull-whackers, mule-skinners, teamsters, even the picturesque yellow-gloved stage drivers who were coining money in wagon freights, hauling Sierra timber up to the mines and ore down to the river mills, all must go! Why should these Jehus wax wealthy on the Comstock when the Bank, with millions invested in the Lode, was feeling the pinch. Why shouldn't the Ring at one and the same time build a railroad to connect with Central Pacific's freight and transportation, with the Carson's river mills and with the Sierra's pine forest? Such a railroad would open up an alluring prospect. Too, it would be a fatal block flung in Sutro's path, one that he could never hurdle. Any obstacle that the Bank could hurl in the way of that persistent Sutro and his two-dollar royalties was worth procuring.

In thirty days the surveys were completed. Ralston gave immediate orders to proceed with the grading.

One day he sent for D. L. Bliss, who had been one of Sun Mountain's pioneer bankers. The proposed Virginia and Truckee Railroad must have the right-of-way through Gold Hill and American Flat. Bliss was dependable. He was delegated to procure these rights. He knew every one in the Cañon. He could manage men and lead them.

Nor was Sharon sitting complacently in his office. He was here, there, and everywhere. Now along the line of the proposed road; now in the Nevada State Legislature securing a charter and right-of-way through State-owned lands for the proposed corporation of the Virginia and Truckee Railroad Company. Now he was buying out the rights of the five moribund companies that had flirted with the railroad idea before the Bank had tackled it. Now he was hoodwinking the counties of Storey, Lyon, and Ormsby into donating $575,000 to the railroad as a free gift. There must be no obligations with these donations. Sharon made that clear. The Bank would not accept them if there were. Ralston and his Ring must be in absolute control. Sharon knew how to weld his iron while it was hot. Now Sharon was compelling the mining companies to hand over the $700,000 they had promised on their honor to pay Sutro to complete his tunnel. If they did not rescind, he had long ago warned them there would be no more loans from the Bank of California. Thus in two months Nevada raised the sum of $1,275,000 and handed it over to Ralston, a virtual gift from the people, with no strings attached.

When Sutro arrived on the Comstock he was disgusted: The Nevada people had been hoodwinked. "The people have been misled," he shouted at every one, "by the false title of the new company: the Virginia and Truckee Railroad." In their anxiety to obtain a connection with the Central Pacific they had overlooked the fact that the bill passed by the legislature was for a road to the Carson River, not in the direction of the overland trains. "Was there ever such a swindle perpetrated before on any people?" he queried of every man he could get to listen.

In the meantime the people's investment promised to pay Ralston's Ring in yearly dividends a sum in excess of $1,375,000. And Sharon laughed at Sutro's mouthings. For the Comstock must have food, clothes, lumber, and wood. Freight charges alone would buoy up Ralston's factories and failing fortunes.

While these things were being accomplished in Nevada, Ralston was placing orders with San Francisco foundries for three locomotives. "Ralston's Iron Horses," Sutro called them in derision: "Lyon," "Ormsby" and "Storey," in honor of the three bilked Nevada counties. The Three Iron Horses which were destined to take the food out of the mouths of bull-whackers and mule-skinners.

Then availing himself of the Bank's tremendous credit in London, Ralston wired to England for the rails. By January the rails were en route to Washoe in British bottoms: T rails, 50 and 60 pounds to the yard with fish joints. Neither did Ralston depend on one shipment. For well he understood the treachery of the sea. In case one lot went down, other steamers, loaded to the gunwales stood ready, at a moment's notice, to plow the waves toward Washoe.

By March, grading and tunnelling on the Virginia and Truckee Railroad had commenced. Night and day, giant powder was exploding. There were eerie spots above the

Carson's rim, where every inch of the way had to be blasted.

By April, 1500 men, mostly Chinese coolies, divided into thirty-eight camps, were picking, shovelling, blasting, tunnelling, and carting their way up Sun Mountain. Other celestials were hewing ties in the Sierra, while still others scattered them like leaves along the proposed road-bed.

On the 28th of September, at Carson City, Supterintendent Hume Yerington drove a silver spike into the first rail, signalizing the beginning of the road. Three hours later, the "Lyon," the first of Ralston's iron horses, was cavorting over newly laid track. Like a shepherd of the hills it was driving ahead a yellow swarm of Chinese coolies to their tasks above the Carson River. Blowing off a Vesuvius of sparks, the cavalcade speeded past the "Mexican's" 1500 stamps, past the "Merrimac," the "Hurd," the "Vivian," the "Santiago," the "Brunswick," and the "Yellow Jacket" mills. By October the coolies were deserting the river ramparts and the track had begun the steep ascent of the foothills encircling American Flat. Past the "American" they raced, past the "Overman." "Crown-Point," "Belcher," "Kentuck," "Yellow Jacket," up, up toward the Divide.

Ralston was there frequently to praise the antics of his Iron Horses. He noted with concern that the yellow men were antagonizing the whites working in his mines. "The Chinese must go," was the cry he heard on every side. It filled him with misgivings.

The turns, tunnels, and convolutions of the roadbed were indescribable. Slowly, surely, like a serpent climbing a rock the rails wound their way toward the Ledge. With an angry look blazing in his eyes, Sutro watched that serpentining line writhing toward him.

"It's the crookedest road in the world," he confided to his cronies. And those men understood him completely: Sutro was referring more to the Virginia and Truckee's financial foundations than he was to the roadbed's physical features.

In Sutro's mind Ralston's road had become a python whose cold, iron coils were wrapped seventeen times around and around Sun Mountain, squeezing the last vestiges of gold and silver out of other people's pockets into his own. Ralston was refusing the means of sustenance to every concern on the Mountain but his own. Such selfishness made Sutro more furious and bitter.

The Virginia and Truckee Railroad was a part of his inquisition—a special device of Ralston's to bedevil him, to harass him. Never did he miss an opportunity of assailing Ralston for his methods. Nothing could escape those deadly steel coils. They would crush everything within reach. They would draw the last drop of lifeblood from the mountain people. But not until he had appealed to the miners.

Nevertheless Sutro was close to despair. When everything was looking particularly disheartening to him, an event occurred which fed afresh the dwindling springs of hope in his bosom. In May, 1869, the Ways and Means Committee of the House of Representatives visited the Pacific Coast.

The members of this committee had been known to Sutro in Washington the winter before. All of them knew of his fight to drive a tunnel to the Comstock Lode. And of Ralston's opposition to it.

By chance, Sutro met these men in San Francisco. At once he saw the importance of getting them over to Virginia City. They were a very influential committee of the House of Representatives, a committee of gentlemen of the highest standing. In them, Sutro recognized a means to his own ends. He urged them to stop over in Virginia City on their return East and let him show them the Comstock Lode and the site of his proposed tunnel. Faithfully they promised to visit him.

Hardly had the committee registered their names at a San Francisco hotel before Ralston descended upon them. They were just the kind of men to advertise California abroad. Forthwith they were driven to Belmont, where a great entertainment was given for them and they met the chiefs of Ralston's henchmen. Too, they visited Burlingame, Ralston's suburban addition to San Francisco, his woollen mills, sugar refineries, wineries, and tobacco factories. Every Ralston industry that might impress the strangers with California was visited, but very little was said of the Comstock Lode which was keeping all these concerns in a flourishing condition.

When the Bank crowd heard of the committee's determination to go up to Virginia City to inspect the Comstock Lode, and the proposed site of Sutro's tunnel, they determined to take charge of the party.

"All right," said Sutro, on hearing of this arrangement. It could not be helped. The committee had fallen into the hands of his enemies. But Sutro had faith in their integrity.

Meanwhile, the Ring tried to persuade the commiteee not to go; the trip was too long, too hard, too dusty. But when they realized that the committee was determined upon making the trip, they decided to accompany them over the Sierras.

On arrival at Virginia City they became the guests of Bill Sharon. On the night of their arrival they were wined, dined, and serenaded by a brass band. As Sutro was persona non grata with Sharon, he did not call upon them. Somehow Sutro got a message through to them. In spite of everything Sharon could do to the contrary, they called on Sutro at the International Hotel.

Sutro wasted no time in preliminaries. He would show the committee what he wanted to do. He took them to the roof of the hotel—then one of the highest buildings on the Comstock. From that vantage point he could give them a good idea of the topography of the sage-clad country. From there he directed their attention to the mines along the Lode. Through a rent in the sunburnt hills, he pointed out the Carson River and the spot, four miles away, where he wanted to begin his tunnel. Still pointing, Sutro showed them how advantageously the Comstock mines could be operated from the banks of the Carson River.

Being intelligent men, the committee saw at a glance that Sutro was correct. He had represented things as they were: the Comstock should be mined from below, from the Carson River.

The fact that Ralston's Ring was trying to denounce Sutro

made these fair-minded men the more earnest in Sutro's favor. They came away from the hotel fully convinced of the justice of his case and the outrageous character of the persecution to which Ralston was subjecting him.

One day Sharon took Governor Blair of Michigan, one of the most distinguished members of the Ways and Means Committee, on a tour of inspection. Down Gold Cañon they trotted in Sharon's buggy, visiting en route several Bank-controlled mills and mines. In an iron cage they sank to the bottom of one of these shafts. There Blair experienced the intolerable heat, the lack of ventilation, and came close to fainting. Back on the surface again, Sharon pointed out the advancing line of the Virginia and Truckee Railroad, which the people were building for Ralston. When the name of Sutro was brought up, Sharon denounced him. The tunnel business must be stopped.

"Sir," concluded Sharon, "the Bank has waved its hand over the Comstock Lode and ordered Sutro away. That's the whole of the transaction as it seems to me."

All the time that Sharon had been speaking he was turning Governor Blair into a Sutro partisan. The Bank would drive Sutro out of the country, would they? They didn't want the tunnel built? They didn't want fresh air, and a dry place to work, and a safe way of escape in times of fire, brought to the miners? Why not?

Sutro was well pleased with the Congressmen's visit. After all, it had been a very fortunate circumstance. Their influence would secure him a hearing that winter in Congress. They were entirely satisfied with his plan for the tunnel. They could see that his contention was right: the terrible heat; the lack of air. It was no place for men to work. A tunnel was the only solution. That fall, when any one would ask the committee what they thought about the tunnel, every one of them would express the same opinion: The tunnel ought to be built, Ralston's persecution was outrageous.

When the committee returned East, Sutro remained on the Comstock. Every day, he could see, was consolidating Ralston's hold on the Comstock.

One day, Sutro looked in the window of Nye & Co., the best jewellers in Virginia City. On a velvet cushion reposed a great silver sledge-hammer. The handle was made of Washoe mahogany; the hammer of solid silver. Every one of Ralston's mines had contributed its quota toward that silver, every one of his mills had participated in its reduction. One of his smiths had cast, another had forged it, and Nye & Co. had brought it to a highly polished state. Ralston was going to use it to drive the last spike into the road he had hoodwinked the people into building for him. That day was only a short time off.

On a November afternoon Sutro followed a procession of Comstockers over the Divide, down Gold Hill to the ramparts of Crown Point Ravine. While massed bands were playing and people were shouting their heads off, Sutro saw the "Lyon," one of Ralston's Iron Horses, round the bend and whistle shrilly. Like Proserpina's bull the engine was all decked out with flowers and garlands. Astride the poop-deck of the pilot house rode Yerington, the Virginia and Truckee superintendent of construction. On the tender, hat in hand, bowing to right and left, stood Bill Sharon. Across the trestle puffed the "Lyon." Amidst a continuous ovation of whistles, shouts and music the engine came to a halt. Champagne was served. Speeches were made. The Virginia and Truckee Railroad was finished. Sun Mountain was wedded to the Carson River with bands of steel. In the twenty-one-mile roadbed there was iron enough to put seventeen rings around Sun Mountain. Such was the answer of Ralston's bank to the threat of Sutro's tunnel.

Sutro was despondent. Ralston had stolen the main reason for building his drainway. Mine and mill were at last united. But Ralston had done nothing for his working men. He was increasing his own riches; but he was not even giving the laboring man good working conditions: ventilation and a dry place to work. He was utterly selfish.

In sheer desperation, Sutro turned to the Comstock miners.

CHAPTER XVI

RALSTON'S PREDICAMENT

1869

Meanwhile, like an infatuated lover, Ralston had lavished all his worldly wealth on San Francisco. His dream had become a force. It had vitality and a miraculous driving power. It possessed, obsessed him.

With his family always in France he had allowed "the city" to become the mainspring of his life. Everything that he possessed, everything that he ever hoped to possess he was using on the city. His one regret was that he did not have enough to offer. Had San Francisco been his mistress, Ralston could not have been more ardent. His one desire was to make the city outstanding. To make her prosperous, progressive, conspicuous for enterprise and big things; to adorn her streets with handsomely constructed public buildings; to develop her natural resources and advance her prestige.

On that altar he had already offered up the Comstock Lode: all the gold, silver and bullion upon which he could lay hands. On that altar he had laid his imaginings, his integrity, ambition, daring and honesty of purpose. On that altar he had prostrated himself.

When it came to San Francisco, Ralston had become a monomaniac. Its growth, its development, its increasing beauty thrilled him.

For the city he had developed a wild, passionate, almost pathetic love. He was like the Medici in their adoration of Florence, or the mad Wittelsbachs in their apotheosis of Munich. What cared Lorenzo il Magnifico, if he impoverished the rich, beggared the poor, or robbed virginity of its chastity, if Florence prospered? What cared Ludwig "der Zweite" what crimes he committed so long as Munich became the queen city of the Eiser? What was immolation, Bavarian bankruptcy, or self-murder if Munich profited? Death was worth its sting if ambition was attained.

What cared Ralston about wealth, money, position or prestige? It was San Francisco and San Francisco alone that mattered. It was his ambition, never himself, that drove him from one vast undertaking to another; that had already converted seven barren sand dunes into a place of pinnacles, domes, stacks and steeples; that had given the town its picturesque appearance. If fewer red corpuscles had coursed in his veins, if his imagination had been less tinged with the splendor of the Orient, how magnificent would have been his sacrifice!

Just as Ralston had hoped, his dream city had developed into another New Orleans: fantastic, fabulous, mysterious, mercurial.

Swept by the violent currents of two rivers and the tide of a mighty sea, Ralston was never through planning for his city. Some of that force about him had gotten into his blood.

Montgomery Street must be another St. Charles Avenue. It must have its opening to the bay. Ralston visualized it lined with trees: magnolia, orange, lemon and lime. Here were open spaces parked with lawns and flower beds. In its bay-ward sweep it brushed Rincon Hill into the sea and scrapped the puny buildings in its environs. In their stead would arise public edifices, pillared and porticoed like those of the maritime city on the Gulf. At one end would arise Telegraph Hill, at the other would lie the blue waters of the bay, the wharves of Pacific greyhounds and the terminus of the Central Pacific. Up and down this main arterial would run a continuous stream of traffic: of California-made vehicles. Children would romp there. Boulevardiers would promenade there. At iron tables under the umbrageous shade of plane trees, they would sip coffee and drink frappéd California wines. It was a magnificent dream that filled Ralston's brain, sleeping or waking.

In no time at all, in carving out this plan, Ralston had found himself involved in dirty politics, lobbying and associating with all kinds of questionable politicians. But Ralston kept his eye on the dream and avoided squalid realities as much as possible. In the end he found himself only partially successful. John Parrott and Milton S. Latham arose in his path and thwarted the fulfillment of his plan. One would not discuss the problem at all. "He would fight it every inch of the way," he threatened. Upon the high price demanded by the other for his property, the boulevard project had finally floundered. By that time, on "Montgomery Street South" Ralston had squandered the best part of $2,000,000 only to find it forever frustrated at Howard Street.

Thwarted as the thoroughfare was, Ralston hid his chagrin by beautifying it. A block of lofty, brick business structures of Mediterranean appearance, their façades featuring Corinthian columns, made its appearance. Their cost was estimated at $400,000.

At the corner of Montgomery and Market Streets, the Grand Hotel, the most sumptuous hostelry in the West, began to rear its white walls. It consisted of two units, three stories in height, French Renaissance in style. The mansard roof of one was adorned by a tall octagonal tower of splendid proportions. The two units on opposite sides of Stevenson Street, were united by a "Bridge of Sighs" reminiscent of the one beside Venetian waters. In this hotel, which could boast of 400 rooms and almost as many private baths, Ralston invested another generous slice of his Comstock fortune.

About this time Lawrence Barrett and John McCullough, the nation's finest Shakespearean exponents, who had been delighting Ralston's eye and ear these many years, with their manly interpretations of Julius Caesar, Iago, Othello, Mark

Antony, and Cassius, received a call to go East. Ralston was amazed at their plan to depart. They were a histrionic asset to his dream city. They were the "Théâtre d'Orléans" over again. One day he sent for them. When they had been ushered into his office in the Bank of California, and comfortably seated opposite him, Ralston propounded a question: how would they like to remain in San Francisco and manage a California Stock Company? Then Ralston went on to outline his plans for the building of a temple of the Muses on California Street between Kearny and Dupont.

McCullough and Barrett were astounded at such a munificent offer, and deferred their departure.

With his usual care before proceeding with extensive enterprises, Ralston dispatched an able architect to New Orleans. He must see Galliers French Opera House as well as other great theatrical centers of the East. They must be studied as regards their adaptability to San Francisco. In the course of time another French Renaissance structure, featuring Corinthian columns, was in process of construction. Then it was finished.

On January 18, 1869, the new temple was opened with a great fanfare of trumpets, and an especially-composed-for-the-occasion overture was played. The Belmont Prince sat in the proscenium box. Red velvet hangings encircled him and his handsome wife like the mat on a gold frame. In the stalls and galleries about him were gathered some 2000 San Franciscans. Francis Bret Harte had composed a poem for the occasion, which Barrett had committed to memory and delivered with telling effect. Then the play, Bulwer's comedy, "Money," got under way.

In the entre-acts, when the drop-curtain was lowered it was found that Ralston had provided a tremendous surprise for his fellow citizens. On it, in resplendent greens and blues, was depicted a scene dear to the Ralston heart: a marine view of the Golden Gate with several stately clippers sailing through on their way to the great sea beyond. There was the well-remembered scene: the great tossing gulf of blue water separating the rocky headlands of Fort Point from the precipitate cliffs of the Marin hills. In the foreground sparkled the opalescent waters of the bay; beyond the Golden Gate swept an infinite stretch of sea.

It was received with tremendous acclaim. Every one flocked about Ralston's box to press his white-gloved hand and congratulate him. It was New Orleans over again.

At the close of the play came the ovation: rounds of applause, cheers and throwing of flowers. Lawrence Barrett became the spokesman of the evening. Acknowledgments were made to the capitalists of San Francisco who had made this home of the Muses possible. This artist was commended for scenic effects, that one for costumes; but not a word of the Belmont Prince from whose brain had emanated the whole glorious setting. Not an allusion. Not because Barrett did not want to pay honors to whom honors were due, but because Ralston would not permit it. He had flatly forbidden any phrase in praise of his name. He was too modest, men said. Not for Ralston were empty eulogisms. It was enough for him that San Francisco could boast of such a temple. It was enough for him that his mines on the Comstock Lode had made it possible.

But neither this sumptuous temple of the Muses; nor the mansarded Grand Hotel with its 400 baths and telegraphic communication between each room and main office; nor the colonnaded stores in the Harpending block; nor woollen factories; nor sugar mills; nor silk-worms; nor Hereford cattle; nor fields of tobacco; nor hogsheads of wine, were warranted by a population of 120,000. The cost of labor, of coal, of materials was high. Advertisement was increasing population; but to keep people busy Ralston had always to be manufacturing jobs.

Such a dream as Ralston had been enjoying could not endure the light of many days. Long since, California's placers had exhausted themselves. And into each one of his cherished projects Ralston had been pouring Comstock silver. Washoe bullion alone had been developing San Francisco, promoting the welfare of the State, and advertising the fame of the Pacific at home and abroad.

In beautifying San Francisco, sterile Washoe had come

into her own. Again, a miracle had happened: the barren staff had burst into effulgent bloom. And Ralston counted on the Ledge's vigor maintaining itself forever.

As yet none of Ralston's industries had become self-supporting. True, his woollen mills had taken a gold medal at the Paris International Exposition of 1867; and A. T. Stewart, the New York merchant prince, had ordered $275,-000 worth of cashmeres, broadcloths and woollen goods. But still his mills and factories were not prospering as Ralston had hoped they would. Always he had the unforeseen to contend with.

One winter the Sacramento River overlapped the levies on Sherman's Island, destroyed the crops and inundated the warehouses. At another time a destructive fire swept Gilroy's tobacco fields. One million dollars' worth of cigars, raw material and appliances went up in smoke.

The Cornell Watch factory, too, was having its trouble. Inefficient Chinese labor drove the company across the Bay. In Berkeley, the dust-laden atmosphere was inimical to the works of fragile timepieces.

But a more terrible thing for the security of Ralston's empire was happening to the East. A thing that he, as well as every Californian, had anticipated as a boon to the Coast was bearing an economic blight. With every hour Union Pacific and Southern Pacific lines were rushing headlong toward one another. At last one day at Promontory, Nevada, East and West were irrevocably joined by bands of steel. Ralston, Stanford, Crocker, and Hopkins were present at that union; but the marriage on which he had counted so ardently begot nothing but chagrin for Ralston.

Now over those polished rails, for whose purchase Ralston had advanced thousands in bullion, there poured down into his empire a very avalanche of St. Louis and Chicago goods. San Francisco markets, California markets, Comstock markets were deluged, then glutted, with woollen, silk and cotton goods, tobacco, furniture, wine and sugar from "the States."

Everything that Ralston had fostered with Comstock gold could now be purchased far cheaper than he could manufacture them in his mills and factories. Many firms failed, some consolidated, some retired from business. Rents in San Francisco dropped like lead. Real-estate values shrivelled up to nothing. The Montgomery Real Estate Company received a knock-out blow.

Imperceptibly the walls of Ralston's empire trembled. Earthquakes could not make the Belmont Prince quail but the rumble of the overland trains filled him with dismay. Many of his ventures in wool, sugar, furniture, silk and tobacco were attended with tremendous loss. But never a word of complaint from the magician of San Francisco. Men wondered how he could maintain his light-hearted manner; but of course these people had never known life on the Mississippi.

If it hadn't been for his tremendous income from the Union Mill & Mining Company and the Virginia & Truckee Railroad, many of his industries would have succumbed then and there.

Now more voraciously than ever his infant industries swallowed up the profits of "Kentuck," "Yellow Jacket" and "Crown Point." But Ralston was sanguine. He saw nothing but ultimate success. He had supreme confidence in the Comstock, confidence in his own judgment, confidence in the future. He possessed the knack of bringing every one to his views. Nevertheless, money was so drastically needed to sustain his economic empire that he and Harpending decided to auction off the properties of the Montgomery Street Real Estate. As soon as the sale was announced the whole city was alert. The offices of the company were crowded with investors eager to purchase at private sale, but they were told that the company would hold an old-fashioned auction and nothing else.

The great day arrived. By consent it was held on the floor of the Merchant's Exchange. Never had such a mob of moneyed men gathered together in San Francisco. Among the throng Ralston had posted many "cappers." Pandemonium broke loose when the first offering was announced. Men fought and raved for it like brokers filling "shorts" on a stock exchange. Time after time the same scenes were enacted, but it became only too evident to Ralston that his "decoys" were picking up everything ostensibly sold. Finally the great sale was adjourned. Ralston realized he had been living in a fool's paradise over the boom that would follow in the wake of the overland trains. They had spelled ruin to his real estate. Not a lot could he sell except to "by-bidders."

To meet demands for money and to preserve his own credit from becoming impaired, Ralston had to avail himself of his position and influence with the Bank to obtain "pecuniary assistance," by borrowing.

On top of that economic blight the ore bodies in "Kentuck" and "Yellow Jacket" began to exhaust themselves: no new bonanzas were being located, and the burden of his indebtedness hung like a sword over Ralston, and anxiety and alarm as to the consequences seized both the Bank and the banker. In this hour of anguish Ralston turned to his agent in Virginia City for some comforting hope of further Comstock developments. He told Sharon the peril which threatened both himself and the Bank.

"Unless the Comstock comes to my aid with a new bonanza," he confided, "I cannot liquidate my large indebtedness and the Bank will be compelled to suspend."

It was a terrible confession to make, a worse one for Sharon to hear. Was he not Ralston's partner in William Sharon & Co.? Failure to Ralston meant failure to Sharon, and Sharon could not face that condition again. After that admission he became less frank with his patron, and invested largely on his own score.

"Do not despair," Sharon bade.

Often now, he reminded his chief of the crisis through which the Bank had, safely, passed in 1864. What had saved the Bank then? The Comstock Lode: the great deposits in "Kentuck," "Yellow Jacket" and "Crown Point," etc. Sharon then infused into Ralston his own faith in developments of ore certain to be found in Gold Hill. He encouraged him with hope of work then progressing in the deeper levels of the "Crown Point." In the "Yellow Jacket" there was a new-found streak of ore that was more than promising. He told Ralston to keep his eye on that "Yellow Jacket streak." In the meantime the profits of the Virginia & Truckee Railroad and the Union Mill & Mining Company, from the milling of low-grade ores, of which there was abundance, were large and would tide him over. He urged Ralston to rely upon these dividends until the needed bonanza could be found. There was no doubt of a rich body of ore about to be discovered in "Yellow Jacket" or "Crown Point."

During this interval Ralston riveted his attention on the "Yellow Jacket" and set himself to work at recuperation. He realized what he could from the enterprises with which he had become entangled. He closed out those which were already unsuccessful, and withdrew from those which could stand without him. The danger of financial catastrophe remained a secret, and a torturing one, between Ralston and Sharon, with the Comstock on one side and San Francisco on the other.

Even with assets freezing about him, Ralston went on paying his 1 per cent dividend a month. And knowing of frigid conditions the directors went on pocketing their dividend. Content to leave the outcome in the hands of the great Ralston, the Magician of San Francisco!

Now the financial and social leader of California became a tragic figure. He found himself standing alone, absolutely alone, no longer leading but pursued by a crowd of dividend-devouring Californians. Not for a minute could he pause. On he must go—lead or be destroyed by the pack behind him, and he preferred leadership to lagging. All the time, a look of sadness was creeping over his face.

All the time, Ralston kept his hopes riveted on the desolate Comstock hills. Out of that sterile earth must come the Aladdin-like power that would save him as well as economic California. Twice before, the Comstock had saved him and not for an instant did Ralston doubt that the Lode would come to his rescue again.

All that time he allowed the thought of the thin streak of pay ore Sharon was unearthing in the "Yellow Jacket" to buoy him up. On that streak depended hope or failure.

CHAPTER XVII

RALSTON'S WORRIES MULTIPLY

January, 1869

While financial conditions in San Francisco were depressing Ralston to the extreme, things took on a more sinister aspect on the Comstock.

Of the eleven ore bodies known to exist at the beginning of the year 1868, the greater number were completely exhausted. None of Sharon's exploratory operations had discovered anything. Long since, the deposits in the "Mexican," opulent "Ophir," and magnificent "Gould and Curry" had "petered out." Not since 1867 had the "Empire" paid a dividend and the "Imperial" only $24,000 in 1869. For years Ralston had been depending on the "Yellow Jacket." Of late that, too, had fallen off—from $2,677,488 in 1867 to $682,000 in 1868. In order to keep the mines going, Ralston's Ring had resorted to assessments. Every chambermaid and demi-mondaine in San Francisco was contributing her earnings toward the running of the Comstock. Of late their earnings had proved insufficient.

No wonder Ralston was worried. But no one would have guessed it. His companionship was just as jovial. His temper just as even. His air of confidence never more infectious. Neither was there any let-up in the scale of superlative entertainment at Belmont, in the number of guests; the speed of his horses; the tempo of the music, nor the frequency of his Neptune Beach swims. Nor was there any slackening in his program for San Francisco's improvement. From all outward evidences times were never more propitious, but within, tension was playing physical havoc with Ralston. His color had become more hectic, the throbbing of his temporal arteries more noticeable. And he had been forced to put himself under the care of Doctor John Pitman. On the Comstock there could be no let-up in expenditure. It took gold to dissipate rust. It took dividends to pay miners and to keep San Franciscans smiling.

Sharon's face grew long in contemplation. Exploration in depth had been disappointing. Sutro was wrong. There was nothing below the water-level. Underground floods were more menacing than ever. There was not power enough in any pump to handle it. The Comstock gangue was changing from predominant quartz to predominant carbonate and sulphate of lime: a deposit hitherto barren. Ore bodies occurred less frequently: none of any extent. What there were had become poor and refractory. By January, 1869, these facts were known to Ralston and his Ring. In San Francisco the Bank's capital had been jeopardized by the finishing of the transcontinental road. On the Comstock his investments were failing from lack of ore bodies. Never had Ralston's financial horizon looked so dubious. One single ray of hope illuminated it: a small vein of extremely rich ore recently uncovered on the 900-foot level of the "Yellow Jacket" mine.

As if the financial depression in San Francisco and a threatened exhaustion of the Comstock were not enough to make Ralston white-headed, he suddenly found himself facing labor troubles in Virginia City; the miners struck for higher wages: $4 a day for all men working underground was their demand. At a time like this Ralston realized the futility of refusing. His only hope of relief came from the Comstock. So the miners were promised a raise, although that meant a loss in dividends to Ralston.

One mine alone stood out against the increase, the "Savage." They would not pay $4 a day to all their workmen.

When the Miners' Union met they considered the case of the stubborn "Savage." One resolution was taken. The president of the Union was instructed to appoint a committee to deal with refractory Superintendent Bonner.

With a grim bit of sardonic humor the president appointed a committee of the huskiest, brawniest men on the Lode: 300 strong. On the following day the committee formed a column. With beating drum and defiant fife they marched on the "Savage," with every step booming at the top of their lungs: "$4 a day." Not to heed that voice was futile. The "Savage" surrendered to the ultimatum. For Ralston that meant thousands of dollars lost in dividends. But it was better to pay $4 a day all around than jeopardize the future of that yellow streak just appearing in the "Yellow Jacket."

Having attained a raise in pay, the miners turned their attention to the Chinese. "They must go." Ever since construction on the Virginia and Truckee Railroad had commenced, Ralston had availed himself of their cheap labor. Along the twenty-two miles of track some 700 to 800 coolies were employed in grading, tunnelling, blasting, etc. The sight had been gall and wormwood to the Miners' Union. One day they sent word to Ralston: get rid of your cheap celestial laborers. Ralston paid no attention to their mandate. The Ring controlled the Comstock. They would hire whom they pleased to operate it.

When rising indignation could no longer be held in check, a "committee" of miners headed by a brass band marched over the Divide and down into Gold Hill. They were going to drive the Chinese graders out of Storey County. Sharon notified the police. Just beyond the "Overman" mine the Sheriff of Storey County overtook the "Committee."

A proclamation commanding the miners to desist was read.

Loudly the sheriff was cheered. A deputy then read the Riot Act from the statutes of the United States.

Came three cheers for the United States in reply. On such men proclamations and Riot Acts were a waste of breath.

Not only had the Chinese seen but they had heard. At the nearer approach of the "committee," coolies with long queues flying could be seen disappearing over the sun-baked hills in all directions. Labor had become king on Sun Mountain. No longer could Ralston's Ring deny its ultimatums.

Ralston heard about that uprising with distress. Not only had he a barren Lode and a general business depression to contend with but a rising cost of operation. Labor had become a potential threat to his plans: no longer could the Chinese be employed on the Comstock. That meant further drains on dwindling resources. But greater calamities were about to be added to the unbearable burden resting on Ralston's shoulders. No matter how chaotic he felt within, he must present a sanguine exterior to the public. No matter how the tempest raged about his boat, the captain must appear calm and reassuring.

John W. Mackay, superintendent of "Kentuck," and James G. Fair, superintendent of "Ophir," chose to select this very time to try to wrest the control of "Hale and Norcross," of which Ralston was treasurer, from the grasp of the Bank Ring.

Both Mackay and Fair were weary of the monster monopoly that had attached its tenacious tentacles to the Comstock Lode and scared all the little fish away. They contended that small fry had as much right to sustenance as the hydra-headed Californian. Not only was the monster sapping the vitality of the Lode, operating it with the cheapest kind of labor, but it was unscrupulously milking the San Francisco Stock Market. False reports of the mines would be made. From the inside, prices would be keyed up. Investors would be tempted. When highest peaks had been attained, adverse reports would be circulated; "Ophir" or "Mexican" or "Gould and Curry" had struck a "horse." Down would go stocks on the San Francisco market. Purchasers would be caught like rats in a trap. Who would profit? Always the same crowd: the Ring.

More than once Mackay and Fair had been caught in that trap and squeezed; more than once it had taught them costly lessons. So powerful had become the monopoly's hold upon the Lode that they despaired of escaping that monstrous clutch. Always they must remain "muckers." Never could they escape the traps. In desperation they had taken their courage in their hands. They set out to plumb the secret of the Ring's success on the San Francisco Stock Market. At last they had solved the problem: only with inside information could a man succeed on the California market. It was a foregone conclusion before you started.

Like twin Jasons, Mackay and Fair determined to go up against Ralston's monopoly and wrest a piece of the Golden Fleece from its clutches. Closely they watched the Lode. One day the coveted opportunity arrived. They pounced upon it like gamins upon a coin. By a code of courtesy recognized on the Comstock, the superintendent of one mine was allowed free access to the internal workings of any other. By this means Mackay and Fair had convinced themselves of a bonanza in "Hale and Norcross." And they intended to get control of the stock on the San Francisco market.

One day in January, 1868, Mackay and Fair saw Ralston's crowd stoop to an old dodge, one they had practiced time without number in the past. Always had it succeeded in milking a gullible public and leaving broken hearts in its wake. On the 900-foot level of their mine they confined twenty-five miners. When the newspapers announced that blankets, food, and drink were being sent down the shaft to the imprisoned men, Mackay and Fair understood their ruse. Either Ralston's crowd had discovered the bonanza on the East hanging wall of which they knew or they were again about to milk the public. Either would be profitable, but milking more so than a discovery.

Just as they anticipated, on January 10, 1868, when the "Hale and Norcross" released the imprisoned miners, it was voiced about the San Francisco Stock Exchange that rich ore had been discovered. Immediately the market responded. Stock, which had been quoted at $1300 per share on January 8, three days later suddenly skyrocketed to $2200 per foot.

So certain were Mackay and Fair of the mine's value that in spite of Ralston's ruse they determined to gain control in the open market. As they could only muster $160,000 between them and as that would not be enough to go up against Ralston's Ring and win, they hurried off to San Francisco to enlist the help of two of their Irish friends: Flood and O'Brien, proprietors of the Auction Lunch Saloon on Washington Street.

Mackay and Fair outlined their reasons for believing that there was a bonanza in "Hale and Norcross." Flood and O'Brien thought well of their discovery. Besides, they had faith in Fair's "fine nose for ore," and Mackay's stability. In their joint account the bartenders had $60,000. They would pool their resources with Mackay's and Fair's. Then the Irish insurgents would go up against Ralston's monopoly and wrest the control of "Hale and Norcross" from them.

On February 8 the great contest for control of the "Hale and Norcross" began on the San Francisco Stock Exchange; bartenders and muckers with $225,000 against the unlimited supply of the California Bank monopoly. Shares opened at $2925. Suddenly the fight veered into a duel between Charles L. Low, a San Francisco business man, and Ralston's Ring. Sorrowfully the Irishmen had to admit the Comstock adage: "When giants are striving for mastery, it is wiser for small fry to stand aside." In the end, the Irishmen came so close to winning that they forced Ralston to pay $7100 for those shares which decided the contest. At that, Ralston would not have won had not millionaire Alvinza Hayward, one of Ralston's friends, arrived on the scene of action in the nick of time. Ralston was so grateful for Hayward's aid in the victory that he immediately raised him to the Bank's hierarchy. He was elected to the Mine's directorate and became a member of the Ring. A move which he would bitterly regret.

Undismayed by defeat, the Irishmen went back to their jobs: Mackay and Fair to the Comstock, Flood and O'Brien to their saloon bar. But all four held to their purpose. Back to his office of many worries went Ralston. Only Sharon knew how close the Ring had come to a loss of their monopoly. He belittled the Irishmen: Flood and O'Brien were nothing but bartenders, Mackay and Fair nothing but "muckers." Soon the Bank would be hiring them at $4 a day. Unforunately those remarks reached the ears of the insurgents and made them more bitter than ever against Ralston. Apparently the Bank's victory was a hollow one. Nothing developed in "Hale and Norcross." No dividends were declared. During the spring and summer, stock fell from $2924 a share to $11.50.

When the stock struck that unprecedented figure the Irishmen pounced upon the market and gobbled up all available shares. One day, Ralston and Sharon were horrified to read in the *Gold Hill News* of February 27, 1869, an item which took their breath away:

"As J. G. Fair and John W. Mackay of Virginia City," it read, "own over 400 shares of the stock, they will be very liable to exercise their controlling interest in influencing the choice of officers for the ensuing year."

Again Ralston saw himself pressed by the four Irishmen. Out of a possible 800 shares of "Hale and Norcross," the quartet held 400. Now it was up to the Bank to get hold of the other 400 shares and stalemate them. It was then February 27, less than two weeks before the annual election on March 10, at the San Francisco offices of the Company.

In the meantime, Sharon proved himself far from idle. If the Bank was to continue its control of the Comstock, it behooved him by hook or crook to get control of the stock. Every share located Sharon purchased at high figures. Price was no object—only the result counted. Shortly before the election of the officers, in whose hands the operation and future management of the mine would continue for the ensuing year, it was found that each side had about an even number of shares. Unaccounted for were only 100 shares.

It was obvious to both sides that the acquiring of those 100 shares would decide the matter. Both parties hunted for them in vain. On the very night before the election Sharon learned that the 100 shares, so earnesly sought by both sides, were in the possession of a San Francsico widow, unaware alike of their value and importance. Immediately Sharon telegraphed to Ralston in cipher, giving the widow's address and telling him to get the stock.

It happened that John Mackay had an ally in the telegraph operator at Virginia City. An ally that hated and detested the very sight of Bill Sharon. By poring over previous Sharon-Ralston dispatches, the operator had been able to work out a key to the cipher used by Sharon. Now he translated the message Sharon had sent to Ralston and handed it over to Mackay.

Half an hour after Sharon had wired the widow message to Ralston, Mackay was sending a similar coded one to Flood.

On receiving his telegram, Ralston, not knowing any hurry was necessary, waited until morning to call upon the widow. At that time he was chagrined to find that Flood had already called upon her and had paid her $8000 a foot for the stock she held.

As scheduled, the "Hale and Norcross" meeting was held. The Bank Ring went out of service and a new Board of Directors was chosen. Among other changes, James G. Fair was appointed superintendent. As a result the product of the mine was tripled in 1869; quadrupled in 1870. An impending assessment was rescinded and $728,000 was divided in dividends among the stockholders.

In these Irishmen Ralston saw a power in embyro—a power that filled him with misgiving. Just how far could four illiterate Irishmen go? Could such men sap the influence of the Bank of California on the Lode? Sharon still looked on the four with disdain. Ralston appreciated worth when he met it. In the quartet he saw a threat to his supremacy—a threat against San Francisco.

Then the Irishmen dealt Ralston another resounding blow. By no means were they disposed to allow the Union Mill and Mining Company to monopolize their profit from the reduction of ore; they began acquiring mill property. First Bacon's mill, and then Sullivan's, and finally, Trench's mill fell into their hands.

Thus in Ralston's hour of need even the dividends of the Union Mill and Mining Company were jeopardized.

Now more than ever he pinned all his hopes on the pay

streak just emerging in "Yellow Jacket." Never had he needed a bonanza as he needed the one he now anticipated.

On the morning of April 7, 1869, the whistles of the "Yellow Jacket" began to shriek. Fire engines from Virginia City and Gold Hill rattled up. With them came an immense throng; men, women, and children. Into the hoisting works, coughing, sneezing, choking, they jammed. Through clouds of smoke, to the mouth of the shaft they fought their way. Desperately they peered down the dark funnel. Forty-five men, husbands, fathers, and brothers, were working down there. They must be saved. While they looked, fumes, cinders, and flame spouted out of the mouth of the shaft and drove them back.

Well those onlookers knew what horrible things were happening down there 900 feet below the very spot where they were standing. Their men were hurtling through darkness. Choking, blinded, suffocated, they were climbing ladders; in desperation, clinging, like human flies, to cracks in the shaft timbering. Up, with a death-like grip, they were clambering. Overcome by flame, gas, and smoke, they were fainting, falling and crashing into the volcano below.

All the time, deadly fumes were gushing out of the shaft. Cinders, chips of burning wood, clouds of dust were flying in all directions. So rapidly did the works fill with smoke that the engineers could not see. One ran his cage into the sheaves. Another lift came rattling up the shaft: 800 feet in twenty-four seconds. Those on it had terrible tales to tell: of asphyxiation; of those who had fainted, had toppled off the platform and been crushed against the timbering and had fallen back into the furnace below.

Up shot another crashing cage. A horrible sight met the onlookers' eyes. On it were the three Bichel brothers. On the floor lay the eldest, dead. Another, unconscious, clung by one hand to the uprights of the cage. In his other he gripped the torso of his youngest brother: head and arms had been decapitated in the lift's up-rush.

When the cage made ready to drop, a lighted lantern was

hung from a stringer. To it Superintendent John P. Jones attached a note:

"It is death to come up from where you are. We shall get you out soon. The gas in the shaft is terrible and produces sure and speedy death. Write a word to us and send it up on the cage and let us know where you are."

In breathless suspense the onlookers watched the indicator. The cage sank. It reached the 800-foot level. For an eternity it waited; but no signal came to hoist.

Up crept the cage with the message and lantern. The light was out. The onlookers groaned. They knew what that meant: mortal eyes had not read the message. Their men were dead.

"The blowers must be stopped," insisted Superintendent Jones. "Steam must be forced into the burning levels. The shaft must be sealed. The fire starved out. It is the only way to stifle such flames." The crowd moaned. Such an act, they knew, meant certain death to all below. Jones did not ask for volunteers. He would go below himself. He was as strong as an ox. The crowd knew that he was an expert miner. He could hit a fly on a wall with the point of a pick. He was the one to drive a metal sheet into the blower and shut off the air.

He stepped upon the cage, one trusted miner and fifteen candles with him. The onlookers watched him sink from sight. They were sick with apprehension; but there were no wild cries or despairing shrieks. With clenched hands and swaying bodies they stared at the indicator. It showed them when Jones had reached the 800-foot level. Breathless, they waited for a signal to hoist. At last, it came. Up rushed the cage. On it was Jones with the unconscious miner in his arms.

In the gallery where Ralston's streak of pay ore had been discovered, the fire blazed on for days, weeks, months. Whenever the drift was opened, unseen coals burst into flames. Eventually forty-two bodies were recovered. Three never were. Wrapped in sheets of flame they were left to guard the streak of pay dirt on the 900-foot level on which Ralston had been banking. One day there was a cave-in. The gallery collapsed and had to be abandoned and block-headed off from the rest of the mine.

That was a terrific blow to Ralston. No one but Sharon knew how desperately he had been counting upon that stringer of pay ore that promised to lead to a new bonanza; that promised to relieve his crippled bank and foundering industries. Ralston realized that the "Yellow Jacket" fire had rendered the condition of the Bank of California a hazardous one.

In the meantime the fire caused a panic on the San Francisco market. Stocks of the "Crown Point," "Chollar," and "Yellow Jacket" crashed. From all sides came cries for "mud." Any number of Ralston's friends were ruined. In the downward dive, the Bank lost thousands.

Ugly stories were circulated: the fire was of incendiary origin. On purpose to depress the Stock Market the mine had been fired. It had been planned, went the whisperings, during the change of shifts. But the flames had gotten away from the plotters and forty-two miners had paid the price of the blunder. From all sides came vehement denials. But the stories persisted.

Aroused to a panic of terror and indignation by the fire in three of the great producing mines of the Comstock and the horrible deaths of forty-two of their comrades, the miners were up in arms against Ralston and his Ring. Proper precautions had not been taken for their safety, they claimed. Ralston was interested only in returns.

Ralston's plight was desperate. Never had his San Francisco finances been at such low ebb. When the mines were in borrasca, there was no work for the Union Mill and Mining Company nor the Virginia and Truckee Railroad. Thus those dividends ceased.

Hemmed in by disaster, depression, and worry, Ralston donated $5000 from his personal funds to the widows and orphans of those who had been lost in the holocaust.

CHAPTER XVIII

SUTRO'S SPEECH

August, 1869

Adolph Sutro was quick to realize the opportunity which the combination of miners and their growing bitterness against Ralston, following the terrible "Yellow Jacket" fire, offered him. Now was the time to strike.

The Union was just the media upon which he could work, for Sutro was at the end of his rope. His four years of heartbreaking labor to drain the Comstock had come to naught, solely through the machinations of Ralston's bank. How many times during that period had he lifted the cup of fruition to his lips only to have Ralston or one of his Ring dash it to the ground? How many times had Ralston pricked the bubble of success just as his eager fingers reached forward to seize it?

Ignominiously Ralston had pushed him to the wall. Now that the Bank had gotten control of the Virginia City papers, not one of their editors dared print an advertisement or a news item if it referred to the Sutro Tunnel.

Sutro looked about him. Ralston had barred every avenue leading to the opening of the tunnel. And what for? Merely because he had dared to dream a great dream, to challenge Mother Earth in the name of humanity. Such power was unbearable.

If the Bank had helped him years ago to push his tunnel through to the Lode, those forty-five victims of the "Yellow Jacket" fire would not now be rotting in their graves in the hard rock. Just as sure as there was a God in heaven, Ralston's ambitions had lighted those funeral pyres. The more he thought of that terrible catastrophe, the angrier Sutro became. Ralston had closed the doors of escape, but thank God! not yet had he been able to silence him!

Now, in sheer desperation, Sutro determined to turn upon his oppressors—to use any weapon against them. Right in their midst, he would stand up, condemn them and appeal to the working miners. He would show up the Bank's rascalities and explain the persecution Ralston had instigated against him. Then he would ask for a "home-indorsement." Right in their stronghold he would teach the Bank crowd a lesson they would never forget.

Somewhere or other Sutro got hold of a private press. At furious pace he printed hundreds of flamboyant posters. These he had distributed to every laborer in every mine in Virginia City and Gold Hill. The posters invited the miners to a mass meeting at Maguire's Opera House on August 19, and announced that Sutro would lay the whole matter of his tunnel before them.

On the designated night, Maguire's was jammed to the doors with working men. It was a friendly audience. The miners admired the pluck of the man before them. They knew that the Bank had some notion of building the tunnel themselves. Hadn't they boasted that when the time came to build the tunnel, they would make their wishes known to Congress. Then, and only then, would the Comstock be drained.

"I have come out here among you, my fellow citizens," began Sutro quietly, "in order to explain to you all about this tunnel business, and while some of the moneyed men of San Francisco look upon the whole thing as a failure, not knowing anything of its history, nor of the great fight of the California Bank Ring against it, I have more confidence in its success now than ever.

"Fellow citizens, I have come among you to propose to the working people of Nevada to join in together in order to start work on the tunnel itself, and thereby give me that solid indorsement at home, from those who live on the very spot, from the men who work in these very mines, and who are supposed to know most about it, which I have lately sought in vain from the mining companies and from the people who should be most deeply interested. Your solid indorsement will be valued highly at Washington; it will annihilate the efforts of that scheming combination: the California Bank."

Then, with bitter eloquence, Sutro attacked Ralston's Ring. Every sentence struck home.

"Fellow citizens, it must now be evident to you that the arch-enemy of this great work is that hydra-headed monster you have reared in your midst, and allowed to grow into gigantic proportions; that enemy of the welfare of the whole Pacific Coast; that incubus upon your prosperity; that crafty concern which resorts to every means to carry out its ends. And why do they oppose the tunnel? Why do they do all in their power of cunning and scheming and planning to defeat it? Why are all their satellites and hirelings told they must defeat and oppose the tunnel project with all their might and power, by fair and by foul means? Why do they threaten to discharge their employees if they take a hand in it? And why are they compelled to do all this in the darkness of night? Why is it they dare not make their motives known?"

The miners were astounded at Sutro's eloquence. Such nerve was not lost upon them. Such courage won their hearts and held their attention. For one lone man, single-handed, to tackle a fortified monopoly like Ralston's bank, was worthy of the best traditions of Sun Mountain. They applauded and listened intensely.

"Fellow citizens, let me enlighten you. Allow me to pierce that darkness and let in a ray of daylight; let me explain to you why these men so bitterly oppose a work which in them, the ostensible owners of the Comstock Lode, should find the strongest advocates; let them show to you why they have turned to the guardians of the Treasury at Washington; let them tell you why they tremble with fear lest work on the tunnel be started; let me explain to you why they make you work in foul atmosphere, which sends half of you to your graves in the prime of manhood; let me show you why they have allowed forty-five of your miners to be foully murdered at the fire of the Gold Hill mines, for the want of an exit through the tunnel; and let me show them to you in their true colors and then hold them up to the shame, contempt, and ignominy they so richly deserve."

On went the deep, insistent voice. The miners recognized that voice: it was theirs, the voice of the common people. The voice of the working man crying aloud against the greed of the monopoly that was exploiting them.

With every sentence the listeners grew angrier and angrier, as Sutro exposed the manner in which Ralston's Ring had victimized them.

"Many of you will be utterly astonished to learn that neither the Bank nor the Mill Ring own more than a few shares in each mine, just about enough to be elected trustees of the companies, while you, the miners and residents of Virginia City, always own a large amount of stock, and sometimes a controlling interest in many of the mines. How is it possible that they can control the elections, put in men of their own Ring as trustees, and manage and manipulate these mines as they please, to further their own ends, if they do not own any stock?"

How? Indeed! And Sutro showed them how they had been gulled and swindled and humbugged, and had allowed this clique, by sharp practice, to carry out their nefarious schemes. "Go and examine the books," Sutro thundered, "convince yourselves, and then wonder how such unblushing falsehood, based on brass and impudence, could have existed so long and not be exposed.

"You all know there is an institution in San Francisco called the Bank of California; they have a branch house in Virginia City over which William Sharon presides. Their capital stock is $5,000,000, with which they do a business of many millions more. They loan out a great deal of money; whether they loan out any of their depositors' money we don't know; but they loan out a great deal. They loan a great deal to their individual members, who are engaged in extensive speculation. Some of them pay, but a great many do not; that money is scattered all over creation, and whether they could pay all they owe, should they be called upon, I doubt very much."

Sutro paused to let this astounding statement sink into the minds of his hearers.

"Now let us see how their control of the mines further operates. There is a concern called the Union Mill and Mining Company, composed of just about the same men as control the California Bank and the mining companies. At the head of that concern, at Virginia City, is the agent of the California Bank. Somehow or other this mill association has gobbled up all the valuable mills in the neighborhood, and, as is stated, by paying a very small portion of the cost of them. Most of these mills were erected by private individuals, depending on a supply of ore from the companies on the Comstock Lode."

Then Sutro went on to tell the startled miners that in controlling the mines, Ralston's bank had seen fit to control the ore. Only those mills which were in his good graces received any rock. The others had to borrow from the Bank of California to tide them over. The poor victim on taking that money signed his own death warrant. As soon as such a mill man was indebted to the Bank, he received no more ore. When he could not pay the interest on his indebtedness, the mortgage on his mill was foreclosed and the man was utterly ruined.

In this wise, Sutro continued, Ralston's bank became possessed of nearly all the valuable mills on the Comstock, costing millions of dollars, at a trifling cost to them.

Neither did Sutro stop there with his exposé. While he was about it, he decided to become aggressive, as well as defensive, to take the war into the Bank's own camp and attack them where he knew they were the most sensitive: in their own pockets. He drew the men's attention to what every one of them knew full well: "their nefarious business methods, as well as their absolutely dishonest and wicked gambling system," and the amazed miners listened as he unfolded, in clearest English, plots and schemes that, as a rule, were never referred to above a whisper.

"There is still another way by which you are victimized," Sutro continued. "Supposing the superintendent and foreman of a mine are pliable tools in the hands of these cormorants, how easy it is, when a rich body of ore is discovered, to keep it secret, and instead of taking it out, start the miners going in the wrong direction, taking out inferior ore or bed-rock, sending it to the mills, involving the mine in debt, necessitating assessments, and then depreciating the stock. And how simple is it for the Bank to gobble it all up again quietly, while it is down, and after a large amount of it is secured, to set all the men to work that can find room and take out the good ore, make a great noise over it, declare large dividends, send up the stock, and then quietly sell out and pocket a million or so.

"How many of you have been bitten in this manner?" Sutro demanded. "What show have you when the cards are thus stacked against you? Have you ever seen a cat play with a mouse? It lets it run a little piece and then catches it again and repeats the experiment a number of times, to its great delight and amusement. But did you ever know it to fail that the cat ate up the mouse in the long run?

"A few of you make a good strike once in a while by sheer accident; that keeps up the excitement, and so you keep on gambling in stocks, pay your assessments, and in the end you will be eaten up like the poor mouse. There is no guesswork about it. It is a sure thing.

"Fellow citizens, do you commence to understand why this Ring opposes the construction of the Sutro Tunnel? They have thus far had things their own way, and have with a high hand grasped and taken everything worth having in the State of Nevada. They, like the devil-fish, have reached out their long slimy arms and taken hold of everything within reach, and nothing can escape their deadly grip. Do you think for a moment that they would allow so valuable a property as that of the Sutro Tunnel Company to escape their notice? Do you suppose that this clique, whose ideas of mine and thine are very confused, would not go to every exertion to obtain so great a prize by intrigue, machinations, and scheming? Do you suppose they would allow a superior power to spring up in their very stronghold, and not make every effort to destroy it? And do you believe that they would allow it to grow at all, but that they would nip it in the very bud?

"The tunnel, they know full well, is the key to this mountain and these mines, and will and must control and own this whole district. If that tunnel is constructed by third parties, their monopoly will be utterly broken up and ended. They could then no longer 'bull' and 'bear' stock, manipulate the mines and mills, and their railroad would be of little use."

With his eloquence exhausted, Sutro turned appealingly to the miners.

"Will you see me crushed out now?" he pleaded. "Will you allow that monstrous combination to trample me under foot? Will a chivalrous people allow one individual to be set upon by a whole pack of hounds? Will you see fair play when one man has the pluck to stand up against a crowd? Will you come to the rescue when I appeal to you in my endeavor to carry out a great and good work? I believe I need not make the appeal. For I know you will.

"Laboring men of Nevada, shake off the yoke of slavery and assert your manhood. The same power which has thus far defeated the tunnel project is crushing you down into the dust; they threaten to take your bread and butter from you if you subscribe to the tunnel stock, but you must act jointly. There lies your power. If you will all come in together they dare not discharge you. Let 3000 laboring men pay in an average of $10 a month, which gives you $30,000 per month, or $360,000 per annum, and insures the construction of the tunnel, carrying with it the control of the mines. That amounts to 33 cents per day. Who is there among you so poor as to miss it? How many of you expend that much every day in stimulants, cigars, and other luxuries? Put that money into the tunnel.

"Laboring men of Nevada, crush out that hydra-headed monster: that serpent in your midst—the Bank of California.

"Rouse up, then, fellow-citizens. You have no Andrew

Jackson among you to crush out the bank which has taken your liberties, but you have the power within yourselves. I do not mean to incite you to any violence; I do not mean to have you assert your rights by riot, force, and threats. That would be unwise, unnecessary and would only recoil upon yourselves. But I do mean to say that you can destroy your enemy by simple concert of action. Let all of you join in together to build the Sutro Tunnel; that is the way to reach them. They do already tremble lest you will act; they know you will form a great moneyed power; and that you will own the mines; they know it will cement you together.

"They also know full well that the first pick struck in the Sutro Tunnel will be the first pick into their graves. That first pick will be the signal for a new era.

"Come forward, then, and subscribe your names. Come at once and you will prove your friendship for the cause."

That speech gained for Sutro the confidence, respect, and adherence of the miners.

It was not that Sutro had exposed anything new to the miners, rather it was his audacity in bringing to their amazed attention the nefarious business methods of Ralston's machine, which heretofore had never been broached in tones above a whisper.

What with the recent fire in the "Yellow Jacket," the loss of forty-five of their number, and the known opposition of the Bank of California to the tunnel and to Sutro, the men were wrought up to the highest pitch of excitement by Sutro's speech. Swept off their feet by his eloquence they filed out into the street. Only one word was needed to set off the fireworks. Only one word and Sharon or any other would have been strung up to the nearest gallows frame. All night they milled about street corners, heatedly discussing the situation. Nothing could persuade them to disperse.

By dawn they had worked themselves up to such a degree that the police had to send for Sutro. Among them he circulated and had to use all his personal influence to prevent an outbreak.

Sutro added to the force of his appeal by showing the miners several effectively conceived cartoons. One represented a rich speculator, undoubtedly Ralston, driving six fast horses at breakneck speed down a country highway and covering a working miner with contemptuous dust; another showed Ralston's big woodpile; and still another the Virginia and Truckee Railroad, labelled the crookedest road in the world. All this to emphasize the monopoly: that the Bank of California controlled the Comstock's transportation and wood supply.

The series closed with a huge double cartoon that Milton might have conceived and Doré might have executed. It was headed "The Yellow Jacket Fire." On one side was a shaft 1000 feet deep, full of burning and falling ladders, timbers, and machinery. A vortex of swirling smoke and flame, with hundreds of miners trying to escape and tumbling headlong into the fiery depths below. Wives, mothers, and children were seen running to the mouth of the shaft and sinking in despair on the ground. It was a horrible conception. Many groaned as they looked at it. In the other half of the picture was a similar shaft on fire, but with the Sutro Tunnel connection made with the burning shaft, and the miners were seen escaping, meeting their wives and children at the mouth of the tunnel.

A few days later, on August 25, 1869, at a joint meeting, the Virginia and Gold Hill Miners' Union adopted some resolutions.

"We, the miners, who are compelled to delve and toil daily in an atmosphere heated and corrupted to such a degree that our health has become impaired, in many instances resulting in consumption and an early death, are the parties most deeply interested in the construction of this great work, which, had it been in existence at the late disastrous fire in the Gold Hill mines, which hurled into eternity forty-five of our brethren, would have given them the means of egress, and thus saved their lives; and

"Whereas: We consider the immediate commencement of work on the tunnel as of the most pressing necessity, and paramount to all other interests of this section of the country; therefore be it

"Resolved: By the miners of the Virginia and Gold Hill Unions, in joint convention assembled, that, as an earnest of our faith in the results to spring from the construction of the Sutro Tunnel, as a great national work, and as a financial operation, we do hereby agree to subscribe to the stock of the Sutro Tunnel Co. the sum of $50,000 in United States gold coin, as a first installment payable immediately and for the purpose of starting work upon the tunnel itself without delay."

Sutro was elated. At last he could set to work. He had a "home-indorsement!"

CHAPTER XIX

SUTRO'S "HOME–INDORSEMENT

October 19, 1869

"Awake! Arm! Arm!"

So read the startling headlines on the hand-bills which Sutro distributed among the miners inviting them to the inauguration of the Sutro Tunnel.

When October 19, the appointed day dawned, it was anything but propitious for such an occasion. Clouds suffused Mt. Davidson and a drizzling mist blotted out the scene of operation on the distant Carson River. Many who had engaged teams and carriages backed out and remained at home.

But not so the Piutes. They cared nothing about Sutro's Tunnel, but plenty of "Chamuk," and roasted pig, beef, and bread in exchange for a "fandango" was worth considering.

So, armed to the teeth with a gnawing appetite, they were on hand in force.

Down the Cañon they clattered in the wake of a "three seater" in which Sutro sat, in white beaver and Prince Albert. At Silver City the cavalcade dropped out of the clouds only to find that it was still drizzling. At Dayton things looked blue for any kind of a turnout. At Cross' Hotel, the Miners' Union brass band took up their position in front of Sutro's carriage. At one o'clock the three-mile march through the rain and the sagebrush, to the appointed rendezvous, started. Music was playing. Sutro, bolt-upright in his carriage, looked like a young Roman on the way to a triumph at the Forum. The pounding Piutes brought up the rear.

Not far from the proposed mouth of the tunnel, a tall flagstaff and speaker's stand had been erected. On nearby tables was the "Chamuk": loaves of bread and kegs of beer. On spits, dug into the mountainside, a "porker" and a whole bullock sizzled in the falling rain. Not a miner who looked at those twenty kegs of lager but shivered. Not a Piute, who listened to the sputtering beef, but his mouth watered in savory anticipation.

At last Sutro alighted. Arising before him in all its somber majesty was the misty mountain he was going to transfix with a five-mile tunnel. On a shelf, 2000 feet directly above him, perched the clustered stacks of Ralston's mines. Straight down from these, to a level with the very spot where he was standing, lay the sumps of those mines which Sutro was determined to drain whether Ralston would allow him to or not.

Between the spot where Sutro was standing and those Comstock sumps lay six miles of rocky escarpments that his tunnel must pierce to reach the Lode. It took a stout heart to contemplate the task and not quail. But Sutro was far from depressed; elation shone from every lineament of his face. Any one, that October day, who marked the jutting chin and the burning light in his eyes, realized that he was gazing into the face of a fanatic and that nothing short of accomplishment could appease him.

A brass band burst into the familiar strains of the "Star

Spangled Banner," a salute was fired, then Sutro cast aside his white hat, threw off his immaculate black coat, rolled up his sleeves on his big arms, took up a pick and threw it across his right shoulder. Then turning about he faced his audience, and made a neat little speech, in which he stressed the importance of the tunnel and the significance of the blow he was about to strike for humanity.

It would be heard in San Francisco. It would be heard in London, Paris, Berlin. For four years he had struggled for this moment: the moment he was to pry open the mouth of the underground drainway and drive his pick into Ralston's monopoly. Numerous branches would sprout from the main channel, Sutro explained. Eventually, there would be a hundred miles of conduits running in every direction through the mountain. It was the inauguration of a great "underground world."

With that, Sutro drove his pick deep into the earth. With a dull thud, a great quantity of earth and rock fell away. But Sun Mountain did not quake, nor did the land tremble; and yet that sound would reverberate on Wall Street, Fleet Street, the Bourse, and Unter den Linden. It was on this echo that Sutro counted.

From the immediate vicinity cheers welled upwards. Anvils were fired and giant-powder was set off. But not a whistle on the Comstock replied. Yet all the time Sutro was smiling and looking as triumphant as Wellington might have appeared at Waterloo or Nelson on the bridge, at Trafalgar.

Not to lose a second while the iron was hot, Sutro waved aloft a great sheaf of certificates that he held in his hand.

"Who will buy this Sutro Tunnel stock?" he cried.

"I takes von share," said a Dutchman.

"One share sold," called back Sutro. "Who is the next man?"

Some one indicated Mike.

"Faith," returned the Irishman, "I bought the first stock that was sold in town, and I'll not be after buying any more." It was three o'clock and Sutro's stock board closed for the day.

Just at that very moment, the sun burst through a black cloud and a radiant rainbow appeared in the heavens to the north. The arch, on account of the hour, was very low. The two ends appeared to be not more than a mile apart. As a bow of promise it was perfect in shape and tint. The west end seemed to rest on the very mouth of the Tunnel. By all, this was hailed as a good omen. Some hinted that Sutro had ordered the rainbow expressly for the occasion.

Due to the storm, the barbecue turned into a fizzle. The beeves were so "rare done" that not even the Piutes could make use of them and the twenty kegs of lager filled all with chilly misgivings.

The next day and the next found Sutro driving his bore into Sun Mountain. Like a frenzied earth-monster he dug his way in. In every direction dust was flying. Rocks were falling, earth caving. A sizeable dump reared its mount along the banks of the Carson. Sutro knew that that blow of his pick had been a nail driven into the coffin lid of the Bank of California.

With all his burning zeal, never once did Sutro realize how pitiful had been his tunnel's beginning. Never once did he see himself as Ralston's press writers did: a pygmy trying to bore a hole through Olympus; a mouse nibbling at the base of Ararat; one single man pitting his strength against the Bank of California. He left those pictures for his enemies to chortle over. To his few admirers he had become a conquering hero: one lone man contending against a corporation's greed.

His speech to the miners had been the stick of dynamite that had torn a way into the mountain. To Ralston's Ring it had been a bandit's torch intended to blast the doors of their treasure vaults and rob them of their millions. His speech and his beginning had antagonized them to the utmost. They would make Sutro regret every word he had uttered against them. Now he would have to look out: the mouse was facing an aroused lion. Roundly Ralston's press denounced his speech. It was the work of a demagogue. They accused him of inciting the miners to violence against the Bank of California. They scouted the idea of his ever finishing his project. He was an underground highwayman trying to rifle the Bank of California's mines. Could they have prosecuted him for his audacity, the Ring would not have hesitated to have sworn out the warrant.

Sutro laughed to scorn the shouts of "demagogue" that Ralston's crowd had raised against him. How could he have started his tunnel without that barrage of words? he retorted. Before them, Ralston's first line of defense had fallen. How could he have raised $50,000 or started those echoes now resounding throughout the world of finance without telling the miners the truth? It was the truth that the monopoly could not endure.

Ralston's methods had made Sutro aggressive. "If it takes my last breath," he swore, "I'll reach the Lode, if only to show Ralston how the Comstock should have been mined and to bring help to my suffering fellow men."

From all sides the newspapers on the Pacific Coast went after him: Sutro was a "humbug"; "a wild-cat swindler"; "a played-out carpetbagger."

"His first pick," said the *Gold Hill News,* "has been heretofore, is now, and ever will be, a pick at the pockets of all honest workingmen and others, whom he can 'bamboozle' into supporting him like a gentleman at other people's expense.

"In December Sutro will go to Washington," went on the tirade, "and 'make a big blow' over yesterday's affair at Dayton—hoping thereby to continue his deception of Congressmen; expecting to get aid from the Federal treasury; but we have printed one hundred extra copies of today's *News,* which we will send to 'the Committee of Ways and Means' of the Lower House of Congress so as to keep them posted. When Mr. Sutro arrives he will find that Congress is familiar with his plans."

In those taunts Sutro recognized the groans of discomfort he was causing his persecutors. Now, like so many drops of rain, they rolled off his back. Barking dogs had never stopped a procession's passing. On he meant to go through the mountain. The important thing to him was that the great Sutro Tunnel, which for four years had been only a handsomely framed blueprint, hanging on dusty office walls, had at last received a "home indorsement." For the time, he was well content.

But not so Ralston's Ring. One October evening Sharon cornered the "Yellow Jacket" miners just at the change of shift and addressed them:

"There is a wrong feeling of antagonism against the Bank of California, which charges it with being the enemy of the working man, and trying to crush labor and grind down wages," Sharon told them. "Yet this is not so. Can these mines or mills be worked without capital? Is it not this very capital that pays four dollars a day to you miners? Is it not better to have an institution that you can depend upon, and capital that can insure wages to working men, than to have to depend upon irresponsible parties? We must all work together for mutual benefit. We are doing the best we can for your interest as well as our own, and we earnestly desire your full confidence and co-operation.

". . . The golden days of the rich ore in the 'Mexican,' 'Ophir,' and 'Gould and Curry' are past, and now we have to put up with deposits of lesser grade. What there is below the present levels God only knows, and we must make the best of what we have got.

"Great God, would you kill the goose that lays the golden egg? Never mind what needy and designing demagogues tell you, but with the good sense you are endowed with, study and work for your own interests and that of the country.

"And now, with regard to the little seven-by-nine tunnel. This penniless adventurer, who does not pay a cent of taxes, wishes to make use of you to make himself rich. Of what benefit would that tunnel be to us on the Comstock Ledge? We can run a drift from the 900-foot level of this 'Yellow Jacket' mine and strike the 'Savage' ground at about the same depth that tunnel would, developing the ledge as we go, and with a mere tithe of the expense.

"That famous tunnel, which was started the other day on a barrel of champagne and 'four-bits,' even if it were finished, would not drain the Comstock Ledge. As you all know, the bodies of water in it are held at various points in the upper workings by cross seams of clay and other matter, every one of which has to be tapped by itself, and by that tunnel it would only be done at a ruinous expense. Many of you have been working at the 900-foot level of the 'Yellow Jacket' in good dry places, with the levels about you filled with water, which it has taken many weeks to get out.

"There, again, Sutro wants to make the mines not only pay $2 a ton for all the ore taken out through the tunnel, but also for all the ore taken from the surface, besides charging you 'two-bits' each for passing in and out to your daily work.

"How many men would the running of that tunnel employ at $4 a day, and how good is the security for your pay? I think you would rather have the Bank of California paper than his. We oppose him and his project; therefore he makes his fight by spitefully slandering us and trying to incite you against your employers. But, as I said before, let no such nonsense induce you to contend against your own interests and those who are of real benefit to you."

CHAPTER XX

RALSTON FACES PANIC

December, 1869

"You're just the man I want to see," said Ralston, drawing Harpending into a chair near him. "If things go on as they are every bank in San Francisco will be closed by tomorrow afternoon. Not one of us can stand a half day's run, and all will go down in a heap. Then look out for hell in general to break loose. This will happen if I don't get a million dollars in coin in the vaults tonight. But I intend to get it, and want you and Maurice Dore to help."

Of late, Ralston's troubles had been multiplying at a terrific rate. No one could realize the hazardous conditions under which his bank had been operating. All known bonanzas had exhausted themselves; the Miners' Union had demanded a higher wage-scale; cheap Chinese labor had been excluded from Washoe; the great fire in the "Yellow Jacket" had wiped out the last promising streak of ore; Sutro had inflamed the working men against the Bank and had actually started his tunnel; the Union Mill & Mining Co. had been given up to rust; the Virginia & Truckee Railroad had nothing to haul. So much for his monetary source of supply. And in San Francisco expenditure had been doubling. Nor was that all.

Sometime since, Ralston had advanced Stanford and Huntington $3,000,000 with which to finish their railroad. Now that amount was a frozen asset. Lately, $2,000,000 had been sent out of San Francisco to finance some South American proposition. Thus, recently, $5,000,000 in gold had gone out of California. A good share of it out of Ralston's bank. At any rate out of circulation.

When, in July, 1869, Jay Gould had cornered "gold" and held the yellow metal at a huge premium and the gold coin in California had been drained eastward as through a sieve, Ralston was filled with fresh dread. Some mornings his bank doors opened with only $50,000 to $75,000 in coin in the vaults. If there were a run, never would he be able to withstand it. No matter how he was racked within, to the world at large Ralston had to present a light-hearted, debonair manner.

During all this time his only comfort lay in the bars of bullion, entrusted to his care, in the bank refinery. A terrible temptation it was to have gold in the raw, yet none available as coin to use over the counters. Worse still, owing to the fact that Ulysses S. Grant was just coming into his administration, the San Francisco branch of the United States Mint had been temporarily shut down. Strangely enough,

President Grant had refused to allow local bankers to deposit gold bars with the San Francisco Assistant Treasurer and receive in return an equivalent in gold coin. Hard pressed as he was for funds Ralston had brought all possible pressure to bear upon Grant but without results: like adamant the President stood between him and sufficient gold on his counters.

To Ralston it seemed ridiculous that he should find himself in such a plight when there was plenty of Comstock bullion in his possession and $14,000,000 in gold coin tucked away in the United States Sub-Treasury right in their very midst.

To Ralston it seemed like a legitimate transaction to deposit Comstock bullion in the Treasury and carry away an equivalent in gold coin. Not only was it legitimate, but under the prevailing circumstances imperative. And right was might. Ralston telegraphed this suggestion to President Grant. But there was no response. Innumerable times, at great expense, he wired the Bank of California's predicament: he was on the fringe of a "run"; on the brink of failure.

As conditions became worse and panic and catastrophe stared him blankly in the face, Ralston fairly burned up Western Union wires with his pleas for executive help. But President Grant remained obdurate. For some unaccountable reason he absolutely refused to sanction the exchange of bullion for coin or even to heed Ralston's cry of need. Yet right was might. And the fate of San Francisco trembled in the balance. A run spelled ruin to the Coast.

All the time, while the uneasy feeling on California Street was mounting, the strain had stained Ralston's face a crimson color and knitted the black brows above his troubled eyes. Nor could a canter on his favorite horse nor a plunge in the cold waters of the bay alleviate the load that palled upon his shoulders.

It was on this day when tension was at its height that Ashbury Harpending dropped into the bank and was ushered into Ralston's office. Ashbury, too, was feeling the financial pinch. He needed funds. He wanted to know something about the outlook. Most of all, he needed a tip or two, and he got it in no uncertain terms.

"Be at the bank at 1 o'clock, and put on an old suit of clothes, for you will have plenty of hard work to do," Ralston said imperatively as Harpending got up to leave.

Shortly after midnight Dore and Harpending met by appointment. They were utterly mystified as to what Ralston wanted of them. Together they tramped through the deserted, dimly lighted streets. To them it seemed like old times in San Francisco—the times when footpads lurked in alleys—when blackjacks flourished in the dark—when a thud on the head was feared—and a splash in the bay followed. Warily they proceeded toward the Bank of California.

They found Ralston in his office with one of his trusted officials. Ralston was in the highest spirits. The spring of youth was in his step, but he counselled caution, no questions, and silence.

Noiselessly he led his mystified friends through darker downtown streets to the United States Sub-Treasury, then located on Montgomery Street between Sacramento and California. Through the shuttered windows a dim light shone. When within a few paces of the entrance Ralston called on his friends to halt. Alone, noiselessly, he approached the door of the Sub-Treasury. To Harpending's and Dore's utter amazement and without challenge of any kind, they saw Ralston open the great bronze door. Whether he had used a key, tapped, or whispered a word, they could not tell. They watched him disappear over the threshold. Noiselessly they saw the door close behind him. Then they were alone on the street, gaping in openmouthed astonishment.

How long they stood there they could not tell, but suddenly the door opened and Ralston emerged half-carrying, half-dragging several heavy sacks.

"Take that to the bank," he ordered the dumbfounded duo, "the gentleman there will give you something to bring back."

Away went Harpending and Dore, bent double with the heavy sacks on their backs.

The trusty official at the bank received the sacks. He was

gone for some time. At last he was back with several bars of Comstock bullion. These Harpending and Dore toted back to the Sub-Treasury. On the sidewalk they found Ralston, smilingly awaiting them with a fresh supply of bulky burlap bags. Over to Ralston they turned the bars and received in return the heavily laden sacks. Not a word passed between them.

Thus at dead of night, passing noiselessly to and fro, they transferred in actual weight, between Sub-Treasury and bank, nearly five tons of gold. From start to finish, from a physical standpoint, it was a heart-breaking, back-breaking job. Continually, Ralston spurred his friends on to greater effort. Work as they would they could not transfer as much gold as Ralston needed, before dawn began to break. Harpending, young and athletic, had stood his end of the Herculean task well, but Maurice Dore, slight and of sedentary habit, was on the verge of collapse. Chest-foundered, he could not pull himself erect. But as long as the streets were wrapped in darkness, as long as Ralston needed them, the duo held to their task. Gladly would these two friends have fallen in the street for Ralston. Gladly would they have died for him, had the banker exacted such a sacrifice. They were idolatrous in their devotion.

During all this time not a person had passed or interrupted them. Well Harpending and Dore knew that that was due to a pre-arrangement with the policemen on the beat. Even the law was ready and glad to connive with Ralston.

When the Bank of California opened next morning a rather ominous-looking crowd whose queues extended far down the street was in waiting. Lines began to form behind the paying teller's windows. Sure enough, the run was on. Ralston, gazing through the glass screen between his office and the bank proper, looked annoyed. Finally he could stand it no longer.

"Why are you making so many of our customers wait, on a busy day?" he grumbled to his head clerk. "Put more tellers on the windows and have your coin on hand."

More tellers appeared at the windows. More gold-laden trays were hustled up from bank vaults below. The crowd saw. Eyes bulged with amazement. Literally, the Bank of California had money to burn. The sight brought general relief. Quickly the news ran along California Street. The populace changed their minds. Abashed that they had ever doubted Billy Ralston, they slunk away to spread the good tidings throughout the city: there are trays and trays of gold on the counters of the Bank of California. Many doubters felt that they should go back to the bank and apologize to Ralston for entertaining any doubts.

When a serious run began on a neighboring bank, Ralston hurried to the spot, mounted a dry-goods box and addressed the crowd: "You are doing the bank and the city a great injustice," he chided, as if speaking to a roomful of naughty children. "The bank is absolutely sound, you need not wait here for a line-up. Bring your books to the Bank of California. We'll accommodate you with the cash."

Again, abashed, the crowd slunk away. How could they doubt Billy Ralston?

Thus Ralston and Comstock bullion averted a tremendous panic. A crash, the consequences of which would have been State and coastwide, had been averted by Ralston's bold front, and a nervy bluff backed by Comstock gold. The only trouble was Grant. What would he think of Ralston's defiance? Luckily three days later President Grant reversed himself and allowed gold to be exchanged at the Sub-Treasury for cash, which settled all anxiety.

But neither Mills nor Sharon, who were leading officers of the Bank, ever knew how Cashier Ralston gathered in nearly a million dollars after banking hours that day. All the satisfaction they ever got out of him was that a kind friend had come to the Bank's assistance. Ralston was locked within himself. There were times when a man could not tell all he knew or feared.

Besides, that foray on the Mint had delivered only temporary help. It tided him over for a time. No new bonanzas were in sight. If anything, the Comstock outlook became more depressing. In 1865 the Lode had delivered $16,000,000 worth of bullion. Those had been marvellous days. In 1866 and 1867 there had been similar outputs of $16,000,000. But in 1868 the production had shrunk to $8,499,769, and in 1869 it had shrivelled to a mere $7,528,-607. At that rate the Comstock would soon be bare. It was that realization which filled Ralston with an increasing dread. A dread that assumed hideous forms: a crippled bank; a despoiled economic empire; ledgers smeared with red ink; frozen assets; a decline in popularity; a loss of power; and a desolate San Francisco. That last thought he could not endure. The city must always be gay and happy.

The very existence of the status quo depended upon continued productivity of the Comstock Lode.

Hardly a mine was paying a dividend. "The Savage Mining Company" issued its last in June, 1869; "Kentuck" in March, 1870; the "Gould and Curry" a speculative and spasmodic one in October, 1870; and the "Chollar-Potosi" a moderate one in 1871. The lately discovered bonanzas in "Hale and Norcross" and "Yellow Jacket" were fast approaching exhaustion. The only promising lead of 1868–69 had been found in the "Yellow Jacket," "Kentuck-Crown-Point" combination. That had been lost in the conflagration that swept the mine, and was now walled off and irretrievably consigned to flame. The Virginia and Truckee Railroad had been built on the strength of that leader. Not a mine except those named had paid a dividend since the organization of the road. The thing that had promised so much had delivered practically nothing.

Anxiety and alarm held the debonair Ralston at bay. But only to Sharon did he confide his inner worries: something must be done to put a stop to Sutro. His tunnel digging was full of possibilities. Suppose he unearthed a bonanza!

CHAPTER XXI

THE REPEAL

March 17, 1870

While bullion was pouring out of his mills and thousands of dollars were collecting in nearby banks, Mackay was filled with ambition to explore "the Bullion" mine, which lay on the Divide between Gold Hill and Virginia City in the very topographical center of the Comstock Lode. By every geological sign, there should have been a "strike" in its workings. Already millions had been invested there in machine, drift, winze, but had divulged nothing. In spite of those failures, Mackay convinced himself of a bonanza. He would find it where Ralston had failed. As "Bullion" stock was knocking around the San Francisco stock market for a song, Mackay bought it up and had himself appointed superintendent. Into deeper explorations he poured many of his lately acquired "Hale and Norcross" thousands but found nothing.

About the same time Fair, with his "fine nose for ore," had himself appointed superintendent of the "Savage Mine," and proceeded to develop it with the same skill but not with the same success he had demonstrated in the "Hale and Norcross." The ablest superintendent could not find ore where none existed but he could spend a large amount of money in proving or disproving his supposition. Such had been the case with both Fair and Mackay. They were learning, but it was high-powered education at the expense of dwindling bank accounts, to say nothing of the exasperation of their city partners.

Flood began to entertain doubts of Fair's "nose for ore" as well as of Mackay's feet being on the ground. After all, they had been nothing but visionary Irishmen. As for O'Brien, the most philosophical of the Fenian quartet, he was glad he had never left the jovial bar at the Auction Lunch nor left off his back-room "penuckle" games with his cronies.

With these failures, Ralston and Sharon began to breathe easier. Anyhow, it had not been much of a storm. The million or so that the four Irishmen had accidentally made in "Hale and Norcross" had already been sunk in the unprofitable "Bullion" and "Savage." Soon their mills would be more silent than their mines. Mackay would be back at the face of a drift at four dollars a day, and Fair, a superintendent of parts, would be useful providing he would give up his notions of being an independent owner. To the Ralston and Sharon mind, Mackay and Fair might just as well join Sutro in the ash-heap of disuse. The Ring didn't intend to give them a chance to jeopardize the coalition.

Although nothing, so far, had relieved the pressure resting on Ralston's shoulders, still he was master of the Lode. But his hands were tied. Not much longer could he sustain industrial San Francisco without help from the Comstock. It took all of Sharon's ingenuity to keep Ralston buoyed up. No longer could he dangle before his chief's eyes the paystreak in "Yellow Jacket"; but now he began to encourage him with another possibility: "Crown Point."

When Alvinza Hayward, avowed friend of Ralston, and one of the staunchest links in his Ring, wanted John P. Jones, the hero of the "Yellow Jacket" fire, appointed superintendent of the "Crown Point," he lent a sympathetic ear. Ralston would do anything for his friends. More than once Hayward had shown his fidelity, and Jones was a clever miner. Perhaps he could re-locate the lost stringer of "Yellow Jacket" ore in the nearby "Crown Point."

While Ralston watched the "Crown Point" for further developments, Mackay and Fair, greatly weakened financially, turned their attention to the 1310 feet of ground between the "Ophir" and "Gould and Curry." Both the latter mines, in their prime, had produced $15,000,000 bonanzas. And it seemed to Mackay and Fair that there must be several plums in the earth between. The idea was an old one. Dan De Quille, mining editor of *The Territorial Enterprise,* had drawn attention to these facts as far back as 1867.

In the spring of 1869 Ralston had grasped at them and had organized "The Virginia Consolidated Mining Company" to include "Central No. 2," "Kinney," "White and Murphy," and "Dick Sides." On these 700 feet he had levied an assessment of $200,000 and had sought in vain for a "plum" to relieve the pressure on his shoulders, but had discovered nothing but water: floods and floods of hot, scalding, ill-smelling water. Ralston had been so discouraged over this influx that he gave up the search and ceased to protect the stock of "The Virginia Consolidated." Shares fell in February, 1871 to $1⅝. At that rate the 11,800 shares of the company were not worth $20,000. When props fell out from underneath, the stock dropped still lower. Some shares were disposed of at 15 cents each. At that price, many a disillusioned miner could afford to paper his cabin walls with "Virginia Consolidated" certificates that had cost him hundreds of dollars.

All this time Sutro had been preaching: "Await deeper developments. Let me drain off the floods and then explore." But Ralston had lost interest and Flood and O'Brien stepped into the San Francisco market and gobbled up the stock of "Virginia Consolidated" for a song. To them it was worth a gamble.

Ralston was satisfied to see the quartet squander the last of their "Hale and Norcross" winnings on ground which he was confident was in utter borrasca. As far as he was concerned the Irishmen were no longer a cause for worry; Sutro was the only active, persistent one. He was worse than a half-dead fly, always buzzing around. At any price he must be smashed. Now that he had opened the mouth of his tunnel, the Ring never knew a moment of peace.

While Ralston was hatching plans to end the tunnel digger's activity, Sutro was digging into Mt. Davidson with all his might. Every month he was making progress through Sun Mountain at the rate of 160 feet. Although he had 4 to 5 miles of burrowing to go, never had he been so sure of ultimate success.

One day in January, 1870, came a telegram from a Washington friend that shattered his hopes. Sutro must come to the capital at once. Ralston's agents had introduced a bill into Congress to repeal the Sutro Tunnel rights and concessions. Sutro was surprised and startled. He could not understand what had occurred. He left at once overland.

On March 1, Sutro arrived in Washington. He had been delayed in the Rockies. There was neither time nor opportunity to interview new Congressmen or draw to their attention the humanitarian aspects of his tunnel. To his dismay Sutro discovered that the Hon. Thomas Fitch, the newly elected Nevada representative, had already introduced a bill into Congress to repeal the third section of the law of Congress which secured him his $2 a ton royalty. Without that royalty, Sutro knew, it would be impossible to pay interest on loans already made or negotiate fresh ones.

In addition to having the Fitch bill introduced, Ralston had dispatched Hillyer, one of the ablest mining lawyers in the West, to Washington to help lobby the bill through Congress. Behind Hillyer, as Sutro knew, lay the unlimited backing of the Bank of California. On March 17, Sutro discovered, the repeal bill was scheduled to be submitted to a Congressional vote. Two weeks ahead! It was a dastardly, underhanded, eleventh-hour move on Ralston's part to ruin him. Sutro did not know which way to turn.

Sutro discovered that the Fitch repeal bill had not been printed, so that nobody would even guess what had been going on. Deliberately the Bank had put their bill in writing. In that form it was unobtrusive. Then they had filed it away among other papers on the Speaker's desk. There it would have remained until the repeal passed, without Sutro ever knowing anything about it, had it not been for one of his wary friends finding it mixed with nondescript papers.

Now Sutro got busy. He intended to forestall Ralston. He had the Bank of California's repeal bill printed at his own expense. Along with the bill, he had some other documents printed tending to show up Ralston's rascalities. These he had distributed among Congressmen.

Not content with introducing the repeal bill, and Hillyer's efforts to lobby it through the House, Ralston's envoys had hired Washington newspapers to abuse Sutro in the most outrageous manner: the Comstock Lode did not require a tunnel to operate, there was no water for Sutro to drain. People were warned from having anything to do with him or the stock in his tunnel. Both were rank fakes. On every hand Sutro found Hillyer making constant efforts to have the law repealed and Sutro stopped from driving his tunnel toward the Comstock Lode.

Meanwhile the Fitch bill was referred to the House Committee on Mines and Mining. Sutro was elated when he discovered that fact. He realized how fortunate it was for him that the Ways and Means Committee had recently visited the Comstock and had seen with their own eyes and heard with their own ears all about Ralston's opposition. Now, to a man, the Committee stood by him. Had they never made that chance visit to the Lode, Sutro realized that he would have been beaten from the start.

Immediately Governor Blair of Michigan and Judge Kelley of Pennsylvania came to Sutro's rescue. Blair told the Committee the whole story: when he had visited the Comstock, Sharon had shown him about. One day Sharon had moved his hand over the Lode in a grandiloquent way: "Sir," he had said, "the Bank has waved its hand over the Comstock Lode and ordered Sutro away."

"Then and there," Blair said, "I arrived at the conclusion that Ralston would do anything in his power to break Sutro and prevent the project from being carried out. He would even try to set aside a law of Congress."

Judge D. M. Kelley, too, made a speech before the Committee, in favor of Sutro and his tunnel:

"I propose to speak for the miners, the men who with

pick and shovel extract the ore, and 45 per cent of whom die of miner's consumption, who die in their youth, in the vigor of their young manhood, prostrated by the heat and poisoned by the atmosphere in these mines. These industrious men are subscribing to the stock. They swarm behind Mr. Sutro, and beg Congress to vest all the rights in him that will enable him to reduce for them the terrible doom to which the Bank of California would condemn them. Sir, I brought with me from one of these mines a bit of blackened ore, blackened by the smoke of a fire that smothered and burned forty-five of these men, in a mine fire. Had there been a tunnel such as Mr. Sutro is constructing, they would have been breathing pure air while at work; and though the timber of the mine might have burned, the miners would have dropped below the fire and escaped."

Those who did not make speeches in favor of the Sutro Tunnel made it a point to tell less-informed representatives that Ralston's effort at repeal was a great outrage.

As a result of the efforts of these friends of Sutro, the House Committee on Mines and Mining reported unfavorably on Ralston's repeal bill. Judge Orange Ferris, Chairman of the Committee, made a last-minute gallant fight against it.

"Repeal this law," he thundered; "strike out that section. Take the heart out of it. Leave nothing but an empty carcass. Repeal and what do you find? The gentlemen from California [the Bank crowd] have told us that when they want the Comstock drained they will do it themselves without any help from Congress. Perhaps they may do things that way out in California, where the power of the corporation is greater than the power of the individual. Not in this Congress but in some subsequent Congress this representative [Ralston's] will appear and ask not for limited rights but rights to which are attached double and triple the demands of Sutro."

In conclusion the judge advised Congress to stand by their plighted troth and give Sutro such monetary aid as would help him to accelerate the finishing of his tunnel.

On the 17th of March, when the Fitch repeal bill came up for final vote, a great struggle developed in the House. The Bank of California brought all its power to bear upon the measure. When the vote was taken and the ballots were counted, Sutro found that he had 124, while the Bank of California could muster but 42.

Joyful as Sutro was over his victory, he dared not leave Washington. He had to keep his eye on Hillyer, Sargent of California and Fitch of Nevada. Too well he knew that if he departed, Bank henchmen would try to steal in something or other and get the bill through Congress in an underhanded way.

With his victory in the lower House secure, Sutro one day appeared before the United States Senate. He must have a provision inserted in a general mining bill to protect his tunnel rights in the future. He asked to have that done.

There, Judge Trumbull of Illinois championed Sutro's rights. Such tactics as the Bank of California had recently employed ought not to be allowed in Congress, the Judge said.

With the rights to his bore protected, Sutro returned to Sun Mountain. But never could he relax his vigilance or enjoy the tunnel. Always he had Ralston in mind. What would the monopolist do next?

CHAPTER XXII

JONES' SICK CHILD

1870

How Ralston endured the anxiety of those terrible months, God only knew, God and the Bay of San Francisco. Every day, during all these weeks, foul weather or fine, Ralston sought relief from his cares, in the sea. For the surf to Ralston was a place of freedom; no worries could reach him there.

Great powerful strokes would carry him through mist and foam half way out to Alcatraz Island. The delight of skimming through opalescent waters, now green, now blue, now gray, was to pass from a sordid world into one of sheer beauty. With even more powerful strokes, Ralston would battle his way back to shore. This conflict with the tide assured Ralston of his mastery, made a man of him again, brought the spring back to his step, the joy of life back to his eye. Invigorated him. Vitalized him. The sea was a never-failing battery.

Once more, renewed in mind and body, Ralston was ready to grapple with his troubles and to listen to Sharon with some degree of assurance and even partake of his faith when he spoke of an approaching discovery in "Crown Point." Again and again Sharon assured Ralston: the Comstock would rescue him just as it had in 1864. Again he would remind him of his desperate condition when the twenty-million-dollar bonanzas in "Yellow Jacket," "Chollar," "Kentuck," and "Imperial" had come to his assistance.

Encouraged by this bold talk, Ralston turned his attention to the work going on in "Crown Point" under the able direction of their newly appointed superintendent, the jovial, ruddy-cheeked, powerfully built Welshman, John P. Jones—the hero of the "Yellow Jacket" fire.

Jones was a man both Ralston and Sharon felt they could depend upon. In fact, Jones owed his position to Ralston. If Ralston had not had confidence in his friendship with Hayward, he would never have agreed to his brother-in-law's appointment, first to "Kentuck's" superintendency, and then to the even better position in the "Crown Point." Often Ralston had tried Hayward out and never had he found him wanting. Hayward was one of the mainstays of his Ring: one of the best friends he had ever had. Hayward had helped him "corner" "Hale and Norcross." As a reward, Ralston had made him a trustee. Hayward was a member of the Union Mill and Mining Company. In many other deals he had been associated with Hayward. Many was the pot Ralston had divided with him. It was just such loyal men as Hayward that Ralston welcomed to his Ring.

Thus, with great confidence in the management, Ralston could turn his attention to the "Crown Point." No one knew better than did Hayward how he needed a bonanza to carry on his San Francisco industries. It was a source of satisfaction to have faith in the superintendent as well as the future.

Up until the "Yellow Jacket" fire, "Crown Point" had been a consistent producer. During the years 1866–68 it had yielded about a million in dividends. But that catastrophe, by walling off the "Yellow Jacket" stringer, had destroyed the promise of both properties. But not in Jones' mind. It was Jones' plan to re-locate the lost "Yellow Jacket" ledge, in the womb of the "Crown Point." It was his contention that that seam of promising ore must extend through the adjoining mine—and he intended to find it.

In the beginning, Jones had confined his exploration to the 1000- and 1100-foot levels. When his work had revealed nothing but porphyry and barren seams of quartz, he had drifted with a cross-cut 800 feet due eastward, likewise without results. After that, further search eastward had been abandoned. At a distance of 360 feet from the shaft, Jones had drifted southward. For the first 200 feet nothing worth while turned up.

Ralston was disheartened at his reports, especially as Jones had used up a $250,000 assessment without locating even a promising stringer. Another assessment of $3.50 per share was decided upon. In December it would fall due. The outlook was dismal. From $100 in June, 1868, shares had gradually depreciated to $2 by November, 1870. With $140,000 invested in mine and mill plant, the entire property could now be acquired for $24,000. Was there ever any outlook, in any mine, more discouraging?

No matter how depressed Ralston grew, Jones never lost faith in his "Crown Point." He began to spend long hours below alone. In this way he learned what the mine was capable of. When shares were knocking around at $2 each he invested all his savings, and all he could borrow from his pals, in "Crown Point." Southward he continued to drift. When he had gone thirty-nine feet farther, indications began to change. The hard rock which had encompassed him in the beginning on every hand, suddenly grew softer. Here and there streaks of quartz revealed themselves. With feverish anxiety Jones raced ahead. It was a will-of-the-wisp he was chasing. Now he had a vein of ore, now he had lost it. It was exasperatingly irregular in its meanderings. Promising one week, vanishing the next. But John P. Jones had greater faith than ever in that last stringer.

Once, in this buoyant frame of mind, he called upon one of his wealthy friends and tried to induce him to buy "Crown Point" stock. But the friend remained unmoved.

"Jones," he replied, "I will loan you the money to buy with, but as for me, I have seen the time when I reached through the holes in my pants and scratched a poor man's hide, and I don't mean to take any risks that will make me do it again."

But the friend had faith in Jones' word. On the Welshman's promise to pay, he loaned him all the money he needed to purchase "Crown Point" on his own. On went his elusive search.

Now Jones noted a new crisis in the character of the hard rock. The porphyry became more decomposed and friable, lighter in color, and seamed with straggling red lines of iron-rust. When he pierced a well defined clay seam and a body of soft whitish quartz was developed which contained pockets of ore, Jones was still better satisfied. He must go to San Francisco for a few days and confer with brother-in-law Hayward.

Jones succeeded in inspiring his relative with his own enthusiasm regarding prospective developments and he prevailed upon him to purchase a large block of "Crown Point" stock while shares were kicking around the San Francisco market at $2 each. Further, he prevailed upon Hayward to carry a generous slice of stock for Jones as well.

Some months before, on the strength of his surmises, Jones had induced a number of prominent San Francisco operators to carry large amounts of stock on his account, upon the agreement to bear all losses in consideration for one-half the possible profits. Now Jones was confident that there were not going to be any losses, but neither he nor Hayward imparted their enthusiasm to Ralston. They decided they would play this game alone. Without causing any flurry on the San Francisco stock market or unduly exciting the women operators, Hayward managed to pick up 5000 shares of "Crown Point" at figures ranging from $2 to $5. Before Ralston or his Ring learned that there was considerable likelihood that the lost ledge had been re-located, Hayward and Jones had almost gained control of "Crown Point," and stock was rising. Not even Sharon had discovered what was going on beneath his feet.

While Jones was still in San Francisco, one of the usual stock reactions occurred. "Crown Point" had struck a "horse," ran the reports. It seemed as if developments were less promising. The rising stock market slumped. Many small investors lost. Some of the timorous holders of stock on Jones' account began to lose confidence: they wanted to get out.

Being on the inside, naturally Jones' faith did not waver, but suddenly he found reasons for exercising more than common prudence: his son Roy had been taken ill in the East, he confided to his cronies. Momentarily, he was expecting a telegram which would call him to "the States" and, perhaps compel him to be absent from "Crown Point" developments for many weeks.

In this frame of mind he went to those operators who were carrying large blocks of stock on his account and told them about the illness of his son. He would probably be away for some time. Probably he would be forced to go East. Before going, he preferred to settle his outstanding accounts by the disposal of the shares of "Crown Point" in their hands. Though he assured those operators of his firm belief in the value of "Crown Point," his action belied his words in their minds. They regarded the story of his son as a lame pretense to explain his stock sales. Scarcely could they refrain from laughing in his face. "Jones' sick child" became a byword in the purlieus of the stock market and of the Bank's privileged circle. When Jones departed, it was the prevalent impression that the real invalid was the "Crown Point" Mine and not Jones' son.

Jones bore these sneers nobly. Back he went to Virginia City and down he sank into the darkness of the "Crown Point" shaft. As soon as he had ascertained by careful inspection that developments as a whole, during his absence, were unmistakably favorable, he had himself hoisted to the surface. At once, without changing his miner's outfit, he hied himself over to the telegraph office and wired Hayward in code: buy all the "Crown Point" stock on the market.

Immediately at the San Franciso Stock Exchange shares shot upward. Brokers for the Jones-Hayward combination bought 700 shares from Charles B. Low around $90 to $120. When "Crown Point" reached $180, they bought 300 shares more from Low.

Now, it was May, 1871. The "Crown Point" company's election was close at hand. Gradually the story of the discovery had leaked out. To their chagrin, Ralston and Sharon discovered that Hayward and Jones already had acquired nearly one-half of "Crown Point's" 12,000 shares. But neither Ralston nor Sharon had been asleep. When they saw their fortified monopoly being threatened, they had quickly acquired 4100 shares. Ralston was hurt. He had trusted Hayward implicitly. He had helped Jones to the superintendency.

At first in their bitterness against Hayward for his defection from the Ring, they decided to fight it out with him in the San Francisco stock market and cripple him. On thinking it over more carefully, they decided it was only a small bonanza. It would be far better to break Hayward's financial back, as it were, by unloading their 4100 shares at a high price. So they offered their 4100 shares for $1,400,000—a little over $340 a share. To their utter amazement Hayward accepted their offer, drew a check and handed it over to Ralston and Sharon. Instead of breaking Hayward's back their step had gone a long way toward breaking that of the Bank of California. Sharon's boast, that he had engineered the biggest stock deal on record, had a hollow sound.

While these stupendous things were happening on the San Francisco Stock Exchange and shares were bounding upward, Jones was delving deeper into his "Crown Point" bonanza. Every day increased his amazement at the enormity of his find. It was pyramidal shaped. During some cataclysm of nature in prehistoric times it had been foaled in the womb of Sun Mountain. Nothing less than an earthquake, or a volcano, could have sired such a bonanza. Its apex towered to the 900-foot level. On the 1000-foot level it had a width of 45 feet; on the 1100th, 58 feet; on the 1200th, 70 feet; on the 1400-foot level it was 360 feet in length and 90 in width. It assayed $75 per ton. What a colossal bonanza it was, with its apex 500 feet above its base!

It was far loftier than the pinnacle of old Cheops. On receipt of these figures, stock soared and soared on the San Francisco Stock Market. Shares skyrocketed to $1825 apiece. The women in black had coachmen and maids. There were diamonds in their ears, diamonds on their breasts, diamonds on their fingers, a sparkle in their eyes and big accounts in the Bank of California to their credit. The swish of their silks could be heard a block away.

Never had Jones faced such a piece of engineering. Hardly was he scientist enough to deliver such a colossal bonanza. None of the machinery needed to handle such a huge body of ore was at hand. The "Crown Point's" shaft was too narrow. Her machinery was out of date; her timbering warped; her pumping apparatus insufficient; her ventilation entirely inadequate.

Before he could proceed, the shaft had to be enlarged and retimbered; a new compartment sunk; double cages, three new 80 horse-power engines, new reels, sheaves, wheels, pumps and bobs were required. Special blacksmith shops must be installed on the 1200- and 1300-foot levels to save the expense of hoisting and lowering tools for repairing.

When all these new appurtenances had been acquired, Jones succeeded in delivering a thirty-million-dollar bonanza. Overnight he had become one of the wealthiest men on the Pacific Coast.

Having always had a hankering for politics, he immediately turned his head toward Washington. He would become a United States Senator like Bill Stewart.

On account of the chilly atmosphere about the Bank of California, Hayward resigned as director to head a bank of his own.

This virtual defeat rankled sorely in the minds of Ralston and Sharon. Never would they forget, never would they forgive the concerted action of Hayward and Jones in wresting the control of this bonanza from the hands of the Ring. Neither could they forgive themselves for the folly of having sacrificed their stock and lost control of the mine without a contest.

Neither would Hayward nor Jones have anything to do with the Union Mill & Lumber Co. Overnight, up sprang the Nevada Mill & Mining Co., a Jones-Hayward concern, to handle the ore from their great bonanza.

It was a frightful blow to Ralston to have one of his own crowd prove treacherous. Just at the time when he needed a bonanza most, he had been betrayed. Never would he have treated a friend like that. Always he had shared with his Ring. Never had he monopolized the gain. He was cut to the core by Hayward's perfidy. More than one melon he had divided with Hayward.

No matter how much Jones' defection smarted, Sharon intended to have his own revenge.

When they had seen the "Yellow Jacket" vein matter continuing into "Crown Point," Ralston and Sharon had taken one precaution. Perhaps the "Crown Point" bonanza would extend into adjoining property. Before "Belcher" stock could soar in sympathy, they had picked up all available shares. In all, there were 10,000 and they bought it at $1 a share, or about ten thousand dollars for the entire capital stock of the mine.

Work of exploration was rapidly pushed in the newly acquired property. In a few months the greatest body of ore which the Comstock had thus far produced was uncovered: "the Belcher"—a thirty-five-million-dollar bonanza. With its discovery, Ralston and Sharon became two of the wealthiest men in the West.

Sharon decided to retire from the mining game and take up his residence in San Francisco again. He had evened his score with the Comstock.

Ralston was himself again, the captain of his ship. Away sailed the bank argosy into unplumbed depths as million upon million in a constant stream of bullion flowed from Carson mills direct into Bank of California coffers.

Now there would be no more worries in carrying out his plans for the industrial welfare of California nor for the beautifying of San Francisco.

But so much wealth taxed him and made him more vulnerable than ever to the plans of designing men.

While he was figuring out means of using it, Sutro was exhausting his resources and journeying East in search of funds.

CHAPTER XXIII

CONGRESS APPOINTS COMMISSIONERS TO VISIT COMSTOCK

1871

In June, 1870, Sutro believed that he was going to be able to borrow 15,000,000 francs from Erlanger & Co., Parisian bankers. All the preliminaries had been arranged. He was to sail on the 20th of July to clinch the deal. At last he had every reason to suppose that he had secured enough money to finish his tunnel.

Out of a clear sky, on the 10th of July, came word that war clouds were hovering over central Europe. By the 15th, the newspapers announced that hostilities had broken out between France and Prussia. The roar of their cannon broke up all negotiations. Not another word was said about a loan. No one could raise $5 for any enterprise whatever in Europe or America.

Sutro was beside himself. After all his Congressional fights; after the injustice of Ralston's persecution and his own subsequent victory; after believing that the battle had been won, that he could borrow all the money necessary to finish his tunnel, the Franco-Prussian War had to break out and ruin all his chances. It was too much to endure. His friends feared that the strain would be unbearable. He would bury his troubles in the sea or blow out his brains. But not Sutro. He was made of sterner stuff. He was inured to disappointment. Soon he was back on the Comstock Lode. He wanted to think in the shadow of the mountain that he intended to transfix.

By December, 1870, as determined as ever, Sutro was back in Washington again. He had given up France for good. All her gold was going to swell the war chests of the Prussian overlords. On account of Ralston, he could accomplish nothing on the Pacific Coast. His only hope lay in inducing Congress to do something. Worst of all, he must stay on indefinitely in Washington. He must watch both California's and Nevada's representatives in the Senate and Congress. If he didn't, he knew what would happen. They would smuggle in some kind of a law designed to ruin him. It was a mortifying condition to find the representatives from the Pacific Coast all arrayed against him. Every last one of them opposed him. They knew the Bank of California was the stronger, and so they helped the Bank. Sutro was the weaker, so they tried to kick him out. Right or wrong, they intended to be on the stronger side. This was a battle of the strong. But he would show them what weakness could do—what the strength of weakness could accomplish.

The Forty-first Congress turned out to be of short duration. Sutro attended daily sessions, keeping his eye on his enemies. Ralston's agents kept up their misrepresentations.

Every representative was notified that Sutro's tunnel was a humbug; the mines had given out; there was no need for a tunnel. It was a hopeless affair. As December waned and Sutro saw that there was no possibility of accomplishing anything he became hopeless. One day he appeared before Congress and before the Senate. He asked that a commission be appointed to go out to Nevada and examine the mines and the tunnel. He must settle this affair. After all these fighting years and attempts to drive him away from the undertaking, a Government decision must be made: as to the utility of the tunnel, its necessity to the Ledge, the cost, possibility, practicability, etc.

"Send a commission out there," he demanded of representatives in the House and Senate, "and let them report upon this question, let them see what there is of it and whether I have been telling the truth or not."

A bill to this effect was introduced and passed both Houses, and the President signed it on the 4th of April, 1871.

For all time, Sutro felt that a commission would settle the question of the tunnel. Gentlemen of the highest caliber would be sent to Nevada to investigate. There would be no more cavilling. The misrepresentations of the bank crowd would be stopped. President Grant agreed to the proposition and appointed Major-General H. G. Wright and Major-General John G. Foster, army engineers, and Professor Wesley Newcomb, conchologist, Commissioners.

In the summer of 1871 when Sutro met these Commissioners at Virginia City, he warned them against the Bank of California. He told them of Ralston's treachery and Sharon's duplicity; that they were determined to wear him down. The Commissioners were friendly, but they had nothing to say. But they let Sutro understand that they were army engineers, as such they were above the petty squabbles between bankers and promoters. Sutro must realize that from the beginning.

All the time the Bank of California was making desperate efforts to draw the Commissioners their own way. Sutro saw that they would be, to a large extent, under the guidance of

Ralston's crowd, as the superintendents of the bank-dominated mines, Isaac Requa of the "Chollar-Potosi," Day of the "Ophir," and Batterman of the "Gould and Curry" were delegated to take charge of them in their mines.

There were no finer men on the Comstock than these engineers: Requa, Batterman, and Day; but knowing that their works were under the thumb of the Ring, Sutro perceived the danger. The Commissioners would not be able to get at the whole truth of the water, bad air, or lack of ventilation questions. But what could he do? The Comstock superintendent told Sutro bluntly that they did not want any interference from him. They would show the ledge to the Commissioners. From that fact alone, Sutro knew that the Commissioners would never see the inside of those hot stifling drifts, nor those that were flooded nor those that were filled with deadly gases. Never would they even hear about them.

The Commissioners remained some time on the Comstock. They were very superior men. The two West Pointers had splendid war records. They were fine mixers, perfect raconteurs, likable men of the world. Sutro had great faith in them. For once the country would get an unbiased opinion of his tunnel.

The Commissioners visited the mines often but always under the guidance of their respective superintendents. From the first, Sharon told them that the Bank of California was strongly opposed to the tunnel. It was antagonistic to their interests. They meant to break it up and crush it. Sutro was trying to exploit the Lode at their expense. He was an interloper.

There were by this time two hundred miles of underground drifts through Sun Mountain. Openly, Sutro accused Ralston's superintendents of taking the engineers only into the dry parts of the Lode, into comparatively cool drifts, but notwithstanding the Commissioners found the temperature in some places as high as 110°.

Several times they went down to the mouth of Sutro's tunnel and examined it carefully. But all the time they were surrounded by Ralston's satellites, who were straining every nerve to prejudice them against the project.

Once Sutro asked General Wright whether he thought the Bank of California would like to set aside a law of Congress.

"Certainly," replied the general, "they intended to break up the tunnel if they could."

"What I want to find out," retorted Sutro, "is, whether they are going to run this government or whether Congress is."

While the United States Commissioners were on the Comstock Lode the agents of a British banking house arrived in Virginia City and got in touch with Sutro. They were interested in his tunnel project, they explained, as a financial investment. Sutro was delighted to find that they had no ties with Ralston, neither social, ethical, nor financial. Sutro showed them the ledge, the mills, the sumps, and the tunnel mouth. Glowingly he talked of the Lode's output and the possibilities of investment when the mines were drained. From every angle the agents investigated his proposition. When they departed for England they promised to report the facts to their principals. In the meantime Sutro forgot about their coming and going. He was used to will-of-the-wisps, promises, disappointments, and intrigue.

One day in August, 1871, a cablegram arrived. It was from the British bankers. Sutro must come to England at once. Perhaps they would be able to arrange some financial matters that would please him, in London.

Sutro debated. There was no knowing when the Commissioners would be finished with their examination. Should he leave them with his enemies or embrace this new opportunity?

On August 15 Sutro started overland for New York. On the 30th he sailed for England.

Sutro was just as convincing a promoter as a Congressional lobbyist. With one idea in mind he talked to the directorate of McCalmont's bank. Of late, said those directors, they had been forcibly impressed by the rich reports of the discoveries in "Crown Point" and "Belcher."

Every year, now, the Comstock was turning over to the world at large $15,000,000 or more in bullion. It looked as if it would go on producing indefinitely and that they could not make any mistake in advancing Sutro capital sufficient to reach such a source of revenue. Without any unusual effort on his part, McCalmont's advanced Sutro the sum of $650,000. It was unbelievable! inconceivable! From such a quarter!

Although that was not the period of airplanes, Sutro fairly flew to New York and from New York to Nevada and the mouth of his tunnel. Now he had money enough to operate on a large scale. He was so excited over his good fortune that he forgot all about the government commissioners whom he had left on the Comstock. He no longer was worried about their report. Engineers of their reputation could not help but see that the only possible way to operate the Comstock was by way of the tunnel, and now he had the money to proceed.

Overnight a mushroom town, named "Sutro" after himself, sprang up about the mouth of the tunnel. There was "Sutro's mansion," a colossal white Victorian structure, lashed to Sun Mountain's hardrock by iron cables, as the Washoe zephyr was still a power with which to conjure. Grouped about it were smithies, foundries, numerous machine shops, a church, a hotel, cheerful bar-rooms, a newspaper, a dance-hall, and every accommodation to promote the driving of a tunnel in a big way. Work progressed night and day. Three to four hundred men divided into eight-hour shifts carried on the responsibilities of driving the face of the header toward the Lode. Vast quantities of machinery were purchased. Mules were brought in droves from California to pull the refuse rock to the dumps. A hospital was built, nurses engaged, a doctor installed. For accidents were frequent and deaths inevitable. Nevertheless an average monthly progress of 76¼ feet was made. During that year the tunnel advanced almost 1000 feet toward its goal.

Before the year closed, four vertical shafts had been located along the proposed line of the tunnel as vantage points to drive the bore from eight points in opposite directions along the survey lines. Before winter, Shaft No. 1, 4915 feet from the mouth, was begun. By July 1, 1873, it had reached the level of the header; Shaft No. 2 was located 9065 feet from the tunnel entrance; its depth to the tunnel grade was set at 1041 feet; Shaft No. 3 was located 13,545 feet from the tunnel entrance and its depth to the tunnel level was 1361 feet; Shaft No. 4 was located 17,695 feet from the entrance with a depth of 1485 feet. During the year work was going on in all four shafts and the tunnel had reached a point 2665 feet from its mouth. A good half mile and only three and a half more to bore!

Ralston and Sharon were paralyzed with surprise at McCalmont's loan. Never had they thought that Sutro would get help from a Scotch quarter. Further, they were dumbfounded at the speed Sutro was making toward their Lode. Every day brought him appreciably closer to those two-dollar royalties. At first Sutro had been a joke, then a threat, now he was a positive menace.

And the four Irish Insurgents were another cause for alarm. But not for serious worry. As long as they confined themselves to that exhausted territory between "Ophir" and "Gould and Curry," the bank crowd were confident that the Irishmen would founder and there would be an end of them.

In January, 1872, when everything was booming in the town of Sutro and along the line of his survey to the Lode, Sutro left for Washington. He must reach the Capital before the Commissioners made their report.

As usual, in the Rockies Sutro's train was caught in a violent mountain snowstorm. Blockaded for days, he arrived too late. Already the Commissioners had presented their report to Congress. While it was being read, Ralston's crowd were hilarious.

Sutro had begun to think that he was entirely out of the woods; that there would be no more misrepresentation now that the government engineers had been out to the Comstock and seen the lay of the land for themselves. But he was utterly dumbfounded when the Commissioners declared that the tunnel was absolutely unnecessary when it came to drainage, transportation, ventilation, or concentration. Only on one point, about which there had been no question, did they agree perfectly with Sutro: the tunnel was feasible. Completed, the bore would cost $3,500,000, but less if proper machinery were installed. To finish completely it would require three to four years. Furthermore, they agreed with Sutro in considering the Comstock a true fissure vein. It could be worked as deep as mechanical means would allow. But when it came to the two most important issues, draining and ventilating the mines, the tunnel was unnecessary. Sutro was absolutely amazed. On seeing that report, McCalmont's would withdraw all help. Nor would he be able to expect further help from the Federal Government.

He began to analyze the report. Quickly he came to a conclusion. The Commissioners had been misled by Ralston's superintendents: Isaac Requa of the "Chollar-Potosi," Day of the "Ophir," and Batterman of the "Gould and Curry." From the beginning they had been inimical to his enterprise. What reliance could he place on their deductions? They had been growing wealthy on bank-management conditions. Of course, they wanted to maintain the present state of affairs. They would be fools to want to have it changed.

Then Sutro turned to the other side of the picture. The Commissioners were old army officers. They had the aroma of age about them. They were not up to modern mining methods. They were not up to the rascalities of Ralston's Ring; nor to their stock-jobbing operations. They took everything for granted. Took it all for Gospel; thought it was all "just so." Not at all were the Commissioners sharp-eyed enough for Ralston's superintendents. The superintendents were young. The Commissioners were old men. They had been deceived.

Their report whipped Sutro into a frenzy. With everything humming in the town of Sutro and along the line of the tunnel, here was this damaging report, every line of it influenced by Ralston's Ring. How they must be laughing now! Also, it struck Sutro that the Commissioners were not positive-minded. They were trying not to offend Ralston, nor hurt him. They had been misled. There was no question about that. They had been utterly imposed upon. Now, there was only one way to proceed to arrive at facts and set matters aright. He would demand a hearing. The Commissioners must be cited to appear before the House Committee on Mines and Mining.

Sutro went to the Chairman of the Committee and made a complaint. The Commissioners were cited. Then Sutro went to the Secretary of War. Never had he talked more forcibly. As a result the Commissioners were ordered at once to proceed to Washington. They arrived. They offered their testimony. Sutro did not leave a stone unturned to show up every point. He acted as his own attorney. For twenty-five hearings, night after night, Sutro quizzed them. The result was 810 pages of printed matter. It showed up everything and was a complete confirmation of everything Sutro had said and written on the tunnel during the past eight years.

Ralston heard of the tempest that was raging in Washington over the Commissioners' report. Immediately he dispatched Sunderland, attorney of the Bank of California and one of the ablest lawyers on the Pacific coast, to uphold the Commissioners and to harass Sutro as much as possible.

Sunderland hesitated at nothing. He brought out all the damaging testimony he could, but he did not bring out one single fact against the tunnel in his whole examination. After the questioning had been going on for days, Sunderland became alarmed. As things were, he saw that he had no case.

So Sunderland appealed to the Chairman of the Committee on Mines and Mining. He must have Isaac Requa, Day, and Batterman brought from Nevada to Washington. Their veracity had been impeached. Sutro and the Committee agreed to the plan. Sunderland telegraphed to Nevada for the three superintendents to come to the Capital as soon as possible.

Disdaining other help, Sutro continued to act as his own lawyer before the Commissioners, the Bank of California lawyers, and the Comstock experts. Alone, he examined and cross-examined witnesses, more than holding his own against Sunderland, the clever and skillful bank lawyer, sent to defeat him.

Sutro proved himself to be a thorough mining engineer. Not for nothing had he studied and visited European mining centers. He had the laws of force and motion "at his finger tips." His calculations were accurate and made with lightninglike rapidity. He demonstrated his familiarity with geology, orology, topography, metallurgy, hydrostatics, mechanics, and engineering. He convinced the Commission that he knew more about ventilation and drainage of mines than either the theoretical experts or the Bank's "practical men."

Sutro met every bank onslaught with watchfulness, vigilance, resourcefulness, and eternal persistence. He proved that the Bank could not purchase mental power enough to dominate and control him. He was more than a match for all the brains the Bank of California could muster against him. The hearing developed into an individual's fight against corporate graft and greed and corruption. Sutro's was the voice of common humanity raised against the man who would ride upon its shoulders and exploit it for his own financial advancement.

His plucky fight won Sutro many friends in Washington. The Committee on Mines and Mining decided to ignore the report made by the Commissioners. So disgusted were they with the treatment that the Bank of California had meted out to Sutro that they themselves introduced a bill recommending that Congress loan him $2,000,000, taking a mortgage on his properties, with which to finish the tunnel.

When they heard about the Congressional bill to loan Sutro $2,000,000 with which to finish his tunnel, Ralston and Sharon realized that more drastic measures would be necessary. In no time at all that two-dollar levy on every ton of ore would be beginning and there would be an end of their profits from milling ores. They must have one of their own henchmen in the Senate when the bill would come up. They must have more expert lobbyists. Sharon must go to

Washington, as one of the United States Senators from Nevada. The bill must be defeated. Now it was defeat for Sutro or ruin for San Francisco.

When McCalmont's bankers heard about that bill they made Sutro another loan of $800,000. Now he had $1,480,000 with which to push the face of his header toward the Lode. But Sutro could only half enjoy his good fortune. Well he knew that success lay only in eternal vigilance. Never for a moment could he relax and devote all his energies to the engineering task ahead of him. Always he had to ask from what quarter would Ralston and his hirelings attack him next.

CHAPTER XXIV

A SACK OF DIAMONDS

May, 1872

Diamonds! Rubies! Sapphires! Emeralds!

A dazzling cataract of flashing stones poured, pell-mell, out of the mouth of the open sack which Harpending was holding upside down, and spilled themselves in shimmering pools of green, red, blue, and white upon his sheet-covered billiard table.

It was an amazing, unforgetable sight! Phosphorescent pools of liquid fire glimmering and glowing in the dim light of Harpending's billiard room.

The stones were of different sizes. Some of the yellow, black, and white diamonds were small, others were larger than dice. For one of the latter, one of 103 carats, Shreve & Co. of San Francisco had already made an offer of $96,000. Besides that huge jewel, there was a sapphire as large as a pigeon's egg; emeralds as round as gooseberries; a ruby that might have fallen out of a hèathen idol's eye. All too valuable for anything but a royal crown. All these gems were lying on Harpending's billiard table, flashing, glowing, burning, in luminous splendor. Ralston and Roberts, Harpending, Rubery and Lent, stunned at the spectacle of so much wealth, looked on in open-mouthed amazement.

One day back in 1871, Philip Arnold and John Slack, two weather-beaten prospectors, had wandered into the Bank of California. With them they had carried several sacks, which, they told a bank clerk, contained property of great value. For safekeeping they wished to deposit them in Ralston's bank. In making arrangements it was necessary to state what the sacks contained. "Diamonds, rough diamonds," the duo blurted out. They had found them in a deserted mountain section of the West. As soon as the receipt was in their possession, the prospectors shambled out of the bank.

Somehow or other news of those sacks of diamonds, reposing in a dark cranny of his vaults, reached Ralston's ears. Immediately his interest was stirred. With mines of gold and silver, and refineries bulging with bullion, the thought of diamond fields stayed Ralston's attention. Look what the Comstock had done for San Francisco. With a diamond mine what might he not accomplish for his beloved city? Ralston saw another chance to invest his Comstock wealth in something spectacular, and he sent for Arnold and Slack to come to his office.

A day came when the two roughly clad prospectors shuffled up to Ralston's desk. They seemed bewildered in his presence. Their attitude said plainer than words that accidentally they had stumbled upon a windfall. A windfall so monstrous that they did not know how to proceed. Being in doubt, they intended to remain silent. Arnold had made it especially evident that he did not wish to talk to Ralston. He was afraid of him, he claimed.

Ralston asked the bewildered duo where they had found the sacks of diamonds.

But the prospectors were ignorant of their United States

geography. Accidentally they had come upon them somewhere out in the great American desert. Arnold pointed a rough thumb towards the East: "Out there." Perhaps it was Arizona, or Colorado, or Wyoming. He didn't know. Anyway, it was about 1000 miles to the east of Ralston's office. Who knew, out in the great desert, where one wandered? Who cared? And the old prospector laughed. They were mining explorers. They had been looking for gold. By chance they had stumbled upon diamonds.

No! they did not want to sell out their rights. True: they had no resources. To get a start, perhaps they would be forced to dispose of a small interest. But only perhaps. On no account would they part with the whole. They did not have money enough to secure title or develop their discovery. Perhaps on that account they would have to take a third party in with them. But they didn't want an outsider.

Ralston could make nothing out of the two shy, cautious, bewildered men before him. So afraid were they of making some regrettable mistake that they didn't know what they ought to do themselves.

Several days passed and the miners, more amenable to reason, returned to Ralston's office. They would part with a half interest in their diamond fields, they told him, to men in whom they had implicit confidence. Patiently Ralston pointed out that negotiations were impossible unless the location of the fields were disclosed and some sort of inspection permitted.

Then Slack and Arnold proposed a strange arrangement. On its face it seemed fair enough to Ralston. If anything, it made the offer more alluring.

They would conduct two men, to be selected by Ralston, to the diamond fields, and allow them to satisfy themselves of their extent but only on one condition: when these men had reached the wild, uninhabited district where the diamond fields lay, they must submit to being blindfolded, both going and coming back.

Full of the adventure of the thing, Ralston agreed. For one of the proposed inspectors he selected David C. Colton of the Southern Pacific, one of the most prominent and level-headed men of big affairs in San Francisco. Ralston acknowledged that he would have absolute faith in Colton's conclusions.

One day Colton departed with the two prospectors. After some time he was back in Ralston's office. He had been to the marvellous diamond country. Both going and coming he had been blindfolded; but there he had unearthed more diamonds than he ever knew existed. There was no doubt of the genuineness of the fields or of their fabulous richness. There were acres and acres of precious stones: diamonds, rubies, sapphires, emeralds. The whole terrain sparkled with them. On hearing this rose-colored report from a sane official of the Southern Pacific, Ralston went absolutely wild. There was one spot to invest his "Belcher" millions. There million would beget million. There would be no end to what he could accomplish for San Francisco. Straightaway he cabled his old friend Harpending, who was in London on mining business, regarding the diamond discovery. The first telegram was so explanatory that it cost Ralston $1100. But he did not care. Ralston wanted Harpending for his general manager. Would he catch the next boat? Harpending demurred. Ralston burned up the cable with messages. Harpending, an unbeliever in American diamond fields, "felt assured his old friend had gone mad." Finally, at great personal sacrifice he gave up several lucrative London deals to go to his old friend's assistance. In the meantime rumors of Ralston's vast diamond field leaked out in London. No less a person than Baron Rothschild sought an interview with the departing Harpending. But the latter was non-committal, although he was still scouting the idea of diamond fields in his country.

"Do not be so sure of that," commented the baron, "America is a very large country. It has furnished the world with many surprises already. Perhaps it may have others in store. At any rate, if you find cause to change your opinion, kindly let me know."

When Harpending saw those sacks empty their contents on his billiard table he kept his promise.

Being a cautious investor, Ralston started an investigation. Who were these two prospectors? Philip Arnold, he discovered, was an old California miner. Originally a California pioneer of '49, he had come from Hardin County, Kentucky. Ever since his arrival he had been mining. Several times George D. Roberts, one of the best-known mining men in the West and a close friend of Ralston's, had hired Arnold to investigate mining properties for him. Never had he been dissatisfied with the honesty of his work. He was an honorable old-timer.

Harpending, too, had known Arnold, and had always found him reliable. As for Slack, he was a plain man-about-town of fair repute. In Ralston's mind there were no longer any doubts as to Arnold and Slack. They were well-known honest prospectors, "Old Forty-niners." Still, all that mysterious hocus-pocus coming and going to and from the diamond fields deserved attention.

He decided to proceed carefully. The supply of diamonds might be quickly exhausted; only a "flash in the pan" as it were. That was not the sort of investment Ralston wanted for his Comstock winnings or for investors. Sensing Ralston's lack of enthusiasm, Arnold offered to go back to the diamond fields, collect a couple of million dollars' worth of diamonds, bring them back to San Francisco and allow Ralston to keep them in his possession as a guarantee of good faith.

That was fair enough. Ralston accepted. Slack and Arnold left San Francisco promising to be back in record-breaking time.

One night, shortly thereafter, Ralston received a telegram from Arnold. He was at Reno. He and Slack were on their return journey to San Francisco. He urged Ralston to have reliable persons meet them at Lathrop: "to share the burden of responsibility." The next morning, after a hurried conference, Harpending, who had just arrived from London, set out for Lathrop to meet the diamond emissaries and accompany them back to San Francisco. Before leaving, it had been agreed that Ralston, Rubery a London friend of Harpending, William M. Lent, and several others interested in the fields would await Harpending that evening in the billiard room of his home on Fremont Street to examine the diamond collateral.

That night an eager group assembled about Harpending's billiard table. Along about nine o'clock the rumble of carriage wheels and the crunching of gravel on the driveway could be heard. A moment later they heard the turning of a key in a lock and the shutting of a door. Then, all excitement, Harpending entered the billiard room. Under his arm was an awkward buckskin-covered bundle. He placed it on the table. He had a lurid tale to tell.

Ralston and Lent drew closer as Harpending began: When Arnold and Slack had reached the diamond fields they had struck an enormously rich deposit. With no trouble at all they had filled two packages, such as the one he laid upon the table, with diamonds, sapphires, emeralds, and rubies. Then they had started on their return. On their way they had been overtaken by a violent rainstorm. They had been compelled to ford a river on a raft. The river had been greatly swollen. Accidentally one package had been washed overboard and was irretrievably lost in the flood. But that had been no loss to the prospectors. There were millions more of precious stones on the fields. But time was pressing. They could not go back for more, so they had brought only one sack with them—the one on the table.

No time was lost in preliminaries. A sheet was spread over the green-baize covering. Ralston, Roberts, Dodge, Rubery, and Lent drew closer about the table. Harpending snipped the elaborate cord-fastenings about the bundle. Taking hold of the lower corners of the sack he turned it upside down. Out gushed a cascade of many-colored stones. How they flashed and scintillated in the dim light! As fiery as pieces of stars! They looked as if they would burn holes through the sheet. There lay at least a million dollars' worth of diamonds, rubies, sapphires, and emeralds. The ransom of a rajah! The loot of a dozen Burmah temples lay before Ralston's startled gaze. The flush on his cheeks turned a ruby red. Such a sight was worth a kingdom.

Having gorged their eyes to the full, Lent tied up the sack

and locked the gems in Harpending's vault for safekeeping. After that, once a week on Sundays, the same group would lock themselves in Harpending's billiard room, spread a sheet over the green baize, open the safe, take out the bundle and spill out the gems. Then they would feast their eyes and speculate over each precious stone; descanting upon its size, beauty, brilliance, and value.

These men had only one fear: there would be a great depreciation in the value of all diamonds, all rubies, all sapphires, all emeralds, when the news of the contents of their sack and of the field of precious stones was given to the world. Sighing deeply, the owners would watch the gems put back into the sack and then into the stronghold until another Sunday should roll around.

So far, no attempt had been made at organization. It was generally understood that Ralston, Roberts, Lent, and Harpending, and one or two others, would be in on the deal by virtue of the large sums of money they had already loaned to the prospectors. For those advances there was ample security in the gems on hand, to say nothing of the unexplored diamond fields. Now without further delay Ralston determined to get the diamond fields on a business basis. For that purpose he called a meeting and outlined his plan of action.

First, a large supply of the precious stones would be sent to Tiffany & Co. of New York, the greatest authority on precious stones in America, for examination and appraisal. If their value were proved beyond peradventure, then a mining expert would be chosen to whom Arnold and Slack would be required to exhibit the diamond fields and permit a full examination. Those were the only conditions upon which Ralston would be willing to handle the situation.

To Ralston's preamble Arnold and Slack readily agreed. Pending the favorable reports of Tiffany & Co. and the mining expert, Ralston agreed to take care of all incidental expenses, which already amounted to several hundreds of thousands. Then Ralston looked up government laws regarding diamond fields. There was no existing one under which diamond lands could be located and held. Therefore a title must be procured and a law gotten through Congress. It would take plenty of money. But, as usual, Ralston shouldered it. Immediately a prominent Washington lobbyist was selected to engineer and pass an act through Congress that would cover the grounds on which their wonderful discovery had been made. After considerable delay and difficulty a bill was finally drafted, introduced, and passed. It was known as "Sargent's Mining Bill," and appeared May 18, 1872. In it the following passage was inserted, purposely to cover the field of precious stones: "Including all forms of deposit, except veins of quartz or other rock then in place."

In the meantime Harpending, who had taken a little bag of the gems to Tiffany & Co., New York, displayed the stones in the presence of Mr. Tiffany, Horace Greeley, General George B. McClellan of Civil War fame, and General Benjamin F. Butler, a lawyer of repute as well as a United States Congressman. Butler had been included because it was thought that he would be of aid in the legislation needed to acquire the diamond fields, as later proved to be the case.

"Gentlemen," said Mr. Tiffany, with the air of a connoisseur, as he picked up a huge gem from one of the piles of stones he had been building in front of him, and held it up to the light, "gentlemen, these are beyond question precious stones of enormous value. But before I give you the exact appraisement, I must submit them to my lapidary, and will report to you further in two days."

Within those limits, Tiffany presented his report before the aforementioned men. The stones were genuine. The lot was worth about $150,000. Ralston was stunned on receipt of that information, as the stones sent to Tiffany were a fair sample of the lot, but composed only about one-tenth of those still in Ralston's possession. It argued a total value of $1,500,000 for the whole.

All that remained now was the choice of an engineer. The name of Henry Janin suggested itself. Henry Janin was one of the best-known mining engineers then living. The John Hays Hammond of his day. As a consulting engineer he was without a peer in the world. His ultra-conservatism was his only known fault. He had experted something over six hundred mines. Never once had he made a mistake. Some complained that he never took a chance. He had not an iota of gambling instinct. That was just the kind of a man he wanted to expert the diamond fields, Ralston explained. One couldn't be too careful with other people's money. Janin valued his services at $2500, an expense that Ralston readily shouldered.

So Henry Janin was dispatched to the region of many-colored gems and made an extensive examination. His report confirmed all that had been claimed for the field of precious stones.

Gems were so plentiful, Janin averred, that twenty rough laborers could wash out a million dollars' worth of diamonds a month.

At least, the uncut jewels were worth the value of all of "Crown Point" and "Belcher" stock combined. Some $65,000,000.

Ralston was so enthused over Janin's report that he telegraphed Harpending that he was ready to make the initial payment of $300,000 as per agreement, to Arnold and Slack. Not having ready cash, he made immediate arangements to sell 100 shares of "Crown Point," which was then bringing $300 a share on the San Francisco stock market.

Ralston now cleared the deck for the formation of his great diamond company. After Janin's return from the diamond fields there was some talk of incorporating in New York, but Ralston would not listen to such heresy. "San Francisco stood ready to furnish any amount of capital required," he wired. Moreover, all gems should be brought to San Francisco. In San Francisco they must be cut. Ralston intended to move the great lapidary establishments of Amsterdam to San Francisco, a decision which caused the Low Countries "no small concern."

San Francisco was ripe for the new company: "The San Francisco and New York Mining and Commercial Company." It was capitalized at $10,000,000. Twenty-five gentlemen, comprising the cream of San Francisco's financial element, men of national reputation for high-class business standing and personal integrity, were permitted to subscribe for stock to the amount of $80,000 each. This initial capital of $2,000,000 was immediately paid into the Bank of California.

The London Rothschilds cabled that they were interested in the diamond discovery. As a result, A. Gansl, the Rothschilds' California representative, became a member of the company. Among other directors were: Samuel Barlow and Major-General George B. McClellan of New York, who were to be resident directors there, where a transfer office was to be maintained. Among San Francisans, the directorate included: William M. Lent, Thomas Selby, whose daughter had married Ralston's brother; Milton S. Latham, Louis Sloss, Maurice Dore, W. F. Babcock, William C. Ralston, William Willis. Lent was chosen president; Ralston, treasurer; Willis, secretary. David D. Colton resigned his substantial position with the Southern Pacific Railroad to become general manager. Such were the men behind the diamond fields. The biggest names in California's Blue Book. The last word in the commercial and financial world. Men who only allowed their names to be used in 100 per cent concerns.

Handsome offices were engaged in San Fransisco. Two or three secretaries were engaged to handle the voluminous correspondence.

The interests of Arnold and Slack were extinguished by a final payment of $300,000 making, with what had been already allocated, $660,000 in all. The capitalists congratulated themselves that $660,000 was an exceedingly small sum to pay for property capable of producing a million dollars a month, to say nothing of a million and a half dollars in value already in their possession. Without more ado, the honest prospectors received their money and faded into invisibility.

Not only in Ralston's office in the Bank of California but in nearly every financial center in the world, the public was keyed up to a point of high speculative craze. "Crown Point," "Belcher," Sutro, Mackay, Fair, and O'Brien retired to the region of limbo.

Suddenly, like a thunderbolt from the blue, came a telegram from a small Wyoming station. It was signed by the name of

Clarence King, the noted scientist, head of the Fortieth Parallel Survey.

Taking assistants, King had visited the diamond fields in order to give official national significance to a notable local discovery. Readily he had located the fields and found diamonds, rubies, saphires, and emeralds aplenty, scattered over a wide terrain. Immediately his admiration had been aroused by the sheer beauty of the ant-hills. Some were powdered with diamond and ruby dust, while others were sprinkled with pulverized sapphire and emerald particles. There were gorgeous things to behold. In the heart of every ant-hill he found a gem corresponding in color to the dust sprinkled over its surface.

On looking about more closely, King found diamonds and sapphires in rock crevices where nature alone could not have placed them. Several times he ran into rubies and emeralds in the forks of trees; but not a gem could he unearth in the underlying bedrock, where, had their occurrence been genuine, the inevitable laws of nature must have placed them.

But when he uncovered a large diamond with the marks of the lapidary's art still upon its face, he realized the moment had come to explode Ralston's bubble and he had sent his telegram: "The alleged diamond fields are fraudulent. Plainly they are salted. The discovery is a gigantic fraud. The Company has been pitifully duped." But how could Arnold and Slack have told that the expert King would examine their diamond field? With any number of unskilled workmen it would have passed muster.

Subsequently some of the "jewels" reached London, where they were recognized as South African "niggerheads." When Arnold's picture was displayed, there were those who remembered him as a buyer of low-grade diamonds and other jewels in the big centers of London and Amsterdam. Thus beyond a doubt the fraudulent nature of the jewel fields was exposed.

Cruel as the blow was to Ralston, as soon as he had been convinced that he and twenty-five other members of the high lights of the city's financial firmament had been duped, he called a meeting of the "San Francisco and New York Mining and Commercial Company." The Tiffany appraisement and the reports of experts Janin and Clarence King were both examined. Then a complete recital was prepared for the public, bringing out the confidence that Ralston and his trustees had reposed in Tiffany and Janin. In conclusion, a complete acknowledgment was made of the fact that every one had been cleverly duped. Ralston intended that not the least of his enemies should ever connect his name with a fraudulent procedure. Then he made up his mind that rather than endure the whinings of faint-hearted partners he would assume the burden of expense himself.

Philosophically he accepted the loss of his own investment. With magnanimity he restored dollar for dollar to the twenty-five stockholders, who had subscribed to the $2,000,000 capital funds. And they allowed him to do so. There remained incidental expenses for lobbying, experting, etc., and the $300,000 that he had paid out of his own pocket to Arnold and Slack: an aggregate of loss not less than $500,000. Thus was expended a half million dollars of his "Belcher" bonanza. This sacrifice Ralston cheerfully assumed. No person should ever even whisper that Ralston had gulled his friends. He would rather sacrifice his last dollar than let any man look him in the face and say: "I suffer through you."

At long last Ralston had the receipts-in-full framed. These he hung upon his office wall, where he might have a continual reminder alike of the faith and the duplicity of man.

Harpending did not get off so easily. Because of innocent activities in London, he was loudly denounced in San Francisco as having "put up the job" on Ralston and others. Already his real-estate block had burned. He now decided to leave San Francisco. One after the other he liquidated his valuable assets. His interest in the New Montgomery Real Estate Company he sold to Ralston and Sharon. With a million dollars in his possession he made up his mind to return to his old home in the South. But before he could get away, friendship would exact another sacrifice.

Sharon was no longer on the Comstock. Ralston's brother

…iser, Sam Ralston, had died. Mills was going to Eu-…pe. Harpending was leaving the West for good. Thus Ralston, at a crucial time in his career, was left without the steadying influence of those ballasting men who could do him the greatest amount of good when emergency required. More locked within himself now than ever, Ralston faced the future with his inscrutable, debonair smile.

CHAPTER XXV

COMSTOCK SILVER COINED IN JAPAN

1872

Now that he was a multimillionaire, Ralston remained just as accessible to bank clients as before. Still, during banking hours, he sat in his office just off the main part of the Bank. Through the glass screen his well-shaped head, alert eyes, high-colored but thoughtful-looking face could be seen.

Like a distinguished Roman he looked: broad-shouldered, immaculately dressed, the bosom of his white linen shirt studded with black-cameos. Other men, in his position in California, might disport diamonds but Ralston clung to the simplicity of his shell-carved gems.

The patrons of the Bank liked to see Ralston moving about his office. His determined-looking expression and the magnetism of his personality were electric. Like voyagers, the onlooking clients liked to know that their captain was always on duty on the bridge. His dash, energy, and success gave them a sense of security.

Ralston allowed himself, now, a bank attendant, "Jim," a distinguished-looking old darky, of antebellum appearance. All patrons of the bank had to do was to make their names known to Jim and they would be ushered into Ralston's presence to pour out their troubles.

One day, Jim ushered Leland Stanford into Ralston's office. Stanford had a complaint to make against Ralston's friend, Harpending. Harpending was planning to run his road-bed, "The San Francisco & Humboldt Bay Railroad," through Marin, Sonoma, Mendocino, and Humboldt counties to Beckwith Pass in the Sierra. Stanford saw in Harpending's scheme a menace to the Central Pacific Railroad. He wanted it stopped. He not only wanted Harpending subdued but threatened Ralston with loss of promised concessions if he refused to do so.

In the dark days of Central Pacific construction, Ralston had been the friend of Stanford and his cohorts. While others had been calling them "swindlers," Ralston had boomed their bonds and sold their securities abroad, and had forced loans to them, as earlier described, from the Pacific Insurance Company as well as other institutions. So grateful had Stanford been, that he had promised Ralston, when the time came, that he should build all their Central Pacific cars. And Ralston had been delighted at this promise and, in his usually large way, had gone ahead and constructed an enormous factory, where all kinds of cars could be built at a moment's notice.

Now Stanford came to Ralston and warned him that unless he could prevent Harpending from carrying out his Beckwith Pass plans, the concessions would be cancelled and he could expect nothing but war from the Four who had become Big.

After Stanford had gone, Ralston sent for Harpending. He admitted to him that he had no right to influence his action. But he confided in him. If he did not get those railroad concessions from Stanford, he would face an enormous loss. Perhaps Harpending would strain a point. Perhaps he would give up his railroad through Beckwith Pass. Harpending paused. He was on the highroad to great success. Yet he would do anything for Ralston, make any sacrifice for him. Finally he yielded and sold out his railroad rights to Peter Donahue, who then and there laid the foundations of his own gigantic fortune. Left to himself, Harpending would have become the owner of the Northwestern Pacific Railroad. As for Ralston, ultimately the Big Four "gold-bricked" him. Never did he receive a car concession of any kind. The great building he had constructed for the purpose remained empty until another project arose by which Ralston felt he could promote the welfare of city and State.

One day I.C. Bateman, a Nevada prospector, was ushered into Ralston's office. "The Northern Belle" mine, Candelaria, Nevada, had reached the point where a mill was needed. He wanted capital on a bond, to complete his development. As Ralston listened he began to tear up paper and throw the pieces into the basket.

"Your scheme looks good," Ralston retorted when Bateman had finished speaking, "but my time is all taken up with the business of the Bank. You go and see General Dodge."

On Dodge's recommendation, Ralston gave Bateman his personal check, with no collateral, for $75,000. On the strength of that help, Dodge and Batemen made several million dollars and posed as great operators. There were no commissions for Ralston, but that was Ralston: always generous, magnanimous, entirely devoid of greed, "permitting others to reap where he had sown." It was a common saying among San Franciscan financiers: "Ralston caught the hares while his friends picked out the fat ones."

Then it was James Lick, California's shabby millionaire, whom Jim ushered into Ralston's office. Ralston was familiar with the eccentric Lick's story. He had been born in Pennsylvania, later he had made a small fortune in Buenos Aires and Rio de Janeiro and had arrived in California in 1847 in time to reap great wealth in real estate. Now that $10,000 had become four to five millions.

Lick was ill. He thought that he was dying. He was about to make his will. He wanted to be sure that eventually his money would be of help to humanity. He had come to Ralston to talk over the terms of his last testament.

With San Francisco ever in mind, Ralston suggested benefactions that would beautify and improve the city; park statuary to commemorate California and national history; an old people's home, to house the derelicts of 1849; free public baths like those in Rome; and an observatory with the biggest lens in the world to crown nearby Mt. Hamilton. But the thing that was nearest the Ralston heart came last: the San Francisco hoodlums.

California's bad boys distressed Ralston. What was to become of them? Were they to be salvaged or scrapped? Were they to be sent to training schools or prisons? universities or reform schools? asylums or the Potter's Field?

While Ralston pleaded for the youth of the city he filled a basket with strips of paper he was reducing to scraps. Finally he suggested that Lick found a technical school in San Francisco where young men could be educated in mechanical arts.

Lo and behold! Several months later when Lick's will was read, he had followed out Ralston's suggestions to the letter. About a half million dollars had been bequeathed to the city to build and endow "the California School of Mechanical Arts." In addition public baths, museums, a pioneer's building, statuary, and homes for the aged had been provided for.

Now it was Daniel Coit Gilman, recently appointed President of the University of California, whom Jim ushered into Ralston's presence.

Ever since 1865, Ralston had been a regent of the State University and latterly treasurer. Heart, soul, and pocketbook had gone freely into its development. Ralston felt that California ought to have an outstanding university: "A Conservator of Civilization," he called it. With all his resources, Ralston backed up Gilman when the young college had to fight the Farmer's Grange and other political enemies.

Ralston always had California's developing boys in mind. It was youth that he would foster. Upon them the future commerce and industry of State and city would depend.

On this occasion, Gilman wanted to provide more adequate dormitories. On the whole campus there was not a decent one. With his generous impulses stirred, Ralston helped to provide for six instead of one. Dormitory space must keep abreast of student enrollment. How better could he invest his Comstock millions than in California youth? To them, some day, he must pass the torch.

After a lunch with his friends at the Union Club, one of the most aristocratic in the young city, Ralston was back in the Bank again. There was never any let-up in the problems seeking his attention.

Endowed with great capacity for work, Ralston had developed a mental prowess in solving other people's problems that would have baffled any ordinary intellect. Quick to grasp a proposition, whether of public or private nature, and to push it with zeal, he infused into business life some of his own passionate interest in San Francisco.

By 1872 Ralston's personality was in evidence everywhere in California. His dream to make Comstock wealth develop San Francisco into a great industrial center was fast maturing. As his plans approached fruition, Ralston could not tolerate anything or anybody which might jeopardize the result. With kindly feelings toward all and enmity toward none, he justified his brusque behavior toward Sutro, Mackay, Fair, Jones, Hayward, Flood, and O'Brien by the thought that they were working toward selfish ends while his goals were for the city's common good.

Although Ralston had powerful enemies, he was thoroughly appreciated by the rank and file of Californians. Everywhere this fact was paramount. Always in the heart of affairs, never on its fringe, he was a part of his woollen mills, part of his sugar refineries, of his vineyards, tobacco fields, granaries, dry docks, railroads, steamships, and all of his bank. It was impossible to think of California or San Francisco and not include thoughts of the great magician.

No public gathering was complete without Ralston. If there was a municipal banquet and an outstanding citizen was required to make a speech, Ralston was pressed into service. If there was an excursion, and horses to drive, the reins were turned over to Ralston.

Ralston impressed stranger and friend with his power, he infused the working man with his energy, he touched the beggar with his generosity, he conquered many an enemy with his magnetism. "His vitality was the flash of steel, his energy the swift flow of a cataract." Said his lawyer of him, "Of all her public possessions, California owned nothing more precious than Ralston."

The great majority of Californians realized this. Fathers held him up to their sons as a pattern of a successful man of affairs; wives quoted him to their husbands as an outstanding business leader. Men baptized their sons "William Ralston"; mothers called their daughters "Ralston"; hoping thereby to bestow on their offspring some of the outstanding qualities which distinguished their fellow citizen.

When new streets were laid out in metropolitan San Francisco, Oakland, San Mateo, Burlingame, Belmont, or Redwood one would receive the name Ralston. Among the new engines on the Southern Pacific line was one called Ralston.

One day a nameless town was created in the San Joaquin Valley and the directorate of the Central Pacific Railroad, in convention there, sought an appropriate name. Some one offered that of Ralston. Could any appellative more suitable for a California town be found than that of the State's central figure, said the proposer.

Ralston himself happened to be present at the conclave. Taken completely by surprise by the honor about to be conferred upon him by the citizens of the undesignated community, he arose and with a considerable display of diffidence declined the honor.

"Too modest," some one repeated. Whereat the name of "Modesto," the Spanish equivalent for modesty, was proposed to honor that reserved quality in Ralston's make-up, which all his friends admired.

The suggestion took the convention by storm. The members clapped their hands in appreciation. And the undistinguished valley town became Modesto.

There were more problems in San Francisco now than ever. Pickering and Fitch of *The Bulletin* and *The Call* had been trying to foist upon San Francisco the Atlantic-Pacific

Railroad. At the very time they were sponsoring the new corporation, Ralston discovered that the company was virtually bankrupt. He called it: "the most dishonest scheme of public plunder ever presented to the people."

When the company asked San Francisco to raise a subsidy of $10,000,000, Ralston countered by organizing a $50,000,000 railroad scheme: The San Francisco & Colorado River Railroad. The line was to extend from the city through the Southern counties of the State to the Colorado River and Arizona—a distance of 900 miles. Ralston did not really want the road. It was merely a strategical move to divert public attention from the Pickering-Fitch project.

Bad blood was immediately engendered. *The Bulletin* and *The Call* became Ralston's staunch enemies and sought in every way possible to visit their wrath upon his head. Living or dead, neither editor would ever forgive him. From then on it became the policy of their newspapers to destroy the idol which San Francisco had set up in her market place.

At the November, 1872, election, Ralston's scheme for the San Francisco & Colorado Railroad was referred to a referendum of the people and was decisively defeated. To Ralston it made no difference. He had accomplished what he had set out to do: to balk the Pickering-Fitch design. Unfortunately, at the same time he had lighted fires of hatred that not all the water in the Bay of San Francisco would ever be able to extinguish.

Now there began teeming in the Ralston brain another plan to beautify San Francisco—a scheme made possible by the "Belcher" bonanza. Ralston aspired to build the most beautiful hotel in the world: a hotel such as no other city could boast. Not even the domed, porticoed St. Charles of New Orleans would compare with it. Ralston pored over architectural books. Pompeii, Roman Coliseum, Athenian Acropolis would all contribute their quota to his design.

Sharon promised to share the expense of the undertaking. The leading architect-contractor in California, M. L. King, was sent East and South to study the question. The plans started out simply enough. But as usual, Ralston's ideas, enriched by the fabulous wealth of the Comstock, grew like Jack's bean-stalk. Finally, they ran completely away with him. But Ralson was not worried. He had the wealth of the "Belcher" behind him.

Nor was there any rest for Ralston at night. Direct from his swim he would plunge into affairs of city and State. Always there were distinguished guests to be entertained. Strangers who could do things for California, and Ralston would not neglect such an opportunity.

One night it was Sinu Tomomi Iwakura, the Prime Minister of Japan: Envoy Extraordinary and Minister Plenipotentiary to the Treaty Powers, whom Ralston had invited to Belmont.

In January, 1872, the Emperor of Japan had dispatched his commission on a round of visits to the Treaty Powers. Their two-year investigation was to begin at San Francisco. In this group were 105 persons including Prime Minister Iwakura; the Minister of Public Works, Yuske Hirobumie Ito; the Chief Minister of Finance, Yussonmi Tossimitsi Okkubo; a Member of the Privy Council, Yussonmi Takaiosi Kido, and many other secretaries, students and attendants. The embassy was especially interested in American education, economics, religion, banking, public works, and construction. Its interests were national as well as municipal in scope.

Ralston saw in the coming of this embassy an opportunity to further San Francisco's Oriental prestige: to stimulate trade, markets, commerce and travel. He did everything in his power to make their trip a profitable one for California and to facilitate the object of Japan.

One day in January, 1872, Ralston sent out invitations for a dinner at Belmont. "A special train will leave the San José depot at 5:30 P.M., returning from Belmont at about 12 o'clock," read instructions.

The banquet was a princely affair. The only toast was a whispered one from one of the Japanese officials: "To the Tenno of Belmont." In it there was a sly humor, but those present preferred to interpret it as a compliment to Ralston: The Great Californian.

Although Iwakura, like all Orientals, was inscrutable in bearing, every one could see that he was impressed by Ralston's occidental hospitality. What other private American dining room could accommodate 110 guests? What other host could boast of such urbanity?

As Iwakura gazed upon the dazzling splendor of the mirrored ballroom he forgot his inscrutability long enough to murmur: "it seems like a dream."

When the Prime Minister returned to Japan he told his Emperor, the Son of Heaven, that Ralston, the California banker, had promised aid in precious metals. Soon, along came a shipment of Comstock bullion. When the Imperial Mint was created it used Virginia City silver to coin its first yen.

CHAPTER XXVI

SHARON'S CONSPIRACY

1872

By 1872 Sharon was consumed with ambition. Next to D. O. Mills he was reputed to be the wealthiest man on the Pacific Coast. Although Ralston had put him in the way of accumulating every cent of it, he now intended to free himself, and use his own wings.

After the "Belcher" discovery, he was finished with Virginia City. He wanted a bigger field of operation. The Comstock was a gambling hole, not a place to reside. Who could be proud of hailing from such a spot?

Acceding to Sharon's demands for retirement, Ralston had appointed his brother, A. J. Ralston, agent of the Bank of California in Virginia City. Sharon departed for San Francisco, through forever, he believed, with the Comstock as a place of residence.

In nine years he had gotten even with the Lode as he had once sworn he would. No one had plundered it to better advantage. But nothing is gained without some loss. In making himself a wealthy man, Sharon had antagonized the Comstockers and warped his own fiber.

Now, along with the Ring, Sharon believed that if he could be elected United States Senator from Nevada he would be able to fight this persistent Sutro to a finish. Never, then, would Sutro be able to get a Government loan. Never once had Sutro gotten the best of him on the Comstock. Rest assured if he were in Washington neither would Sutro get the best of him there. He would find the way to end Sutro's influence with the lawmakers.

No one knew better than Sharon how necessary it was to protect the Bank's monopoly on Sun Mountain against Sutro. Now the latter was working night and day to reach the Lode and capitalize on his $2 royalties. If he had more capital he would be making greater speed.

So it was decided that Sharon should be the next United States Senator from Nevada. In years past such proposals had always been foregone conclusions. California decided on Nevada's candidates. All the Sage-brushers had to do was to elect them.

No Comstocker could call his vote, his decision, or his soul his own if it conflicted with a Bank decision. As Ralston controlled a majority of the mines on the Lode, no concern was felt about Sharon's election. If all else failed, the Bank could elect him.

The term of James W. Nye, whom President Lincoln had made Nevada's Territorial Governor, and who had afterward become her first State Governor as well as one of her first United States Senators, was just drawing to its close. Nye wished to be re-elected. He felt he was entitled to it. He had merit, had acquitted himself well in Washington and had been a staunch supporter of Ralston there. He had even espoused the Bank's enmity against Sutro. But he had not been able to stay the latter's popularity.

In spite of favorable factors, the Ring felt that the time had come when Nye must be sacrificed. Sharon could serve the needs of the monopoly to greater advantage. So in May, Sharon announced himself as a candidate for United States Senator from Nevada to take Nye's place.

If it took half of his "Belcher" millions, Sharon boasted, he would wrest the Nevada toga from "the Gray Eagle," the name the miners had once applied to Nye. Not only must ambition's needs be served, but Sutro must be put where he would no longer be a menace to the Bank Ring.

Unfortunately, Sharon's ambitions did not appeal to Joe Goodman, the wily editor of *The Virginia City Territorial Enterprise*. Goodman loved the Comstock and its turbulent, rollicking spirit. No one had done more to mould that Comstock soul, if it had one, than Joe Goodman. Throughout Nevada he wielded the power of a Tammany boss.

If there was one man on the Mountain Joe despised, it was Bill Sharon. To him, Sharon was not a Comstocker at heart. He was a plunderer, a grasping, avaricious, unscrupulous interloper, who always thought of Sharon first, his friends afterward. These sentiments were warmly seconded by every miner.

In spite of all the millions the Comstock had bestowed upon him, Sharon looked down on, rather than up to, the mountain that had made him. Never had he shown a strain of gratitude. Never would Joe allow such a man to be the representative of the generous, openhearted, loyal Comstockers. Never while he was dictator of *The Enterprise's* policy and boss of the Comstock.

As soon as he discovered that Sharon was returning to Virginia City, ostensibly to begin his campaign, Goodman prepared the opening shot, an editorial "Welcome" that appeared in his columns the very morning of Sharon's arrival.

"Your unexpected return, Mr. Sharon, has afforded no opportunity for public preparation, and you will consequently accept these simple remarks as an unworthy but earnest expression of the sentiments of a people who feel that they would be lacking in duty and self-respect if they failed upon such an occasion to make a deserved recognition of your acts and character. You are probably aware that you have returned to a community where you are feared, hated and despised. . . . Your career in Nevada for the past nine years has been one of merciless rapacity. You fostered yourself upon the vitals of the State like a hyena, and woe to him who disputed with you a single coveted morsel of your prey. . . . You cast honor, honesty, and the commonest civilities aside. You broke faith with men whenever you could subserve your purpose by so doing."

That editorial pleased the miners. It bespoke their feelings better than they could have worded them themselves. Sharon was a double-dealer. Of all men on the Coast, Sharon was the one man whom they would not have represent them in Washington. Neither did they want Nye. Their loyalty to him was ended.

Now their candidate for United States Senator was a representative from their own ranks: the doughty John P. Jones.

Jones was a real Washoe pioneer. Had he not been with them since the golden days of '49? Many had bivouacked with him in Calaveras, Tuolumne, and Trinity. He was one of them: jovial, reckless, carefree, bone of their bone, a Comstocker to the core. Never *had* he been afraid to tell any man to his face exactly what he thought of him, never *would* he be afraid. Jones would make an ideal Washoe Senator. When his name was proposed, his supporters dubbed him "the Nevada Commoner." Heart and soul they were with him: their avowed champion in their endless Laocoönic struggle with the hydra-headed California monopoly.

No one had been better pleased than their pals when Jones and Hayward had worsted Ralston in the recent "Crown Point" deal. Anything that loosened the monster's grip on the Comstock was applauded. Besides, Jones had risked his life to save that of his comrades in the recent "Yellow Jacket" fire. That piece of sublime heroism had enshrined him forever in their hearts. Not only had it enshrined him but it would go a long way toward sending him to Washington. Then, too, these men were anxious to see the Sutro Tunnel accomplished.

Had Ralston helped Sutro when he should have, their comrades need not have died in the "Yellow Jacket" holocaust.

When Sharon realized that his "Belcher" millions were insufficient to override the prejudice against him, he resolved to crush Jones by other means. First he would ruin Jones financially. A loss of wealth would mean political incapacity. When he had him crippled, he would sweep him off his pedestal—by destroying the faith which had placed him there. So vindictive had Sharon grown that he would stoop to conquer. He began to hatch a plot in which Ralston had no part. Sharon worked on the principle that when a man is to be destroyed the fewer who know the details the better.

The Jones-Hayward, Sharon-Ralston feud had grown more bitter during the winter of 1871–72 when the two former had wrested control of "the Savage" from the Bank Ring.

That victory had meant a loss of votes in the election for the United States Senatorship. For mine control and blocks of votes were inextricably mixed on the Comstock Lode. No one had realized that fact more bitterly than Sharon.

On top of that rebuff the "Crown Point" management had refused to allow "Belcher" ore to be brought to the surface through their new shaft—refused when they knew that Sharon had no other means of handling his great bonanza.

That refusal had been the last straw. It had delayed "Belcher" production, increased Sharon's enmity, and made the thought of revenge sweeter than ever.

When Sharon discovered that Jones and Hayward held the big block of their "Savage" stock "on margin" and hence were vulnerable, he knew exactly how to proceed. He would break the San Francisco stock market. Down with the market to ruin, financial and political, would go John P. Jones, Hayward and all their financial adherents. Even advocates must go the way of perdition. When he got through with those Bank turncoats, Sharon assured himself, "the Nevada Commoner" would be forced out of the Senatorial race.

He would make a pariah out of him. For, not only would Jones be ruined financially and hence unable to run for the Senate, but his character would be so besmirched that he would be fit only for a penitentiary cell. Even the miners would be finished with "their Commoner."

On May 7, 1872, Comstock mining stocks were at their zenith for the year. Their value on the San Francisco stock market was estimated at $81,000,000. The supposed bonanza Jones had uncovered in the "Savage" had inflated them more than ever. Hayward and Jones had "bulled" the stock up to $700 a share.

As soon as prices had reached the highest peak Sharon threw a large block of his own "Savage" stock upon the market. The impact was terrific. For a moment the Exchange rocked under the strain. Valiantly Jones and Hayward fought to sustain prices, but to no avail. The market had been dealt such a deadly blow that it tottered and fell. The collapse was fearful to behold. Wreckage was strewn all over San Francisco's financial area.

Listed stocks shrank more than $48,834,000. Between the 6th and 8th of May, "Belcher" dropped from $1525 to $850; "Crown Point" fell off 200 points; "Savage" lost 260 points. Over night, millionaires with paper fortunes became paupers. Business was crushed. Thousands were thrown out of employment. Jones and Hayward were crippled: the one lost a cool million dollars, the other twice that amount. While the great "bear" Sharon, salvaged $5,000,000 from the debacle. Never had brokers found him in a more playful or prosperous mood.

But while he could count his gains in millions, he had impoverished many a widow and woman operator and had increased the number marching toward "Paupers' Alley." Gone were silks and satins, jewels and laughter; through painted lips they hurled anathemas at Sharon. Men as well as women damned him. He had thrown enough stock on the market to break every margin operator. But he had only singed his antagonists.

Not content with setting in motion a series of events that

Ralston would feel until 1875, Sharon now made ready to slay Jones politically.

On May 8, 1872, there appeared, in *The San Francisco Chronicle,* an article accusing Jones of incendiarism. He had been privy to the act of firing the "Yellow Jacket" mine which had snuffed out the lives of forty-two men.

The fire had been lighted, so ran the accusation, to knock the San Francisco stock market, so that Comstock stocks would collapse and thereby enable Jones to gobble up "Savage" at its lowest figures and make a greater fortune.

One Isaac J. Hubbell, underground foreman of the "Crown Point" on the night of the disaster, had first voiced these accusations. At the time Sharon had taken heed. It was just the sort of material he needed. To clinch the matter, he had brought Hubbell to San Francisco, paid his railroad fare and all attendant expenses and set him up at the Occidental Hotel.

On arrival in the city, Sharon had had an interview with him: with several witnesses present he had promised to pay him $50,000 if he would swear to an affidavit charging John P. Jones with the crime of setting the "Yellow Jacket" mine on fire.

Perhaps the story was not true. Sharon was counting on the fact that "a charge preferred is a charge half proven." Whatever happened afterward, "the stigma of accusation" would be fastened upon Jones. Not all, but at least part of the mud slung was bound to stick. Forever Jones would be besmirched. Some men would always remember that Jones had been accused of the crime. In the reaction Jones would be defeated in the Nevada elections and Sharon would be swept into the Senate.

Immediately on reading the newspaper report, Jones sought out Sharon. Several accounts of what happened are extant. All of them are tinged with melodrama. Finding Sharon with Ralston in the latter's office in the Bank of California, Jones had presented Sharon with a pistol. Taking another himself he had bellowed: "Now let's settle this matter." But Sharon had declined the opportunity. He was not a duelist.

The publication of this story found its repercussions in the stock market. Prices took a steadily downward trend. There were more suicides, more ruin, more women headed toward "Paupers' Alley." Before three weeks had elapsed, shrinkage in stock values amounted to $61,000,000. This proved such a terrific drain on Ralston's resources that he was doubly incensed at Sharon.

On the Comstock the news created a profound sensation. Old stories, regarding incendiarism in the "Yellow Jacket" fire, were revived. Always it had been the settled conviction of the community that the mine had been fired. Now through set teeth the miners began to curse.

But when they learned of Sharon's attempt to bribe a man to swear the crime upon their hero they were ready to fight. Even Jones' enemies claimed that "the Commoner" would not be guilty of a crime so monstrous, while Sharon's personal friends boldly admitted that he had gone too far in his effort to crush his political rival.

As an upshot of the Hubbell accusations, the Storey County Grand Jury indicted Sharon for conspiracy. Among other things he was accused of sending Hubbell money with which to travel to San Francisco and of promising him $50,000 if his accusation would involve Jones.

Ralston and Mills were so disgusted with the whole procedure that they announced that unless Sharon could completely exonerate himself from the charges, he must leave the Bank of California.

Sharon had scarcely a friend left in Nevada or California. The feeling against him in San Francisco was increasingly bitter. *The Stock Report* admitted that Sharon's mode of warfare did not exhibit "the generosity of an honest man." "Rich in purse but poor in spirit" ran another comment, "such a man should be brought within an improving acquaintance of the walls of San Quentin." Some declared that they would "go for him" on the streets when the opportunity offered. While Joe Goodman, the editor of *The Enterprise* claimed that a man capable of conspiracy so damnable, ought to be lashed naked from the haunts of civilization.

"It is plain to every one on the Comstock," ran his editorial, "that Mr. Sharon has resorted to this atrocious means of alienating from his formidable competitor the support of a class of citizens whose numbers render them, when united, an almost resistless political power. In this act, malice has reached the very acme of baseness and cowardice. Malevolence has never suggested a means of vengeance more monstrous. Nor has hatred ever struck with fangs so envenomed."

The story that Sharon had hatched to destroy his rival acted like a boomerang.

In June, when the Storey County Grand Jury investigated the whole subject and rendered a decision exonerating Jones of all complicity, Sharon was done for.

On the 16th of August, Sharon announced his withdrawal from the contest. He was sick, he wrote, too sick to continue his candidacy for the United States Senate.

Ralston, it was rumored, had forced this decision.

It was better to let Sutro get his $2,000,000 than to involve the Ring in such a scandal. That was not all. Sharon's accusations had injured the Bank of California and had shaken public confidence in their management of the Comstock mines. As a result, Eastern and European capitalists had withdrawn large quantities of capital from the stock market. In consequence, Ralston had been forced to call in heavy loans, causing a serious setback, not only to the stock market but in all branches of trade. Ralston feared if the same state of affairs continued much longer it would result in a disastrous financial crisis.

Sharon must give up his ambition for the Senate. The Bank must find a fairer weapon to use against Sutro. So Sharon surrendered, but there burned in his bosom a fire that not even Ralston could ever quench.

The race for United States Senator from Nevada now lay between Nye and "the Nevada Commoner." Jones' popularity had been greatly increased by Sharon's conspiracy. The miners felt that their candidate had been made to suffer in their behalf. Nor could they be blinded to the fact that Sharon's malice had been prompted more by Jones' success in wrenching the "Crown Point" and "Savage" from the grasp of the Bank of California than by politics.

In the Nevada Legislature of 1873, Jones received fifty-three votes out of a possible seventy-two.

And Nye, the discarded "Gray Eagle," left for his Eastern home by way of San Francisco.

A few days after his arrival in the city a number of men who had known Nye in the early days gathered in Ralston's office in the Bank of California to talk over recent events with their chief. While he listened to the conversation, Ralston was tearing old papers into very fine pieces and letting them fall upon the floor.

"I'm sorry for old man Nye," mused one of those present. "He is old and poor and now his office has been taken from him. He's too old to renew the practice of law. On my soul, I am sorry for him."

Ralston had been listening quietly to these comments. The floor about him bore witness to his interest. He, too, was profoundly grieved for the Senator. He was old, now he was discarded. In days past Nye had been a devoted friend of the Bank. No one could be more grateful for services rendered nor more sympathetic toward a friend in need than Ralston. Poor old Nye.

While the others were occupied with their talk Ralston swung his chair round to his desk, picked up a pen, and began to write. Then tearing off the paper he had been writing upon, back he wheeled towards his visitors holding a check aloft in his hand.

"I am sorry ten thousand dollars' worth," said he reflectively, "how much are you?"

Then and there Ralston raised $100,000 to speed the rejected old Senator towards his New York home.

CHAPTER XXVII

THE PALACE HOTEL

1872–1875

When Ralston laid the foundation of the Palace Hotel on the margins of a two-and-a-half acre tract, bounded by Market, New Montgomery, Jessie, and Annie Streets, he told Sharon the cost would not exceed $1,750,000. And Sharon was content. But the first thing Sharon knew that amount had been sunk in the sand in the twelve-foot-thick masonry foundations. Another million dollars would be required to raise the first story; still more millions would be needed for the second, third, and on up to the seventh. About one million of Comstock bullion, Sharon discovered, would be required to raise each story. Sharon grew dizzy contemplating the result. Never had he conceived of such an expenditure. The next thing Sharon discovered was that Ralston was buying a ranch for a large sum of money.

Sharon expostulated: "Of all things, why a ranch?"

He needed some oak planking for the Palace floors, Ralston explained. Barker's place abounded in the finest specimens of oak he had ever seen. Under those conditions there was nothing for Sharon to do but assent.

When Ralston failed to use a plank from those felled trees, Sharon demurred, but said nothing. Construction on the Palace had already begun. He had too much pride to withdraw. But when Ralston bought a foundry to forge nails and tools and the "West Coast Furniture Company," a colossal factory, on the northwest corner of Bryant and 4th streets, came into being for the purpose of turning

California laurel into Palace furniture, Sharon grew desperate. Again he went to Ralston's office.

"If you are going to buy a foundry for a nail, a ranch for a plank, and manufacture and build furniture, where is this thing going to end?" he complained.

"It does look ridiculous to you," Ralston returned quietly.

"Yes," snapped Sharon, "worse than that; it looks pretty bad."

Feeling irrevocably committed, Sharon would not retire; but he complained to his cronies: "Ralston is inclined to scatter. When he goes into anything there is no end to it. Never will he beat a retreat until he strikes the ocean."

When Ralston needed hardware, and founded a lock and key factory as a necessary Palace adjunct, Sharon became downhearted. There was to be no end to this thing. But what could he do? Having abundant means of his own and knowing that Ralston must be equally well off, he reluctantly yielded the construction to Ralston's sole administration.

Along with all San Francisco, Sharon watched, fascinated, as the white foundations of the palatial structure, like the fronds of an enormous budding lotus, emerged from Market Street's sand-dunes and slowly unfolded themselves in regal splendor.

Up, on all four sides of a square block, arose the marble walls: a combination of low arches with Doric columns and embrasures for enormous bow-windows. But those plain walls were only the hard outer tegument of the Palace's inner glory.

Within, a colossal, lofty-pillared, grand-central court of matchless beauty and splendid proportions disclosed itself. For seven stories, 112 feet, arose wide colonnaded balconies, one above the other, to enclose a hollow quadrangular court, 144 by 84 feet.

Over the court was thrown an arched roof of glass. On the ground floor was laid out a circular driveway, wide enough for a coach-and-four to turn, and paved with marble. It was a magnificent, ethereal tower of space, surrounded by illusive white columns and delicately turned balustrades. About it there was something unreal, dreamlike. It gave a feeling of vastness. With its physical properties robbed of all sense of weight, the court had the tenuous fragility of one of those hymeneal towers so dear to the confectioner's art. It possessed the same symmetry of movement, the same rhythmic expression, the same chaste aloofness as those frosted conceptions.

At night when the standards with their multicolored globes, mounted on the balcony railings, were aglow with light, the court became a scene of pagan splendor. It was Ralstonesque. Over it always brooded his proud, manly spirit.

Through the great entrance portals carriages and horses could drive into the court and disgorge guest and luggage. Separated from the driveway by carved screens as light and airy as any in the Taj, was the great Palm Court, paved with alternate blocks of white and black marble, and heated by gigantic bronze braziers filled with glowing coals. Against the colonnades, orange, lime and lemon trees in parti-colored, Italian earthernware pots, ripened. Interspersed among them were tropical plants and palms of exotic beauty. Afternoon and evenings there was gypsy music, and the beaumonde and demimonde swished their silken trains over the marble floors.

On the wide seventh floor was the court's crowning glory: the crystal roof garden. Here all was glass, bronze, thick red carpets, flowering shrubs, hanging baskets, great chandeliers. On pedestals at the garden's corners rested four white marble statues: spring, summer, autumn, and winter. Chaste Dianas in poses as rhythmic as Canova's dancers. Over the lofty parapet they seemed to lean and to gaze down in marble-eyed serenity into the glowing eyes of the bronze braziers seven floors below. At night when there were beautiful women, music, dancing, and the incense of many-hued flowers, Ralston's court became an unforgetable experience.

On every floor Ralston had a desk and attendant installed. Each had an annunciator or speaking tube, and slots into which to drop letters, and pneumatic tubes for packages, direct to the main office.

Off the court on the ground floor opened a ballroom of splendid proportions. The dining saloon could seat 1200 guests. The china was imported: egg-shell Haviland from Vierzin, France; the silver bore the stamp of Gorham & Co., New York; the glass was cut crystal, and the linen: Irish flax. All designed especially for Ralston, all monogrammed "Palace Hotel." The kitchens were a wilderness of polished metal: iron, nickel, copper, tin, steel, and brass, in bewildering array. A special chef presided over every imaginable department, from soups to ices.

On the second floor was a series of committee rooms: "Where one could draw to a pair of aces," and seven private dining rooms, where one could entertain a lady with painted lips and pallid brows without fears of molestation. From these, on up to the seventh floor were single bedrooms and rooms in suites. Each with its connecting bath, each with an especially designed Axminster rug from Glasgow, Scotland; each with a great bay-window that looked out upon the gray veiled city. But each with hangings so heavy that they could, at will, shut out the moan of the sea and the everlasting wail of the foghorns.

On the mantel of every fireplace "tick-tocked" a handsome timepiece made especially at Ralston's Cornell Watch Factory at Oakland. The furniture was California laurel—a light-colored hardwood with wavy lines of mahogany-like texture susceptible of taking the highest polish. Every stick of it was turned out of Ralston's factory, the "West Coast Furniture Company." Even the horsehair that filled the mattresses and the goose-feathers that softened the pillows were Californian in origin. If possible, Ralston would contract for none other. From the looms of his "Mission Woollen Mills" came the thousands of pairs of fleecy, blue, green, and red-bordered blankets that lay upon every bed. Upon the body of each, Ralston had had emblazoned, in block-letters, "Palace Hotel." And the silk that clung to the windows and was spread in such voluptuous folds over beds and divans came from California cocoons and was spun in Ralston's factory.

On every door was a lock, to every bureau a key. Those,

too, were welded in foundries over which Ralston presided. There were four breath-taking passenger elevators, and one for freight. The passenger ones occupied the four corners of the structure. They too were manufactured in a Ralston foundry. The panels that lined their walls were of polished California wood. And the elevator shafts were lined with California baked adobe.

Under the marble flooring of the great court was a thing of special pride to Ralston: a tremendous reservoir of water, fed by four artesian wells, and capable of supplying 28,000 gallons an hour. So enormous was the reservoir, that a boat could have floated upon its surface.

In and out of the court's wide portals flowed an endless line of traffic: hacks, tallyhos, phaetons, surreys, stages, and trucks. Kings of empire, queens of tropic isles, presidents of South and North American republics, Oriental potentates, premiers of foreign realms, generals of armies and admirals of navies; Indian, French, Italian, Spanish, and Chinese; members of the yellow, black, white, and red races; blue-bloods, black-legs, beautiful ladies, painted houris, scarlet courtesans, mining magnates, and brothel pimps: the flotsam and jetsam of international society rolled in and out, night and day. Many of the conveyances in which they rode were of Ralston manufacture. And the horses, some were foaled by his mares and sired by his stallions on the Belmont Farm.

Listed on the wine card in the dining rooms were red wines and white, bubbling champagnes, delicate sherries and stout ports, distilled from grapes grown in the Ralston vineyards.

Even the tobacco that was featured at stands in the foyer, could be traced direct to Ralston's fields at Gilroy. The Palace was a world in itself. All these things, produced directly under his supervision, the Comstock had made possible for Ralston. Every morning, often at the crack of dawn, he was at the Palace, inspecting, organizing, and interviewing. The workmen adored him. Before banking hours, he was come and gone. For these were troublesome times. Mackay and Fair, Flood and O'Brien, and that persistent Sutro were all trying to undermine him. The one thing that Ralston dreaded was the discovery of a bonanza which would threaten his supremacy.

The ascendancy of Ralston's industrial empire rested squarely upon his monopoly of the Nevada Ledge.

CHAPTER XXVIII

THE HEART OF THE COMSTOCK

1872–1875

It was only a seam of ore, a thin dark stratum in the gray porphyry, not thicker than a piece of black thread.

But Fair followed his discovery with feverish excitement. For days he had been digging, by permission of the owners, through the hard, barren rock on the 1167-foot level of the "Gould and Curry" mine. For days discouragement had perched at his elbow. Then he had drifted northward, through 224 feet of "Best and Belcher" ground, likewise with the permission of the owners. Just before he had gone over the boundary line into the "Consolidated Virginia" section, Fair's experienced eye had seen a slight change come over the hard rock before him. Where a moment since all had been gray, certainly, now, there was a dark line running through the porphyry. Hardly thicker than a knife-blade, yet there it was.

Inch by inch Fair followed that knife-blade line with unalloyed agitation. Not more desperately did Theseus follow his thread through the dread labyrinth of the Minotaur than Fair tracked that slender clue through hundreds of feet of vein matter. Like Theseus, Fair was despairing. If he did not find something at the end of the line he would be lost. Both he and Mackay would have to go back to "mucking." Flood and O'Brien would never be able to discard their white aprons.

Sometimes the thread narrowed to a fine film of clay. Sometimes it "pinched out" and Fair would be desperate until his eyes, in the dim glow of the candles, could again pick up the dark line of silver sulphurets as it stole through the hard clay. For more than a hundred feet of "Consolidated" ground Fair pursued that slender clue without finding a quarry. He began to feel that he was chasing a will-o'-the-wisp.

Already he and his cohorts had squandered more than $200,000 in their search for a bonanza. Now that their combined treasury was nearly exhausted, Mackay, Fair, Flood, and O'Brien were practically ruined. Further assessments would be necessary.

At this crisis worry and hard work took their toll. Fair was taken sick and was obliged to leave the work to others. During his absence his miners lost the thread he had been following so assiduously. Far to the east, for many hundreds of feet, they had drifted without relocating it.

At the end of a month Fair was down in the shaft again. He was still feeling weak. Sure enough, the clue was lost. He went back to the beginning, carefully he searched through the vein matter. Finally he picked up the lost black thread. In the meantime, the value of the mine, which had greatly increased when the four Irish insurgents had gained control, began to decline. Fair, as well as every one else, realized that the stockholders would not stand for another assessment.

While affairs were at this ebb and Sharon was rejoicing that the four Irishmen had come to grief, and bragging that the Bank would soon have them back digging in his mines, Fair pushed his drift slowly ahead, never for an instant losing sight of that slender clue. Once already it had been lost. Never would he allow it to get out of his sight again.

By February, when he had progressed just eleven feet beyond the point where he had renewed work, the black thread slowly widened, to a shoe-string, to a cord, and then into a black breadth of sulphurets. Seven feet from side to side it measured and assayed $60 to the ton. On he dug. By March 1, 1873, the main ore vein had widened to twelve feet.

In San Francisco, by February, 1873, the Bank of California's capital had not that liquidity which was pleasing to Ralston. A meeting of the directors, for the 19th of the month, at which President Mills was present, was called. And Ralston put the facts on the table. He wanted all the directors to be fully cognizant of his operations. Capital of the Bank, at that time, was supposedly $5,000,000. Of this there was due the Bank from George P. Kimball & Co. (carriage builders), $578,580.46; from the New Montgomery Street Real Estate Company, $1,971,696.56; from the Pacific Woollen Mills Company, $967,900, a total of $3,518,-177.02.

These loans, from the Bank's capital, had been made to the owners of the properties, William Sharon & Co., in which Sharon and Ralston were equal partners. Now these companies were not paying the interest on their loans, and the Bank could not collect.

Money was stringent in February, 1873. Ralston was worried not only about the condition of his companies, but also about the Bank's assets, and he wanted the directors to know exactly what was going on. When the directors heard this distressing news, they were far from cheerful. The price of Bank stock was high. The directors wanted to keep it that way. But how could they when two-thirds of the assets were frozen? Every month they were getting a good dividend. Naturally they did not want that income cut down.

The discussion that developed was not a particularly agreeable one. The directors were nettled with Ralston. They did not like to see their incomes threatened nor the Bank jeopardized. Ralston's information had hit them in two vulnerable spots: pocketbook and pride. But facts were facts, and Ralston pointed them out plainly. What did the directors want to do about it?

Mills objected strenuously. Why keep three such accounts

in the Bank's portfolio? They were not income-yielding securities. Hence they should be thrown overboard.

So much dissatisfaction developed that Ralston was forced to "assume personal responsibility." When the loans had been made the directors had been pleased enough with the investments. For years afterward the three had paid good dividends and had enriched them all. Had it not been for the Southern Pacific trains they would still be paying. Now that they were freezing, Ralston must assume full responsibility. How often Mills had required that!

Nine years before when Ralston had wanted to establish an agency of the Bank of California in Virginia City and had suggested Sharon as agent, Mills had objected until he had been assured of "personal responsibility" on the part of Ralston, and he had gotten it. Since, Mills had had no cause for complaint. Hadn't the agency proved a gold mine for Mills as well as for every other man concerned?

If in the future the Kimball Company, the New Montgomery Street Real Estate Company, or the Pacific Woollen Mills, turned out profitable investments the directors would be willing to share the profits, but never would they share liabilities. Long ago Ralston had learned that lesson. "If you make money for these people," he had confided to his brother, "you won't get any thanks, but if you lose money you will be cursed for it."

The directors made themselves plain. If Ralston wanted those loans he must protect the Bank during the prevailing money stringency by assuming full responsibility for them. On February 19, an agreement to that effect was signed by J. D. Fry, Ralston's father-in-law, and D. O. Mills, president of the Bank, and ratified by the directors.

Daily, without comment, twenty-five tons, assaying $60 to the ton, were taken out of the "Consolidated Virginia" mine. Underground, Fair was jubilant. On the surface he became a poker-faced gambler. Never for a split second was that expression allowed to relax. Sharon interpreted both silence and appearance entirely wrongly: the Irishmen had found nothing. All the time, on the San Francisco stock market, "Consolidated Virginia" shares were dropping in value. That falling market could not have pleased the insurgents better. Ralston's crowd would be completely misled. They would lose interest in their shares and disgorge.

While Sharon continued to laugh up his sleeve, Flood and O'Brien laid aside their aprons long enough to go into the market in search of stock selling at low figures. Not content with their own efforts they hired one or two little-known brokers to buy up "Consolidated Virginia" and "California" on the quiet. With pockets bulging with stock, back they would go to the "Auction Lunch" to listen to what the stock sharks and mining experts had to say of the falling market. It was very depressing.

While mining shares were looking lugubrious on California and Pine Streets in San Francisco, Fair was down 710 feet with the new shaft he was sinking on the 1167-foot drift of the "Consolidated Virginia." Down it was going at the rate of three feet a day. At the same time the drift from the "Gould and Curry" was being rapidly pushed to the north. Unbearably foul, due to lack of ventilation, grew the air. By October, 1873, the shaft reached the level of the drift and a current of fresh air shot through. Stimulated by the draft, Fair drifted southeasterly a distance of 250 feet until he reached a deposit of rich ore.

Within fourteen days he had cut a chamber out of the ledge from 30 to 54 feet in width, 20 feet in height and 140 feet in length. Walls, roof and floor, assaying from $93 to $632 per ton, would have staggered Aladdin with their riches.

As for Mackay and Fair, they remained absolutely mum on their discovery. Even the workmen, instructed to hold their tongues, divulged nothing of what was going on on the 1167-foot level of the "Consolidated Virginia." Thus the people on the surface and those in San Francisco knew less than nothing of what was occurring in their very midst.

All this time Ralston was looking as serene and unconcerned as if he bore no added weight upon his shoulders. In October, Mills resigned the presidency of the Bank of

California and Ralston was elected in his stead. Mills said he wanted a respite from business to travel abroad. Some onlookers claimed that his resignation was prompted by the lack of liquidity of the capital funds of the Bank. The "freezing" of some of the William Sharon & Co. accounts had hastened it. On the contrary, Mills announced that never had the Bank of California been in better shape: "all the investments were sound."

Be that as it may, on retiring, Mills insisted on selling his 5000 shares of bank stock. Ralston remonstrated. The name of Mills, at the head of his list of stockholders, had a potential value. Resign if he must but retain his stock. But Mills was insistent. Much against his wishes, Ralston took over Mills's certificate of stock, paid him in cash and speeded him on his round-the-world tour. Mills departed, believing that he had severed all ties with Ralston's bank. But somehow or other Ralston neglected to remove Mills's name from the books. To do that, at this time, he told himself, would have had a bad effect in banking circles in San Francisco.

Even after he became president, there was very little difference in the Ralston program. Every month the 1 per cent dividend went over bank counters. Every morning, shortly after dawn, Ralston, debonair and smiling, was at the Palace Hotel. There was no let-up in outlay. Every noon he was lunching at the Union Club. Some evenings he swam off North Point. Others he dispensed a princely hospitality at his Pine Street residence or at his Belmont villa.

Never had there been such a person in San Francisco. "A more genial, liberal or charitable man never trod God's earth," men said. "He was humble; he was simple in his everyday life. It was as easy to approach W. C. Ralston, president of the Bank of California, on business or on a mission of charity, as the most humble hod-carrier in the city."

Morning, noon, night and day Ralston received a public ovation at the Palace, on the streets, at the club. Everywhere he was greeted with a glad eye, a warm clasp of the hand, a lifted hat. No Grand Duke in his prime could have attained a warmer acclaim from his people than California's first citizen was receiving hourly in his capital city. Generous to the needy, to the widow, to the orphan, to unfortunates, to the homeless, and to the bereaved, he was hailed everywhere as the friend of the poor; as a patron of art; a commercial "tycoon"; a great banker; and philanthropist.

San Franciscans loved, respected, all but worshiped Ralston. The poor blessed him as he passed. Children ran after him. Some men hated him for his success. Some were envious of his popularity. A few condemned his manner of life; but no man feared William C. Ralston. Many men are great, some are good, few are both great and good, but Californians believed all that of Ralston.

Who, in 1873-75, that noted Ralston's confident stride, his determined air, his serene brow, smiling lips and kindly eyes as he swung along California Street, could have believed he was worried? But he was.

Again he felt the need of another bonanza. A need that was pinching in its urgency. The Palace was costing far more than he had anticipated. To maintain the major chord of San Francisco's industrial music was costing money. To keep the workingman's bucket filled, his children clothed and happy, to raise the walls of new buildings, to spread abroad California's fame, to keep San Francisco flourishing, cost Ralston anxiety, sleepless nights and more money. To escape the pressure, Ralston found relief in skimming through the surf or in running his horses at a wild gallop down the King's Highway. But never could he find freedom except in the swell of the sea.

Somehow or other hints of what was occurring in the bowels of the "Consolidated Virginia" penetrated the Sutro tunnel. With air-compressors and diamond drills Sutro was battling through the hard rock just about a thousand feet below where Mackay and Fair were operating. Anticipating their bonanza the Irish quartet had aligned themselves against Sutro. They'd be damned if they'd pay him two dollars a ton toll on every ton of their bonanza ore! They'd see him in Hades first.

They began hurling one obstacle after another in Sutro's way. They were ready to invoke any legislative or Congressional aid that would stop him. More and more Sutro realized that it was now or never. The last bonanza would exhaust itself before he could reach the Lode. Every atom of strength, cunning and endurance was being utilized to the full in his fight with the earth. Often with drills he would make as much as thirty feet a day. Many times, day and night, stripped to the skin, he was at the breast of the drift, working, exhorting, encouraging his men.

No one knew what was going on in the depths of the Consolidated Virginia but Mackay and Fair, Flood and O'Brien, and they were not telling anybody. They wanted great wealth for a world-moving lever. Great wealth they meant to have. But they did not intend to spread the news of their discovery.

Carefully now they explored their body of ore in all directions. Drifts and cross-cuts were run through it. Winzes were sunk upon it. Up-raises were made. Lower dropped their shaft, first to the 1200, then to the 1300, 1400 and 1500-foot levels. Everywhere was the same rich ore, tons and tons of it. Millions and millions of dollars' worth. No one had ever dreamed of such a colossal body of ore.

Had Sutro known that such a tremendous bonanza existed only a few hundred feet above the very spot where he was working he would not have relaxed night or day—nor would Senator nor Congressmen until they had promised to come to his aid with a loan.

Had Ralston dreamed what was occurring he would have trembled for the safety of his industrial empire. Banks, hotels, manufactories, mills, steamship lines, railroads, vineyards, wheat fields, ranges, were lubricated and fertilized by Comstock bullion and depended on its monopoly. Not for a month could they function without its bolstering. The Comstock provided California's heart's blood. The wealth in sight in the "Virginia Consolidated" was a menace to existing conditions in California. A power greater than his own was arising, all unawares, at the very source of his own industrial vigor.

Would the bonanza in the "Consolidated Virginia" extend below the 1500-foot level? That was the question that was agitating the Irish quartet. No one could predict. Cross-cuts showed its center was richer than its outlying surfaces. The mind refused to grasp so much wealth. The fancy of the coolest brain ran wild. The bonanza was known to extend into "Consolidated California." A few there were in the secret, who prophesied that it would extend far into "Ophir." No such wealth had ever been known on the Comstock or in the world, before.

It was December 31, 1873, yet no one grasped the situation but Mackay and Fair, Flood and O'Brien. It was the spring, then the summer of 1874. Still, no one was privy to their secret. Their eyes were dazzled by the sight of so much gold and silver but their brains were cool. Why let other people know what they could see for themselves? Why brag when they could enjoy? They were miners not speculators. They didn't care anything about reaping the stock market or exciting envy.

Tutankhamen's tomb could have been no more stirring sight than the scene now enacted within Sun Mountain's imperial chambers.

Cribs of timber pyramided in successive stages from base to topmost rung, four hundred feet above. Everywhere, candles, like stars in azure heavens, pricked the darkness. The walls were black with a metallic luster, now steel-gray, now green, now glittering as though studded with millions of diamonds. But it was not gold or silver that glittered but iron and copper pyrites everywhere mixed with the ore. Here and there they formed themselves into beautiful regular crystals, every facet flashing with the fire of precious stones. In the heart of Sun Mountain nature had unclasped the lid of a jewel casket.

Here were nests of beautiful, transparent stalactitic quartz-crystals several inches long, as blue as sapphires, as violet as amethysts, as evanescent as diamonds, pinker than sea-anemones, greener than olives, more purple than grapes. Here were nests of wire-gold and coils of silver. Here were metal and crystal prism in vast profusion. Here were the hues of emerald, tourmaline, chrysoprase, opal, lapis-lazuli, all scintillating and sparkling against a black background.

On all sides was terrific heat. Red-hot rocks and scalding water, bubbling out of the earth. The flames of hundreds of candles, blazing wicks of hundreds of oil lamps, licked up oil at one end, oxygen at the other. Between man and flame, the air was vitiated faster than the compressors could supply it.

Miners, naked except for loin-cloth and shoes, could be seen rushing back and forth through clouds of hanging smoke. In their treasure house, Mackay and Fair would employ none but perfect specimens of manhood, picked youths that neither drank nor smoked nor carried combustibles in their shoes. They had no intention of endangering their bonanza by careless or dissipated workmen.

"Have you a match?" Fair, with an unlighted cigar in his mouth, would ask a workman.

If the miner had, he was immediately discharged.

If he smelled liquor on any miner's breath, never again would that man be allowed to enter the "Consolidated Virginia." Safety at any price became the underground slogan of the superintendent.

As a result, Fair had none but trained athletes working for him. Pick-swinging, drill-hammering, ladder-climbing, timber-carrying, had trained his men into models for a sculptor. Continual darkness had bleached their skins whiter than alabaster; perspiration had rendered them smoother than marble.

With every swing of their picks waves of muscle could be seen swelling over arms, flanks and backs. Beneath white skins, their hot, red blood glowed like a light behind a marble globe. They dripped with water, reeked with vapor. Ridges of sweat slid down their slippery flesh into the cloth rims about their waist. The bonanza in "Consolidated Virginia" had developed them into a troop of underground athletes.

Never had Praxiteles found such models. Over the perfection of such physiques, Michael Angelo could have sung a paean of praise in marble. On every shift the galleries of the

"Consolidated Virginia" displayed pick-swingers, ore-shovellers, and hammer-drillers, to vie with the discus-throwers, wrestlers, or runners in Louvre or Vatican museums.

To facilitate the work of exploration an arrangement was made in October, 1873, by which the entire section of 1310 feet lying between the "Gould and Curry" and "Ophir" was divided into two portions, the southerly part, 710 feet in length, being held by the "Consolidated Virginia Mining Company." The northerly section of 610 feet was assigned to the re-incorporated "California Mining Company." The stock of each company was divided into 100,000 shares. "Consolidated Virginia" sold at $45 a share. By September, 1874, California had reached $37.

All this time, with millions of dollars beneath familiar Virginia City streets, Comstockers were not excited. And the shrewdest of San Francisco stock dealers, following Sharon's lead, spoke belittlingly of the discovery as well as of the four Irishmen.

The Fenians were expending gigantic energies on a small ore body, a Ring member would say. Two of them will never leave the "Auction Lunch," another would add, the other two will soon be candidates for Bank jobs. Who ever heard of bartenders or "muckers" becoming mining magnates overnight? Even in mushroom camps such things never occurred. It was silly to consider four ignorant miners as a menace to existing conditions.

Sponsoring such propaganda, Sharon played perfectly into the hands of the Irish quartet. While he was depreciating their discovery and stock was falling they were picking it up for a song and consolidating their interests.

As soon as Mackay and Fair were assured of their control, they became less wary. One day they invited Dan DeQuille, the most astute mining reporter on the Comstock, to visit the 1200-foot level of their mine. They were weary of Sharon's abuse. They didn't care what capital DeQuille made of his reports. After Dan DeQuille had finished his examination he wrote up his findings in *The Territorial Enterprise:* There was not the slightest doubt in the world of "Consolidated Virginia's" bonanza. Conservatively, the two mines would yield at least $3,000,000 per month—$36,000,000 a year! Not for one year or two years but for ten years at least. In which time $360,000,000 would be extracted.

After those staggering figures were given to the mining world, Fair invited the director of the United States Mint to make an inspection, confirming or denying the DeQuille data. Fully those figures were endorsed. The two mines would yield, he reported, at least, $300,000,000. I. E. James, a mining engineer who had made himself famous on the Comstock, estimated there was $275,593,200 worth of ore in the mine.

Then came Philip Deidesheimer of Darmstadt, one of the most outstanding Western mining experts of his day. After a close personal survey of the bonanza he estimated the bonanza's probable yield at not less than $1,500,000,000.

Ralston was aghast at the magnitude of those reports. Sharon had advised him badly. At a crucial time for San Francisco they had allowed the greatest bonanza in its history to slip through their fingers without making an effort to stay the catastrophe. Billions of dollars in two mines, and the firm of William Sharon & Co. had sold their shares! The damage was irreparable. But Sharon was not unhappy. Well he knew that his millions were safe and sound; perhaps Ralston's were jeopardized. It would take thousands to sustain them. But there was that little agreement in the vaults of the Bank of California: that always filled him with misgiving. It made him liable for Ralston's debts.

Rapidly the news of the Irish bonanza spread to San Francisco, to New York, to London, to Paris, to Berlin. The heart of the Comstock had been reached; it had turned out to be pure silver. Immediately on hearing those bad tidings, Bismarck demonetized silver in Germany.

Sutro capitalized on those fabulous reports. On the strength of them he was enabled to borrow a million dollars from his Scottish bankers. Now began such a race through Sun

Mountain as had never been dreamed of. He must get to the Ledge before this Irish bonanza exhausted itself. If Deideshei-mer were right and there was $1,500,000,000 in bullion in the bonanza, think what that would mean with royalties at two dollars a ton! Never had an earth-monster made such a frantic effort to burrow through the earth and catch a prize as Adolph Sutro was now making with his diamond drills, and air-compressors and dynamite.

Upon the opening of this bonanza and its development northward through "California" ground to the south line of the "Ophir," Sharon induced Ralston to believe that the "Ophir" contained the richest part of the great bonanza. Hadn't that been true of the "Crown Point" bonanza? Hadn't the richest part of it extended through to the "Belcher"? Hadn't they picked up the stock for a song? Hadn't William Sharon & Co. made millions in that maneuver? Out of those millions had emerged the Palace Hotel and the palatial Pine Street residence. Out of them had come a great stimulus to the growth of San Francisco and California.

Ralston was aware of all these facts. Besides, out of the "Ophir" had come the Comstock's first bonanza. It had been a surface one. But with deeper development, as in the "Virginia Consolidated" and "California," it stood to reason that there would be more. By such reasoning and with previous example to back the argument, Ralston was induced to believe that history would again repeat itself: The "Consolidated Virginia" and "California" bonanza would continue itself into the "Ophir" just as the "Crown Point" had done in "Belcher" ground.

Ralston was in dire need. There were all his offspring to think about: those "personal responsibility" notes; the New Montgomery Street Real Estate Company; the Pacific Woollen Mills; the Kimball Carriage Company; the Cornell Watch Company; as well as a hundred other responsibilities to consider. Above all, there was the Palace Hotel, half finished. Another bonanza was urgently needed.

With so many obligations outstanding it was a bad time to go into the market. It would take thousands to control

"Ophir"—hundreds of thousands, but it must be done. Ralston could read the writing on the wall: already the "Virginia Consolidated" bonanza had endangered his money power. The greater wealth of the Bonanza Kings, as the Irish quartet were now called, would eclipse the supremacy of the Bank of California. He must discover a greater bonanza.

Fortunately there was little chance of doubt. Hardly a risk. Experts assured Ralston of the continuity of the bonanza. So William Sharon & Co. went into the market to buy "Ophir" at bedrock prices. Whatever it cost, "Ophir" must be controlled.

CHAPTER XXIX

SUTRO'S GRAVEYARD

Not only had Sutro continual monetary struggles, Bank opposition, and the animosity of Ralston and his Ring to overcome, but always there were elemental problems: earth, water, heat, fire, darkness, and death. One obstacle after another to contend with him for right of way, through Mt. Davidson. Human strength he could gauge, but who could plumb that of hard rock or hot water or foul air?

Now, inch by inch, Sutro had to fight his way forward with explosives. First he had to drill a dozen or twenty holes, charge them with giant powder, explode the blast, then wait for the smoke to clear before he could go forward and cart away the debris. Under Washoe's hard-rock conditions, he was making more rapid progress than had been made in the Hoosac, Mont Cenis, St. Gothard, or any other tunnel.

Then there was the question of transportation. As steam was fatal to life underground, Sutro had to solve those problems by using other power. First he tried horses. But they didn't work. Every time equine ears touched overhanging rock, up would go a head and crack would go a neck or skull. Finally he gave them up. Then he tried mules—stubborn mules. When the roof of the tunnel touched hinny ears, down would go heads. After that, Sutro used nothing but mules to do his hauling. Seldom were they as obstreperous underground as they were upon its surface. Apparently, darkness, rich earthy odors and oppressive air took all the mulishness out of their hides. In no time at all they became docile miners' pets. As the shift-mules passed the lunching men, one would proffer a piece of bread, another a slab of pie and a third a cup of coffee. Gulp, and food and liquid were both gone. When a signal was given to fire a blast the mules understood quicker than the men and got out of the way faster.

So accustomed did they become to underground darkness that when they went into the daylight they could scarcely see. And vice versa, when they returned to tunnel blackness they could not tell where they were going. As these conditions endanger their sight, Sutro was forced to place a blinder over one eye, when his mules were going into the open. There he would keep it until the animals returned to the dark underground world of the tunnel.

Then there was the clay. Always Sutro had to keep guard over Mt. Davidson's clay. It was the most obstreperous thing he had to encounter: swelling clay. Often it would slow down his progress from 150 to 50 feet a month. The moment picks were driven into this ground, out, like so much blood, would ooze the soft, white, swelling kaolin. Like blood, too, when it struck the air, it would thicken and clot.

No matter what size posts and caps Sutro would use to restrain this ground, the swelling clay would exert a counter pressure so much greater that the post would be driven through the caps as if they were matches. Nothing could be devised to resist that pressure. In one place, on seven different occasions, the track swelled up for a foot or more. As a result, instead of pulling their loads over a perfect level, the mules had to drag them over a bumpity, bumpity road, worse than any New England corduroy turnpike. Finally Sutro was forced to post miners with long sharp knives in these places. The moment the swelling clay would begin to poke its nose through the loose seams down they would come. After a time the ground settled down to its natural state and needed no more heroic treatment.

Then there was the heat and foul air: two of the most fearful things to contend with underground. When he had progressed less than a mile through the mountain, Sutro saw something must be done to carry off the bad air. So he sank his first air-shaft from the surface. Down it went to tunnel level. For a time his men worked in fresh air; right-lustily fighting swelling clay, overpowering heat and darkness.

When he had reached a point 9000 feet from the tunnel entrance again Sutro was halted. Once more he realized that something drastic must be done. To his lode-goal there were 11,000 feet more to go. Sutro could not understand how mules and men could endure such conditions.

Then he sank shaft No. 2: 900 feet from the surface to the tunnel level. Immediately conditions began to improve and Sutro continued blasting his way through the mountain until he had reached a point 17,000 feet from the mouth. Now he had only 3000 feet more to go. Daily, sometimes hourly, Sutro was at the front encouraging his men. Only 3000 feet more and he would tap the great Comstock Ledge!

But the nearer he drew to his destination the more obstacles Sun Mountain strewed in his way. The more obstreperous became earth: the more vile the air and the hotter the water. Suddenly one day air-shaft No. 2 filled up to the brim with 900 feet of water. As an air-shaft it had to be abandoned. Not a pump was there on the Lode that could drain it. As a result the heat became so oppressive and the air so foul that working conditions were intolerable. Sutro sought relief in huge blowers, air-compressors, ice helmets, and cold drinks. Still, at times, the air was too stagnant to support life.

Now, not longer than twenty minutes could the miners work at the face of the drift without reeling back to the cooling stations. Drugged and intoxicated by the deadly carbon-dioxide fumes, they would stagger about like drunken men—incoherent of speech, laughing like maniacs, crying like babies. Often they would sink in their tracks or fall in a deep swoon at the face of the drift. Often Sutro wondered if reaching the Comstock Lode was worth all the physical suffering that the mere digging of his tunnel was inflicting on him and on his men.

The further Sutro went into the mountain the fainter became the light of his candles. There was not oxygen enough in the air to support the feeblest kind of flame. Perhaps man must work under such conditions but candles could refuse to burn. And they did. Still, nothing could be accomplished without light. In the sickly glare of their lanterns the miners were stumbling, weak and sick, toward the goal Sutro had set.

Like the failing light, the mules began to balk at being driven forward under such hellish conditions. For the first time, some animals absolutely refused to budge. Straight for the air-pipes they would lunge. From there they could hardly be driven away.

Lights might fail, mules balk, men falter and faint but Sutro, like the hard-rock, was adamant. The tunnel must reach the Ledge. Only 3000 feet to go. Night and day it must be driven forward. There was no time to lose now. Resolutely on he drove.

Now Sutro sought not only that two dollars tax per ton, that pound of "underground flesh," but most of all justification. Justification for time involved, for insult, for humiliation inflicted in San Francisco, Washington, Berlin, Paris, and London.

Often, with his great torso stripped to his dark skin, perspiration streaming from every pore, Sutro would take his turn at the face of the drift, giving his men an example in endurance, with every drive of his pick forcing the header of his tunnel that much nearer to the Comstock goal line.

There was one mule that not even Sutro could push away from the air-pipe. The miners beat him, yanked at his halter, spurred his flanks with sharply pointed rowels. Better had they used feathers than force for not an inch would the old mule give. In all his glory, he stood with his head poked in the pipe, monopolizing the air-stream as it gushed forcibly past him.

Sutro was summoned. Blows, curses and spurs were re-applied but to no use. Up and down in the pipe-opening bobbed his old gray head. Sutro could hear the air whistle past him; but he could not get near the pipe himself. Finally Sutro gave orders for the mule to be tied by his tail to other mules. Thus he was dragged stiff-legged to the mouth of the tunnel. Never after that could the hinny be coaxed or driven into the black hole again. But the miners had no choice. Economics drove them from the mouth of the tunnel, through swelling earth, caves, fetid, foul air up to the header. There, under any conditions, their job was to push it through to the Lode.

The air-pipes were made of galvanized iron. To prevent leakage the joints had been wrapped with canvas covered with tar of white-lead. So important was that life-giving stream of oxygen that Sutro tolled off Garnett, a man in wretched health at the time, to watch those joints. For a leakage meant death to the men working at the face of the bore.

One day after a blast had been fired, Garnett, already on the point of fainting, stumbled forward to the end of the air-pipe. Before he reached his goal he fell down in a swoon. Unaware of the man lying on the smoky ground, the blaster went forward to examine the blast which had just been made. Two of the holes had not exploded, so he reconnected them, refired the gunpowder and ran back to get out the way of flying rock. Followed a tremendous crash: dirt, splinters, rock and pebbles flying in all directions.

Not until some time later was Garnett picked up riddled with rocks. Over a hundred large and small fragments had been driven in his flesh, one big piece of stone was found embedded in the back of his head. At the time, it did not look as if Garnett, in wretched condition at best, could live ten minutes. But that "application of Mt. Davidson rock" worked wonders with him. Afterward, in speaking of the matter, Garnett claimed that the confounded explosion had cured him.

Then there was the water. Not on the whole Comstock was there anything more terrible than the water in the Sutro Tunnel. At every step it held Sutro back. Hot, ill-smelling, torrential. Unsuspecting men would put in an explosive. Out would pour a perfect deluge. Man and mule would be forced to run for their lives. Nor could Sutro go back to work until the flood had subsided.

One day Sutro's men bored a diamond drill, whose rod weighed several hundred pounds, into air-shaft No. 2, which had been abandoned ever since it had filled up with water. When the drill hit the 900-foot column of water a terrific racket filled the bore. So great was the pressure of water that the rod was shot like a cannon-spear several hundred feet into the tunnel.

Then came a cave. Some timbers broke down. Word was rushed to Sutro that a miner had been caught in the falling avalanche and killed. Sutro with a doctor started on the run to the spot. All work had been stopped. The man, who had been working in the ditch which was being constructed in the floor of the tunnel to carry off the hot water, had been pinned to the ground up to the level of his chest by a mass of loose, fine gravel. Sutro made an examination. The man was not dead. His pulse was beating. But with every minute the hot water was packing the loose gravel more tightly about him. By the time Sutro reached him he could move neither hand nor foot.

Four miners were down on the ground beside him, trying to scoop out the dirt with shovels, then with their bare hands. But it was no use. As fast as they dug, the gravel would cave in. Mud was rising about his neck. Soon it was up to his mouth. One of the miners threw a dam across the tunnel to hold the water back and to divert the flow. Three or four hours passed. Sutro could see that they were making no headway. Steadily the water kept rising about the man. Finally Sutro decided that it was better to pull the man out by force than let him drown by inches. A rope was passed around his body. All the men tugged in unison. The miner yelled in pain but not an inch did he budge. When Sutro saw that the man was about to drown, he again gave the order. They finally jerked him out. More dead than alive they rushed him to the hospital.

On account of such cases, Sutro had set up a hospital. To support it he docked each miner's salary three dollars a month. Shortly thereafter, he had the Miners' Union on his neck. If he wanted to reach the Comstock Lode, they warned him, he must pay all men four dollars a day. No docking for medical fees or any other reason, would be permitted. At this stage of the game Sutro realized that he must not get into trouble with the Union. So he yielded. No matter what the price he must reach the Lode as quickly as possible.

Death was always a stumbling block to progress. So far Sutro had suffered only twelve fatalities. Not a bad record, when the Hoosac Tunnel had sacrificed 185 lives. But Sutro dreaded a burial more than a death. The loss of one man or twelve men did not hold up Sutro's progress nearly as much as the grand wake which preceded every miner's journey to the grave. One wake would keep as many as seventy-five to one hundred men off their jobs for one or two days. If festivities were violent and whiskey plentiful, for a week. And the men would return to the tunnel too dazed and unstrung for such dangerous work. Thus death spelled delay.

Sutro determined that not even the grim reaper should be allowed to impede him for a day. When burials became too much of a nuisance Sutro decided to put a stop to them. He would lay out his own cemetery and require that all funerals be held near the town of Sutro.

"Why can't we have a graveyard of our own," he proposed to his men, "and bury our dead here?"

The next time there was a fatality Sutro had a grave dug in the sage-brush near-by.

"We will not bury our comrade here," said the dead man's friends.

"Why?" came back Sutro.

"It's too lonely," retorted the mourners.

That seemed ridiculous. But Sutro did not want to stir up trouble over a funeral. So over and over again there would be grand obsequies up in Virginia City, with plenty of whiskey, brass bands, carriages, headaches and jitters for days following.

At last two miners got killed who had not paid their fees to the Miners' Union, and had been discarded. Hence there were no friends to object to a funeral near-by. Sutro saw his chance. He had two graves dug and gave the departed a dignified funeral in the sage.

After that the miners could not object to the loneliness of Sutro's graveyard.

And work on the tunnel, unimpeded by wakes, and jitters, rushed that much more swiftly towards its destination.

One day in 1874, Sutro learned that the Bank of California was going to run William Sharon for the United States Senate.

When Ralston's crowd discovered that Sutro stood a good chance of getting a $2,000,000 loan from the Government, they realized that Sharon must be elected and the loan defeated.

This time there would be no slip-up in the election.

CHAPTER XXX

BATTLE OF MONEY BAGS

November, 1874

Speculation in Comstock stocks sped on at a crazy pace. Murder, suicide, and sudden death failed to cause more than a momentary flurry in the wild on-rush of San Francisco.

One day one of Ralston's closest and wealthiest friends was caught in a stock-market jam and irretrievably ruined. On the spur of the moment the unhappy man swallowed an overdose of poison and died. It was a terrible blow to Ralston to see one of his best friends weaken. He did everything in his power to hush up details and keep facts from the papers and the distracted widow. Through the press, he attempted to put a different complexion on his friend's sudden death. When he discovered that the widow had been left penniless, out of his own account Ralston drew a check for $35,000 and carried it to the unhappy woman. He did not offer the money as a gift. "It was all that could be salvaged from her husband's estate," Ralston explained, "all else had been lost."

The widow marked the amount on the check. Ralston was cheating her. Her husband had been a wealthy man. This was a pittance. Furiously, she tore the check into small pieces and threw them at the feet of the astounded Ralston.

Monthly, from May, 1875, "Consolidated Virginia" and "California" were distributing $300,000 in dividends among their stockholders. Every week their ore bodies were reported larger and wider. For nearly two months, the aggregate value of Comstock shares rose on the market at the rate of a million dollars a day. The year closed in a fever of speculation. While stocks were "bulled" up with the most consummate skill and reached incredible figures, the community became virtually frantic. Brokers were driven almost insane by the volume of business. When Ralston's struggle began for "Ophir," "Consolidated Virginia" and "California" sky-rocketed in sympathy. Now, there was no rest for them night nor day.

In the Stock Exchange, the atmosphere was surcharged with excitement. Great events portended. Hell-broth was brewing. Inevitably there would be a clash on the San Francisco Stock Market. Caesar was threatened. Brutus, mad with ambition, was nursing a dagger in his bosom. And Antony was looking on with stricken eyes.

So good were commissions that every broker had horses and carriages to drive. When things slackened, Ralston's crowd might have been seen putting their steeds through their paces or occupying seats in the grandstand at the race-course at the foot of Lone Mountain. No one sitting there, absorbed by events on the track, had an eye for the Cross on Lone Mountain just opposite, nor for the graves that scrambled hit-or-miss up the sandy slopes towards its outstretched arms. No. All ears harkened to hoofbeats. All eyes were glued on the whirling hands of stop-watches.

About this time Ralston decided to enlarge his stables at his Pine Street residence. On it he squandered a huge sum of money. Not with his usual care were plans drawn nor foundations laid. He needed stalls for new horses—needed them quickly. First he would lay a plank, then spike it down. On top of that he would lay another plank and spike it down. Then another, and so on. His friends warned him: such a stable would never withstand an earthquake.

But Ralston couldn't afford to wait. So rapidly was he acquiring horseflesh. Weekly there were Lucullun banquets at Belmont, with his particular cronies and their lovely ladies as guests. On these occasions there would be music, dancing, flowers, wines, and savory foods. Oft in the course of the evening's entertainment, befuddled guests would wander into the wrong sleeping rooms to the great embarrassment of the host.

Some nights fifteen or twenty of Ralston's crowd would meet at a favorite restaurant. One would order dinner, another wine, while a third would engage a loge at the California Theatre, where Edwin Booth was playing Richard III, Macbeth, and Othello. About this time Adelaide Neilson, the celebrated English prima donna, came to San Francisco for a limited engagement. So delighted was Ralston with the exquisite quality of her interpretations, that he deluged her Occidental Hotel rooms with flowers and one night presented her with a diamond necklace that had cost thousands of dollars.

On another occasion he gave a banquet in honor of Madame Neilson. Newspapers spoke of it as the most sumptuous ever served in San Francisco.

Up until this period, Mackay and Fair had always kept their checking account in the Bank of California agency. Out of it they had paid their mine and milling expenses in Virginia City. At one time, Mackay had on deposit with Ralston, $1,800,000. Lacking a place of their own, the Irish quartet had stored their "Consolidated" and "California" bullion in Ralston's refinery. Even then, they had $400,000 in bars deposited there in his care. But they decided to change all this.

In the spring of 1875, there arose rumors of a disturbing nature to Ralston. The bonanza quartet announced that they needed a bank of their own, and a refinery in which to deposit their bullion. On a piece of San Francisco property, bounded by Montgomery, Pine and Summer streets, lately acquired by Flood and O'Brien, slowly arose an imposing edifice. It was to be called the Nevada Block, to commemorate the source of their great wealth. Its first floor would house the Nevada Bank of San Francisco, of which Mackay, Fair, Flood, and O'Brien would be directors. Their president, a fifth member lately admitted to their circle, would be Louis McLane, originally an incorporator of Ralston's bank, later president of Wells Fargo Express Company and of the Pacific Mail Steamship Company. Locked up in their bank vaults would be their capital stock: $5,000,000 in Comstock gold.

Of all banks in the world the Nevada was to be the only one with a paid-up capital of yellow metal: that alone was a threat to Ralston whose investments required a wide circulation of money. But the Irishmen were using no aggressive tactics. Every move was as logical as a child falling off a log: they needed a bank to handle their San Francisco Stock Market operations. They had the capital. Therefore they had founded the Nevada Bank of San Francisco. They wanted complete independence of California banking houses. Every move was as inevitable as the day of doom.

Yet the very presence of the Nevada Bank on Montgomery Street, the removal of the bonanza crowd's checking accounts, a new center of stock-dealing operations, was competitive and therefore threatening to Ralston.

Ralston noted these changes with alarm. Where before there

had been only one financial sun, clearly, now, he could see another arising over San Francisco's horizon. A sun whose inevitable course across California's commercial firmament he had been unable to stay. A sun that was giving forth tremendous light, warmth, and animation. Toward its rays, old adherents were stretching forth eager hands: in welcome, in obedience, in obeisance. It was distressing. Look at Louis McLane: once an original incorporator of the Bank of California; now an adherent of the Irish insurgents. With dread foreboding, Ralston read a writing on his bank walls. Not "Mene, mene, Tekel," but words more significant. Supremacy was doomed. The Irish insurgents were eclipsing him. It was a bitter sight. Fresh alignments were being made, new allegiances demanded. The old order was changing, a new day was dawning, he must be ready to re-adjust himself.

If he was to continue as the financial Caesar of San Francisco he must look to his laurels. He would not yield. He must win out. When his old followers came to Ralston's office seeking financial advice, he was ready for them. As debonair and light-hearted as ever. He had two superb offerings to make. Either of them were excellent investments: buy "Ophir" or buy "Spring Valley," or both. One would control a Comstock bonanza, the other would corner San Francisco water. On neither could his friends make a mistake.

The discovery in the "Consolidated Virginia" and "California" had forced Ralston and his Ring to open the dormant "Ophir" which lay next door to that fabulous bonanza. When they had done so, they had convinced themselves of a bonanza. Not only an extension of the one in the "Consolidated" and "California" mines, but a separate, distinct one. In shape it was not unlike an egg. Narrow at the top and gradually widening out as it descended.

It was the physical presence of that bonanza that had added conviction to Ralston's advice regarding "Ophir" and he was determined to control and share it with his friends.

Another bonanza, Ralston realized, was imperatively needed to keep up the enterprises which had absorbed all his means and from which he could not withdraw without disaster. Also, he had implicated himself. In a way he had fallen into Sharon's power; to complete the Palace he had been forced to borrow $2,000,000 from him. Besides that, availing himself of his position in the Bank, he had drawn freely on its resources. Worst of all, there were all those notes for frozen assets. Not yet were they paying a cent on the principal involved. Once more solvency depended upon the Comstock. With confidence Ralston turned toward the Lode. Twice before, Sun Mountain had rescued him. He had come to believe that whenever he needed a bonanza the Comstock would send him one. Always it could be depended upon. Neither did he doubt Fate this time. Eagerly he turned toward the "Ophir"; eagerly he directed the attention of his Ring in that direction; even Mills who had lately returned from Europe harkened to Ralston's slogan: "Buy 'Ophir!' " or "Buy 'Spring Valley Water!' "

Many others, notably "Lucky" Baldwin, had arrived at the same conclusion: The "Consolidated" and "California" bonanza would undoubtedly extend through to the "Ophir." Now they, too, entered the lists. Of these, already, "Lucky" Baldwin was the largest holder of "Ophir" stock. Ralston realized that he could only gain control of the mine by buying them out. There were 108,000 shares. Of these, he would have to have more than half. Enthusiastically he laid out his plans for the coming campaign.

In all of these moves Sharon had aided and abetted Ralston. On his own, he had proclaimed his confidence in the "Ophir" mine as a permanent investment. Statements to that effect he had circulated upon the street and whispered in confiding ears. *The Territorial Enterprise* in Virginia City and *The Gold Hill News*, both now owned by Sharon, had written up the mine as one of tremendous value. Recent discoveries had been played up to startling proportions. These highly wrought descriptive accounts of the extent of ore bodies, and the richness of assays would have justified investment at the highest prices.

Thus Sharon & Co. entered heartily into Ralston's plan to control "Ophir" before the December elections.

In the spring of 1874, Sharon had, again, announced himself as a candidate from Nevada for the United States Senate. Sutro stood a good chance of getting a two-million-dollar loan from Congress. The Committee on Mines and Mining had already recommended it. According to the Bank, this Sutro loan must be defeated.

This time Sharon announced that he would run on the Republican ticket to succeed William T. Stewart—dynamic Bill Stewart. Stewart had made an enviable reputation for himself in Washington. Faithfully he had listened to the supreme voice in San Francisco; obeyed to the letter all behests; even to resigning the presidency of the Sutro Tunnel Company. But now Sharon, consumed by ambition, was getting out of hand. No longer could Ralston stay him with a crook of the finger. Already the Bank had one enemy in Jones in the United States Senate. Not knowing what might happen, Ralston regretted seeing an old retainer like Stewart pushed aside. But he could do nothing about it. He must have Sharon where he could defeat Sutro.

When Sharon announced his candidacy, he promised his constituents to outdo Jones in the extent of campaign expenditures. Unjustifiably, as events had proved, Jones had squandered over half a million dollars on a foregone conclusion.

As the campaign developed, Sharon kept to his promise. His lavish scattering of money throughout the State before the election dazzled the West. By many it was considered a disgrace to Sun Mountain. During this period, Nevada earned the reputation of being a rotten borough. But as a publicity stunt, this debauch was a huge success. It attracted the attention of California newspapers, and was fully discussed in political circles throughout the country. No less than $800,000 of Comstock wealth, it was claimed, had gone into Sharon's publicity fund.

Neither had Sharon any intention of distributing all that money without reasonable prospects of good returns.

Early in his campaign Sharon had given out the information that a deal in "Ophir" stock was to be consummated during the fall of 1874. Into the ear of every legislator he had whispered a confidential tip: "buy all the 'Ophir' possible, keep buying, but, above all things, do not hold the stock after it has reached $300." That "confidential tip" spread throughout the sagebrush country. Every one to whom it was confided hastened to buy "Ophir." When it was known that Sharon himself was buying heavily, his confidants spent every farthing they owned for "Ophir." At the same time in San Francisco, Ralston was trying to gain control of "Ophir" as quietly as possible. Sharon's "tip" and buying caused a premature rise in the market price. As the campaign continued, every share of "Ophir" began to cost Ralston more and more.

As soon as Sutro learned that Sharon was a candidate for U. S. Senator from Nevada he was violently opposed. Not for an instant would he have Ralston's right-hand man go to the Senate where he could use his position to cripple the tunnel enterprise. Consequently Sutro entered the lists himself, determined at all hazards to "tunnel Sharon's prospects." He made up his mind to run on the Independent Dolly Varden ticket, for the United States Senate.

During the campaign, Sutro and the Independent Party chartered Piper's Opera House in Virginia City and thus forced Sharon and the Republicans to hold their mass meetings out in the streets.

Again Sutro resorted to pictures. Cartoons had started the tunnel. Pictures would send him to Washington. The eye coupled with a proper amount of oratory would be hard to beat.

Sutro had magic-lantern slides painted in the East. They depicted Sharon in various rôles: as a man who had prospered on the misfortunes of others; as the instigator of the crookedest railroad in the world; as a profiteer in Sierra lumber and water. All day-long free exhibitions, one after the other, like a popular cinema, were given to crowded houses.

To counteract these picture shows, Sharon engaged Tom Fitch, the greatest spellbinder on the Pacific Coast. His job was to wither the Sutro movement. He went about it with strangely clothed metaphors, biting wit, and scathing satire.

"The Sutro Tunnel Bill," he declaimed, "was an autogenous scheme to plunder, one of the worst in our official records!"

He predicted that the tunnel would be finished "in about two centuries, but if Congress would assist Sutro in his unscrupulous plunder scheme, he might live to enjoy the honor and fame of being the founder and finisher of one of the most disgraceful enterprises in the United States."

In addition to these oratorical outbrusts, Sharon carried on his campaign through the press of California and Nevada. This time he had not dared to trust his campaign to Joe Goodman, editor of *The Territorial Enterprise,* who during the previous one had made him the laughing-stock of the Comstock Lode by alluding to him as a "hyena" and accussing him of throwing honor and honesty to the winds and breaking "faith with men" whenever it suited his purpose. To avoid such a repetition Sharon had bought *The Territorial Enterprise* outright. It had cost him many thousands of dollars, but the new editor had given the political aspirant a "character" according to his lights:

"Mr. Sharon has lived in Nevada for ten years," he wrote. "By his sagacity, energy and nerve, he has amassed a fortune. This is his crime! Never once," he went on, "has Sharon broken 'his plighted word' or violated one principle of business honor."

That eulogy had cost Sharon several hundred thousand dollars. Goodman's editorial hadn't cost a cent; but similar ones would have cost votes. Hence the tremendous slush fund.

But Sutro did not let Sharon off scot free. *The Sacramento Union* compared him to the Colossus of Rhodes, "Who stands with one foot in San Francisco and the other in Virginia City, astride the Sierra, looming up toward the Great Bear—and shouting towards the National Capitol: 'I am coming—I am a Republican.' "

"Sharon is not coming nor is he a Republican," replied the inspired editor of *The Virginia City Chronicle.* "He simply is the possessor of an enormous fortune with which he has already purchased the Republican machinery and now proposes to buy enough votes to pack the Legislature which will send him to the United States Senate.

"When the people send a man to the Senate because he is

rich enough to buy votes as well as his office, they must reasonably expect that he will sell them, his office and his country for money."

CHAPTER XXXI

CONTEST FOR "OPHIR"

December, 1874

At first Ralston tried to induce "Lucky" Baldwin to combine with them, and then the triumvirate, Ralston, Baldwin and Sharon, would control the "Ophir" stock together. Toward that end Ralston made overtures.

"No, sir," retorted Baldwin. "I prefer to paddle my own canoe."

In September, Ralston sought the assistance of James R. Keene, one of the most able operators on the Board. He must control "Ophir," he told him.

Keene was looming up as a rising star in the firmament of 'change. He was considered one of the shrewdest, most daring, and well-balanced operators on the Board.

"Give me carte blanche to get control of the mine," replied Keene, "and I'll do it for you."

"You can have it," retorted Ralston, although at the time there was an immense inflation consequent upon the "Consolidated Virginia" and "California" discoveries.

Nothing loath, Keene went to work and sold all the stocks on list at any price he could get. "Ophir" was consequently depressed and Keene's brokers had bought between 20,000 and 30,000 shares before any inkling of his design leaked out. The election was scheduled for December and Keene bought cash stock at $75 and $80 a share, instead of purchasing, as usual, at $60, seller ninety days. With the election only three months off, Ralston could not afford to wait the ninety-day period. As he intended to control the election he was willing to have Keene pay 15 or 20 points more per share in order to have the use of it at once.

The last 5000 shares Keene bought, at $60 each, caused a boom in the price. As his reasons for purchasing so heavily were suspected, the stock shot up to $150 a share. Now at any time 100 shares of "Ophir" could be loaned for $20,000.

Even at $150 a share, Keene continued buying. Then Ralston's hand was seen. So magnificent was his faith in what he had been led to believe and so determined was he to have control that he bought heavily without reserve. Cash "Ophir" went by 5's and 10's from $150 to $195 in December, 1874, with seller 90 still lagging at $75, $85, and $90. In January, "Ophir" reached its zenith at $350 a share. The price paid showed that "Ophir" had risen to over $31,000,000 in value. Yet, at this time, a liberal estimate of the actual available capital on the Pacific Slope for mining speculation did not exceed $20,000,000. "Ophir" was valued at $11,000,000 more than that!

During Ralston's struggle for "Ophir" in the second week of December, "Consolidated Virginia" rose in sympathy from $230 to $710; and in the first week of 1875, to $790. San Francisco was frantic with speculation. Nothing was too insane for people to do. Many who had escaped previous excitements, now hurled themselves headlong into the maelstrom.

The scenes at the Stock Exchange for the first weeks of 1875 were wild in their excitement; brokers crying one to another, like the unseemly harpies of Dante's hell; every cry carrying the Comstock higher. Not only at the exchanges, but on the street, the wild bidding for fortune's favors went on. At almost every dining-table in the city the day's advances in stock were canvassed anew.

When top figures had been reached, Baldwin sold out to Ralston and cleared a couple of millions by the transaction. As Ralston did not have the ready cash to pay such an amount, he gave "Lucky" a note for $3,600,000, that portion of the purchase money which still remained unpaid.

A few days later, while visiting Los Angeles, Baldwin lost his pocketbook containing those notes. Luckily for him his brother-in-law, passing along the street, picked it up and returned it to the owner.

On the strength of the money Baldwin had made in "Ophir" he erected a sumptuous hotel and theatre on Market Street: The Baldwin. Near Pasadena he laid out the Santa Anita Rancho and racecourse.

Keene had also been gifted with the same foresight as Baldwin. On his own account he had been acquiring "Ophir," then selling it to Ralston at a big advance: thereby making many of his own millions, and laying the foundations of his enormous Wall Street fortune.

But Ralston was happy. He was not counting the cost. He had set out to control "Ophir." He had succeeded. With this bonanza he felt his struggles would be at an end. In addition he had the Spring Valley Water Company to think about.

Now Sharon played his trump cards. Besides the shares Ralston had bought for the joint account of William Sharon & Co., Sharon had been buying "Ophir" on his own. By fall he had quite a block of stock and so had every politician in the State of Nevada. The latter could hardly wait for the day to come when "Ophir" would reach $300, and they would each make a nice little nest-egg of their own.

In November, as soon as the Nevada elections were over and his United States Senatorship was assured, Sharon began to unload his "Ophir" stock. Some he sold as low as $200 a share, some as high as $250, until it was all gone. Then he "shorted." "When he filled his 'shorts' he got back all the money he had spent in his Senatorial campaign and several hundred thousand dollars more." His coup had been successful. The market broke just as he had expected. Many operators, suspicious of Sharon's design, condemned him for the wicked way in which he had betrayed his political supporters.

"If this be true," cried De Long, one of his dupes, "the man is a demon and deserves destruction."

Unaware of the cause of the market break, Ralston tried to sustain the market. He was in a desperate position, but never for a moment did he lose his composure nor his confidence.

Now, all of his available assets were tied up in "Ophir" or Spring Valley Water Company. He could neither sell the shares of "Ophir" that he had purchased nor could he sustain their market value. There was not in his bank nor on the whole Pacific Coast capital sufficient to support the stock at the figures at which he had purchased it. He had to be content to watch it fall.

Then the "Bears" started a rumor. Ralston's "Ophir" bonanza had given out. It was not an egg-shaped one as experts had declared, that would broaden out as it descended. At the top it had widened, then it had absolutely flattened. It was only a small part of an egg, less than a quarter. When crosscuts had been run, it was found that it had pinched out and was a failure. Like the second shock of an earthquake those bad tidings shook Ralston and the stock market to their foundations.

The Exchange was demoralized. All stocks fell with a resounding crash. "California" in the second week of January, 1875, dropped 200 points. By the end of the month it had lost 170 more. During the same period "Consolidated Virginia" passed from $710 to $595 then to $452. "Ophir" dropped from $315 to $183. Not even at that figure could Ralston sustain it. In the third week in January it sank to $133, and in the fourth week to $116. Finally, absolutely unsupported, it fell in utter collapse, to $50 a share.

San Francisco staggered financially, morally and commercially under the strength of the blow dealt Comstock stocks. Men as well as women were ruined. The march toward "Pauper's Alley" became a procession of ragged and hopeless people. So intimately associated was Ralston's industrial empire with the Comstock Lode that the Coast was demoralized.

Values were destroyed. Confidence was weakened. Men distrusted their fellow men. Where before had been happiness and security, hate and loss of faith took their place. The worst phase had not yet dawned on San Francisco. There were known bonanzas in "California" and "Consolidated Virginia" but there was less than nothing in "Ophir." Nothing, and Ralston had squandered a good $3,000,000 in seeking control.

All this time Ralston's bank, like the sturdy ship she was, rode the financial gale. At times there was an ominous sound in the vaults as gold and silver gurgled out in a steady stream. But skillfully and apparently unperturbed, the debonair Ralston viewed the wreckage about him. When the storm was over, he guided his ship into more quiet waters. "Ophir" was finished.

Now he threw himself with all his wonted enthusiasm into the Spring Valley Water Company. On that water scheme Ralston cast all his faith. After all, water was a man's best friend.

CHAPTER XXXII

THE MAYOR OF SAN FRANCISCO

1875–1878

"Faster! Faster!" Sutro exhorted his workers. "Every ton of ore taken from the big bonanza loses our company two dollars."

Never were men nor machinery handled with greater skill than Sutro used them in his wild underground dash to the Lode. Every moment of night and day, picked miners, in short shifts, drove the incessant drills, like machine guns, against the invisible enemy. Skilled timber men, armed with long knives, held the swelling clay at bay. Young athletes threw shovelfuls of hot rock into iron trams. Trains of mules, lights swinging over their headgear, rushed the cars through the darkness to the dumps. Neither darkness, nor heat, nor foul air, nor stubborn mule nor fainting man held Sutro back. Night and day, month after month, winter and summer, with one idea in mind relentlessly Sutro drove the face of his bore toward the Lode.

Almost hourly, stripped to the waist, Sutro worked with his men, displaying indomitable energy, here, there, everywhere. By strength, courage and example, he kept his men encouraged. Though every foot of advance was gained at the price of pain and danger, onward he worked with passionate eagerness.

Although two powerful Root blowers had been installed in the summer of 1875, the temperature at the face of the leader steadily increased, and the air became unbearably foul. The aroma of perspiring mules grew stifling. It seemed to lurk in the very crevices of the hot rock. As fast as the bore went forward and heat increased, just that much more overpowering became the stench of mules. The stalls of Augeus, before the turbulent waters of the Alpheus and Pineus rivers flushed them, could not have been more foul than the heading of Sutro's tunnel became. Candles flickered with a sickly glare in the stagnant air. Back from the drill-carriage, workmen staggered weak and faint. Now their daily dread was of being entombed by the swelling clay in an airless passage.

All the time that Ralston, a thousand projects of freeing himself in mind, was writhing in the toils of the San Francisco Stock Market, Sutro, with one single idea in mind, was cutting his indomitable way toward the Lode at the rate of 16½ feet every twenty-four hours. In those seventeen tragic days between July 22 and August 8, Sutro made a run of 279 feet. While Ralston was making his December struggle to control "Ophir," Sutro was making the greatest progress he had ever made in a single month—the extraordinary run of 417 feet. By the end of the year he had brought the header to a point 8079 feet from the mouth.

While Ralston was making his most heroic efforts to right his bank by calling in loans and disposing of his personal property, Sutro was making an average monthly progress of 310 8/12 feet.

On the 13th of August, when the heat at the face of the bore had become unendurable, Sutro installed a powerful double compressor built at Kalk, near Deutz, on the Rhine. The blowers were worked to their utmost capacity. The pipes that supplied compressed air to the drills were opened at several points. Even those heroic measures were insufficient to contend with poisonous gases, animal emanations, and insufferable heat.

All the time that Virginia City was burning, as it did in October, 1875, when tongues of flame licked up the Comstock Lode from north end to south end and reduced it to a smoldering heap of hot ashes, Sutro never let up on his drills. When the "Ophir" caught fire and burned and the "Consolidated Virginia" and "C & C" shafts became smoking volcanoes, Sutro redoubled his efforts. He must reach the bonanza before the shafts were retimbered and work resumed. The great holocaust blazing above him was granting a respite.

Steadily the temperature rose from 98° F. the first of March, 1878, to 109° the 22nd of April. During the same period, at the face of the heading, it mounted from 110° to 114°. Under such insupportable conditions it seemed impossible to complete the work, even to work at all, but in spite of them Sutro kept hammering away. One single purpose in mind. Now two or three hours of work was all that the most hardened miner could stand. At that, endurance was strained to the last shred. Man after man dropped down and was carried babbling and incoherent to the outer air.

Thus, the nearer Sutro drew to his goal the slower became his progress and the more arduous the conditions under which he toiled. With every foot of advance the swelling clay became more treacherous. Often after being cut through and exposed to the air it would swell, displace the railroad track and snap the stoutest timbers like reeds. Now constant vigilance was required to prevent accidents. Continually timbers had to be replaced, the clay, behind them, eased up and lagging, driven ahead of the bore.

Only the slightest kind of blasts could be used. Sometimes no powder could be fired, so great became the danger of knocking down timbers.

When the header entered the broad Comstock mineral belt the heat from the solfataric springs became so intolerable that two drills had to be taken off the carriage. From then on, Sutro could not average more than 250 feet per month.

After the first of May, Sutro had to change shifts four times a day instead of three. Conditions became so oppressive that the toughest-fibered mules rebelled. They could hardly be driven toward the header. Enough they had seen of that battle-scarred face. Enough they had heard of the rata-tat-tat of the drills. More than once a "rationally obstinate" mule thrust his head into the end of the canvas air-pipe and had to be literally torn away by main strength. When other means failed, the miners tied the tail of the refractory one to the bodies of two other mules in the same train and forced them to haul back their companion, snorting viciously and slipping with stiff legs over the wet floor.

In comparison with failing flesh the Burleigh drills knew no weariness nor pain. Night and day, ceaselessly, they churned away at the face of the header, driving great fractures into the rock. Now Sutro was about 20,000 feet from the mouth of his tunnel. Less than one hundred to go!

Finally the steady rata-tat-tat of the advancing drills attracted the attention of miners working on the 1640-foot level of the Savage Mine. Sutro was knocking on the door to the Lode. Distinctly they could hear the explosion of the blasts as one redoubt after another was conquered. Louder and louder grew the intensity of his attack. It could not be long now before Sutro reached the "Savage." The miners on the latter began to fear his blasts. Each might be the one to knock a hole into the spot where they were working.

By the 8th of July, only a few feet of igneous rock separated the two parties: the workmen in the "Savage" from the tunnel diggers. When Sutro heard the blasting of the "Savage" miners on their side of the rocky partition he could scarcely contain himself. Now he knew that his surveys had been exact. Straight as a die he had come through 20,000 feet of hard rock to his destination. Only a few feet of syenite separated him from his goal. The ambition of eighteen years was about to be realized. Jubilantly, he wired Superintendent Gillette of the "Savage," then working on the opposite side of the wall:

"Should your men succeed in knocking a drill hole through, let them stop and not enlarge it until I am fully notified. There should be ample time given for your men and ours to retire, for I am afraid a column, several thousand feet in length, of hot, foul air, suddenly set in motion, might prove fatal to the men. I shall telegraph again at 9:30 and give the report of the shift, which will then be out.

ADOLPH SUTRO."

On the same day, Sutro's apprehensions were verfied: a drill from the "Savage" penetrated the rock partition, between the mine and the tunnel. Up through this hole shot a rush of air with a loud hissing sound. A "Savage" miner put his eye to the opening. Immediately he recoiled: the air was hot; but he had seen a glow of light at the other end. Presently a voice came up the passage. He put his ear to the opening.

"How's everything?" came a clear voice.

"First rate," he shouted back through the burrow.

Every sound arose with startling distinctness but it required the force of a cannon's roar to make itself heard above the sibilation of that hissing air current.

Immediately along came another dispatch from Sutro to Gillette:

"The men report a drill hole knocked through near the north side. Put in your blast, and let your men retire to the incline. Will be at the header at 11 o'clock.

ADOLPH SUTRO."

At a little before that hour word shot up the drill opening: "Mr. Sutro was ready."

Gillette of the "Savage" replied that they were about to blast. Signals were exchanged: Gillette pounded on the rock partition with a sledge-hammer. Some one in the tunnel beat back a reply.

The "Savage" miners shoved eight Rigorret powder cartridges into as many prepared holes. On his side, Sutro sealed the bottom of the drill hole with clay. Again Gillette used the sledge-hammer signal: the blast was about to be fired. Fire! struck back Sutro's hammer—all hands withdrew. Tom Tengilley of the "Savage" lighted a fuse.

A dull roar shook the earth. Down the Savage stope swept a stygian gale. Followed a blinding rush of smoke and a gust of noxious air so hot that the miners were convinced that they had blasted an opening into the infernal regions. Lanterns went out. One after another stope-lights succumbed. They were left in a drift blacker than Erebus and hotter than Hell. Without being able to see what their explosive had accomplished, the "Savage" miners knew that an opening had been made into Sutro's Tunnel. The wind stifled—sickened them. They clapped both hands over nose and mouth. Even then they were almost overpowered by the noisome stench of perspiring mules. Knowing full well what lay in wait for them in that hot corrupt atmosphere, they "stripped to the buff." Naked, gamely, they faced foul air and overcoming heat. At times sheer desperation drove them to the end of the compressed-air pipe where they gulped down the current of fresh air as eagerly as the parched swallow water. Again and again they lighted their candles. Again and again they saw them extinguished by the violent gusts of wind sweeping about them. Carefully through the whirlwind they groped their way forward. Finally they came to a great square hole with jagged sides which the blast had torn out of the rock partition between the "Savage" and the tunnel.

Through the gap swept clouds of pulverized earth and a hot solfataric gale. From the jagged edges fell a mist-like curtain of dust. Through it glowed the bright lights of the tunnel. As the miners gazed, perspiration started from every pore and ran in muddy rivulets into their shoes.

A ladder was rushed forward. Down it was dropped to the floor of the tunnel ten feet below. Up the rungs crunched hurrying feet. Suddenly Adolph Sutro, flushed, sprinkled with powdered rock, half-naked, stood framed in the jagged opening. Like Mephisto, with flashing eyes, he paused. Dust flying about him. The light from the tunnel glowing red behind him.

Suddenly the terrific force of the wind sucked Sutro through the opening and dropped him against the opposite wall of the stope. Bruised and bleeding, Sutro picked himself up and shouted with joy. Vigorously he shook every hand within reach. Then he hurried forward to the cooling station on the 1640-foot level of the "Savage," almost overcome with excitement.

An American flag was placed in the giraffe. In the great draft of air sweeping up the "Savage" its folds unfurled. Up the shaft the colors pointed as stiff as a piece of tin.

Pennants flew from the hoisting works. Beer was served in copious drafts. Every man drank a flagon in honor of the great event.

At the mouth of the tunnel, 20,081 feet distant, cannon were booming. Plainly the roar could be heard in Virginia City, and the light of bonfires reflected from the mountains beyond the Carson River could be seen from every street. After nine years of struggling with Ralston, banks, halls of legislation, Sutro had reached his goal: the Comstock Lode. The dream of 1861 had materialized seventeen years later. Behind him lay the development of a single idea.

Sutro's troubles did not end when he reached the Comstock Lode and made the "Savage" connection, rather they began afresh. All the mine owners insisted that they had no need for the tunnel nor would they ever use it. To bonanza king and mine owner alike, that two dollars a ton royalty was a sore point. Not a cent would they ever pay Sutro. Every conceivable weapon in the way of law and legislation was resorted to in their final effort to thwart him.

One day the pump rod in the combination shaft of the "Hale and Norcross," "Savage" and "Chollar-Potosi" broke down. Immediately those mines were flooded with water. To save his underground workings, and without asking Sutro's permission, the superintendent set hundreds of men to work to turn his flood waters into the tunnel. Water at a temperature of 130° surged down its trough toward the Carson River. Unwarned, Sutro's miners and mules, almost overcome by steam and hot water, fled for their lives. The "Hale and Norcross" was in a fair way of being drained when news of the mishap reached Sutro. Immediately Sutro began the construction of a water-tight bulkhead. Unless the "Hale and Norcross" desisted, he threatened to hermetically seal the tunnel. In the meantime, by a bit of Sutro ingenuity, the flood waters were returned to the combination shaft, upon the source from which they came, and their pumps pumped and re-pumped the same water into the tunnel. When the trick was discovered an injunction was sought to prevent the use of the bulkhead. Followed an underground battle between "Savage," "Hale and Norcross" and "Chollar-Potosi" miners on one side and Sutro Tunnel workers on the other. Picks, axes and shovels came into play. Luckily before any fatalities occurred, water aligned herself definitely on the side of Sutro. He had proven himself master of her underground floods.

The Julia Company struck a reservoir. Capitulation or ruin stared the company in the face. Surrender was inevitable. The officials of the combined "Savage," "Hale and Norcross" and "Chollar-Potosi" sought Sutro out and sued for peace. Then "Belcher" found herself unable to cope with the rising floods. They too came to Sutro with the white flags of surrender in their hands. Then "California" and "Consolidated Virginia" passed their dividends. Stocks, like a violently thrown rubber ball, bounced up and down on the San Francisco stock market. Said engineers: The only hope for the Comstock lay in deep mining. "Deep Mining" became the slogan of the Comstock. Sutro was the solution of deep mining. He was the master of the drains. The only one who could keep water in subjection and the mines working. One by one, crest-fallen directors of various mines took off their hats, and sought Sutro's favor. Would he give their shafts an opening into the tunnel? Even the proud Bonanza Kings joined the procession. On all sides was capitulation. Sutro had solved the Comstock Lode's water question. He alone could vanquish the floods. He was master of Washoe's unplumbed underground seas. He was the keeper of the water gates: to keep them open would resuscitate the Lode; to close them would mean speedy death.

With all mining owners and Bonanza Kings paying their devoirs and imploring his help, Sutro became the King of the Comstock: the fourth dynasty to rule the Lode. His mastery of underground floods had made his victory complete. A compromise was effected with all mine owners. New contracts were drawn up. Like adamant Sutro stuck to his royalties, but in victory he could afford to be magnanimous. In a heated conclave, he agreed to accept a $2 tax on all ore assaying $40 or over to the ton, $1 on all ore assaying less than that amount.

At last, necessity had compelled his enemies to recognize his genius and his devotion to a single idea. The new contracts terminated the long struggle of one tenacious spirit against that enemy hardest to beat—"a soulless corporation."

With dispatch Sutro completed his laterals. A wide covered drain was excavated down the middle of the tunnel to accommodate the floods. When completed, there was an underground tramway through Mt. Davidson, over six and a half miles in extent. Daily Sutro drained 3,500,000 to 4,000,000 gallons of water into the channel of the Carson River.

Now all the mines were supplied with fresh air, transportation, means of egress in fires and a cheaper method of milling on the Carson. Some months the Sutro Tunnel brought to the company $200,000 in rentals.

For two years Sutro enjoyed his Comstock ascendancy. When everything was booming in the tunnel and stock was commanding a high price on the San Francisco Market, Sutro sold out his interests to the stockholders for a million or two and retired to the city.

There, one day, his championship of the cause of humanity would make him the Mayor of San Francisco.

CHAPTER XXXIII

WATER BONANZA

1875

All the time their stocks had been shrinking, both "California" and "Virginia Consolidated" had remained in bonanzas. Every month they had paid a regular dividend to their stockholders that totalled all the way from $1,000,000 to $1,500,000. But "Ophir" was a drug on the market.

Aside from their menace, the output made no difference to Ralston. It was the stock shrinkage that was playing havoc with his bank. In eight months he had seen values decline $100,000,000—equivalent to the loss of as much available security. Such a shrinkage continuing could have but one result. None noted the concern behind Ralston's composure, nor the flushed appearance of his face as he countered these facts.

All the time stocks were falling, brokers were calling for more "mud" to cover margins. To meet these demands, every hour of the day saw money flowing out of Ralston's bank. Now a trickle, now a steady stream. There was no styptic to staunch the hemorrhage. The savings of lifetimes were being hurled under the wheels of the triumphant juggernaut that was grinding up and down the financial district: grinding out fortunes; grinding out hopes; grinding out lives.

To meet the inevitable, Ralston began stripping himself of his individual means.

Among the first transfers of property noted was Ralston's magnificent 16,000-acre Kern County estate, one of the finest tracts of land in California. He had received it as a bequest from his old friend Fretz. That went at a sacrifice of $90,000 a little more than the customary unimproved value of $50 an acre, to Col. J. D. Fry. To Sharon went his interests in the crowning achievement of his life: the Palace Hotel.

Prudent men watched these transfers with concern. Nicholas Luning sold his bank stock. Sharon reduced his to a nominal figure. There was new ground for inquiry, but only for momentary concern. Ralston's method of life reassured onlookers. He was swimming wholeheartedly, unconcernedly, in Bay waters. He was tallyho-ing distinguished guests back and forth to Belmont. He was chartering a special train to accompany European capitalists to the San Joaquin Valley. He was sleeping, dining and wining them in a palace car. He was being photographed while driving them with a six-horse coach through the gigantic trunk of a Sequoia on the rim of the Yosemite Valley. He was astounding the visitors with the magnificence of mountain scenery, the girth of big trees, the singing of falling waters, the vast fields of San Joaquin grain; but above all with the princely character of his hospitality.

Sharon's daughter was marrying a distinguished lawyer, Francis G. Newlands. Ralston was master of ceremonies. The papers reported that he was presenting the bride with some choice Venetian mosaics. The reading of this random gossip revived confidence in Ralston's invincibility. His supply of money was as inexhaustible as Monte Cristo's. He was a money magician.

Once more Ralston was electrifying California with the magnitude of a business operation. People smiled when they saw the daily accounts. Smiled in commiseration when they read the onslaughts of the *Call* and *Bulletin*. They hoped Ralston would succeed. The city needed more water. They admired Ralston's dash and enterprise. As always, he captivated hearts. They hoped he would control the water supply of

San Francisco, in spite of everything that Fitch and Pickering could do to the contrary.

And Ralston intended to control the city's water. No matter how many millions it cost, he would corner water. All the time that Comstock stocks were falling, and money to cover margins was gushing out of Ralston's vaults, and "Consolidated Virginia" and "California" were dividing a million-dollar melon monthly and the juggernaut was grinding its worshipers into the dust, Ralston was buying up Spring Valley stock. He seemed to have any amount of money. There were 80,000 shares. Of them he must corner at least 36,000. Then he would add Calaveras Valley to the city's watershed, increase production by piping around the head of the Bay, and sell the whole works to the supervisors. He had it all arranged, even to the selling price.

When Ralston didn't have funds enough of his own to accomplish his Spring Valley goal, it was easy to acquire more. One day, Michel Reese advanced him between three and four million dollars at 6 per cent interest. The rate did not disturb Ralston. He was confident he could swing that. The important thing was the control of Spring Valley. At all costs he must accomplish that. It would be a desperate attempt. But he must retrieve his old position. If it was the last card, he would not hesitate to play it.

As winter waned, Spring Valley stock certificates increased in Ralston's vaults by the hundreds and thousands of shares. Still he was never satisfied. When the Reese loan exhausted itself, Ralston borrowed from San Francisco's savings banks and gave as security shares of Bank of California stock. In this way he turned over some 13,000 shares for value received.

At last Ralston was ready to act. The election of supervisors, in whose hands the power to purchase the Spring Valley Water Company would lie, was scheduled for September 1. To accomplish his ends Ralston had had to dabble in politics. The newly elected supervisors must be sworn to support Spring Valley. On account of the growing population, the demand for an adequate supply of water for the city, and the great devotion of all classes to Ralston, there seemed little doubt of the result. And that little doubt was expressed in the person of James Otis, Mayor of the city, who had vetoing power.

By this time, Ralston had acquired some 49,608 shares of Spring Valley water stock. Besides his own, Ralston had control of all those shares held by different members of his Ring.

Upon Spring Valley Water Company, Ralston had put a value of $14,500,000. With the Calaveras Valley attachment, he had added another million, making a total of $15,500,000. At that price he offered the Water Company to the city.

Immediately on reading these figures the *Call* and *Bulletin*, their editors Pickering and Fitch, and Simonton of the Associated Press, were up in arms: Ralston was a masked highwayman. He was an old hand at the hold-up business. Among other things, they claimed he had engineered the Colorado Railroad swindle. Carelessly he had used men and thrown them away, either they had had to help him or find themselves out of power. He would gag the people, the papers warned, tie their hands behind their backs and rifle their pockets at leisure. All the time that Ralston had been posing as San Francisco's benefactor, secretly, he had been plotting to plunder the people for profit. If the 60,000 property owners of the city would be kind enough to constitute themselves into a bonanza, Ralston and his high-toned Ring would mine them for their own benefit.

Ralston was a banker become politician. Imagine the financial leader of San Francisco, running candidates and manipulating politics to consummate his own ends!

"Ralston's Ring is entrenched behind bank-counters and installed in comfortable chairs," warned an editor. "His ring is powerful by reason of wealth. It is above the law. The influences which it yields are not of the bar-room, ward-gathering or sailors' boarding-houses. Its methods resemble Washington rather than New York. Its head is depraved. It hatches the worst designs against its own body. Its dangers smack of the villa, bank and palace rather than the back-alley and slum. For all that, its bite is more vicious than that of New York's Tweed Ring."

On and on went the abuse. In 1874, claimed *The Bulletin*,

the city could have bought Spring Valley water for $6,000-000. Now that Ralston had gained control of the stock it would cost $15,500,000, so that Ralston and his ring would make a profit between $8–9,000,000. For what? For the City? No. For himself and his crowd. For more villas, more palaces, more Lucullan luxuries; for more fast horses; for more dust for his chariot wheels to hurl in the faces of the people and blind them from seeing the low estate to which they had fallen. Ralston was a traitor to public interest. He was making San Francisco water as expensive for the consumer as the champagne that he drank at his Belmont banquets.

As Ralston perceived that the possession of a controlling interest in the Spring Valley stock would be of no avail unless supervisors and Mayor approved, he redoubled his efforts to control the election.

Stocks were affected by these press accusations. By June "Consolidated Virginia" had dropped to 421; "California" to 60; "Ophir" to 61.

By June 15 "Consolidated Virginia" had fallen to 390; "California" to 58.

By July "Consolidated Virginia" had reached the low level of 309; "California" 56; "Ophir" 45.

In June "Consolidated Virginia" and "California" produced $1,502,600 in bullion; in July, $1,604,000. Of this they distributed the best part of $6–8,000,000 in dividends. Men said the Irish quartet were giving stockholders the most honest management the old Comstock had seen. Nevertheless, every day saw fresh batches of certificates hurled on the crumbling market. Confidence was ruined. Neither "Consolidated Virginia," "California" nor "Ophir" could sustain themselves. The quartet didn't even care. They had known bonanzas. Some accused them of throwing their own stock on the market. They would break it down still lower. Ralston watched these falling prices with consternation. The drain on his resources was in direct proportion to their fall.

Now the Bank of Nevada building was finished and the Bonanza Kings were getting ready to open its doors. Gold was getting tighter and tighter on the San Francisco market. Ralston's friends accused Flood and O'Brien of locking up $5-000,000 in their vaults, so as to cinch the market. With money growing scarcer and scarcer Ralston grew more and more bitter toward the Irishmen.

One day Edney S. Tibbey, who had been Ralston's receiving teller in 1864, met W. S. O'Brien on the street. O'Brien had been drinking a little and was over-chatty. He drew Tibbey aside and confided some details of the Nevada bank which they were just opening.

Locked up in Donohoe and Kelly's bank, Ralston's early partners, was a million and a half in coin, he said. "With it, when they started their bank, they were going to break the Bank of California."

Being devoted to Ralston, Tibbey believed that he should make these facts known to him.

The next morning he called at Ralston's office. Although O'Brien had said the facts were confidential, Tibbey related the conversation in toto.

All the time Tibbey was speaking Ralston in his nervous way was tearing up papers and letting them slip through his fingers to the floor. As Tibbey finished, Ralston looked up with a smile.

"I am not afraid of them," he replied.

"If you are in the same condition you were in when I left the bank, it behooves you to take in everything you possibly can and sail close to the wind," Tibbey warned.

"If you hear anything more about this come in and let me know," Ralston replied.

The nearer election day approached, the more acrimonious became the columns of the *Call* and *Bulletin*. Every day readers were warned afresh that Ralston was not engaged in a legitimate banking business. His assets were carried in manufacturing ventures, in the wildest and most dangerous stock speculations like "Ophir" and Spring Valley water. Every day both dailies grew more determined that never should Ralston put his water scheme over. One day they called Ralston a marauder, a marauder struggling to force the Spring Valley water on the city at a profit of over $6,000,000. Ralston would even pollute the purity of water!

"If Spring Valley had been an individual," claimed *The Bulletin* editor, "long ago it would have found itself in a striped suit behind State prison bars. It has been guilty of every crime known to our laws except murder. False pretenses are made to appear justifiable, robbery as an innocent prostitute, extortion as a virtue."

So angry did these onslaughts make Ralston's friends that, of their own accord, they withdrew their advertisements from those periodicals' columns. Every cancellation added venom to the next day's attack.

In the midst of his financial difficulties, Ralston grew morbidly sensitive to the newspaper tirades to which he was daily subjected. But who, that watched his imperturbable expression, would have guessed it? Apparently he was oblivious to every assault of printer's ink. After banking hours, with the ribbons of his tallyho in his hands, Ralston would go galloping down the King's Highway to Belmont. The worse the onslaught the faster he drove. When pressure of business prevented these Belmont excursions, Ralston would be found measuring his strength against the tides at North Beach. Only in the sea could he find complete independence.

But not for long was there escape. When he would get back to the city the newsboys would be yelling "Extra!" In the editorial, Ralston would find fresh tirades against himself: He would debase Spring Valley water to his own evil ends.

Slowly the market recovered. The bullion product from "Consolidated Virginia" and "California" had encouraged popular confidence. About the first of August, stocks began to show added strength. No longer was Ralston in doubt regarding weathering the storm. "Consolidated Virginia" was selling at $360, "California" at $75 and "Ophir" had gone up to $77.

On the 19th of August, *The Bulletin* seemed resigned. In his editorial the editor advised San Francisco citizens to march to the September polls and sign away their homesteads. "Vote a mortgage on whatever you possess," he suggested, "for the millions you are going to give away are going into the pockets of the unconfessed owners of Spring Valley water stock."

On August 23 *The Bulletin* propounded a question: "Shall San Francisco be saddled with a $20,000,000 debt solely for the benefit of Ralston and his water ring?"

At the same time Simonton, of the Associated Press, had been wiring New York information of a type designed to effect Wall Street. The next thing Ralston knew, *The New York Commercial Advertiser* was predicting bank troubles in California. "There is something of an uneasy feeling in certain quarters," the papers hinted. "We are afraid that a good many of the Pacific Coast dollars will be found stuffed with straw before their $5,000,000 hotel, $20,000,000 water works, $100,000,000 railroads, and big bonanzas generally are all settled up. Some of their banks are 'kites,' with very long tails, and it would be well for these rich men to pause in the mad career of their fancied prosperity before adding electricity to their movements."

Just as the *Call* and *Bulletin* had been undermining confidence in California, Associated Press dispatches had succeeded in impairing Ralston's credit, not only in New York, but also in London.

By Monday, August 23, Ralston was well aware of the damage the Associated Press had accomplished. On that day he sent for Bell, one of his oldest friends, then agent for the London Oriental Bank.

"Money is very scarce," Ralston confided. "Flood and O'Brien are preparing to open the Nevada Bank and are locking up all the coin."

As he spoke, Ralston placed in Bell's hands a large amount of bills receivable and asked Bell to cable to the Oriental

Bank in London that he had the securities and to request credit for the bank for them.

But already reports, denouncing Ralston for manipulating politics, and organizing a water ring to swindle San Francisco, had reached the staid London money magnates. A report that he had taken to "bucking faro" could not have inspired more distrust.

To Ralston's chagrin, the Oriental Bank of London failed to answer Bell's cablegram. But he was not discouraged. He had made up his mind to win out and he would.

Ralston turned to another never-failing source of help: The United States Sub-Treasury. In times of financial stringency, like the present, the Bank of California had always been able to get, in New York, an order for a transfer from the Sub-Treasury of at least a million dollars. Now, Ralston telegraphed the Treasury. He needed a million dollars to tide over an immediate crisis.

For the first time in his experience the request was refused.

Like the arms of a cuttlefish closing around him, Ralston could feel the toils of his enemies. He could hear their loud-mouthed gulpings as their hold tightened. But never had Ralston appeared more light-hearted. Never had his laugh had a merrier ring. He would fool his foes.

On August 25, George L. Upshur, Flood and O'Brien's clerk, was ushered into Ralston's office with a sealed note. On reading it Ralston flushed scarlet.

"My son," he said, "do you know what is in this note?"

"No, sir," came back Upshur's swift reply.

"Well, you go back and tell Flood that I'll send him back selling rum over the Auction Lunch counter!"

Out went the clerk. Back he came within a few minutes.

"Mr. Flood," he repeated, "says that, in a short time, he will be able to sell rum over the counter of the Bank of California."

Ralston's face paled as the clerk finished speaking.

Fifteen minutes later the perturbed Upshur ushered Ralston into Flood's private office on Montgomery Street near California, and retired, leaving the door between Flood's office and his own slightly ajar. In passing, Upshur had picked up a

Derringer pistol, with nine nicks on the handle. Once it had belonged to the desperate gunman, Jim Dodson. If Flood was in danger from this hot-headed Ralston, as he suspected, he stood ready to protect him. Upshur fondled his gun and listened.

It appeared that Flood and O'Brien had a large sum of money deposited in the Bank of California. Flood's note notified Ralston that they were about to withdraw it.

"Flood, you will have to let up on us," began Ralston.

"What's the matter?" retorted Flood.

"We have not enough coin to pay that check," gave back Ralston.

"When can you pay?"

"In three or four days."

"If I put it in three checks," asked Flood, "to be drawn, one Thursday, one Friday, and the last on Saturday, will it be satisfactory?"

Ralston replied that it would.

The checks were drawn and Ralston hurried past the astounded Upshur.

As per agreement, the first check was presented by Donohoe, Kelly & Co., Ralston's old partners, on Thursday morning the 26th. Immediately the check was paid. Shortly afterward, Mills came to Flood.

"If we cannot get relief," he said, "the bank will have to go under."

"I do not see," retorted Flood, "how I could render any assistance." And Mills departed.

But Flood did not deposit his two remaining $100,000 checks. He called off the arrangements with Donohoe, Kelly & Co. He did not want to rest under the imputation of having closed the doors of the Bank of California. Rather, he concluded, he would lose that amount than press the payment.

On August 25 *The Bulletin* continued its onslaughts. This time it accused Ralston of using money to deceive the people. To accomplish his wicked ends he had subsidized both *The San Francisco Chronicle* and *The San Francisco Ledger.*

But now editors Fitch and Pickering had gone too far.

The people of San Francisco were rising against them. Not half of their accusations would the people believe. Ralston was the idol of San Francisco. He would do no wrong. They loved to hear of his banquets; to see the notables of the day flash by in his shining coaches. Ralston was doing what they, were they in his position, would like to be doing. To them he was a symbol of a successful business career. He carried off his laurels well. They cherished nothing but pride. They were proud of the great Bank of California, proud of Ralston's industrial achievements, proud of Ralston himself. He was the creator of San Francisco. He had made the city the center of Pacific Coast activity. He was the friend of the working man, the artisan, the poor man. He manufactured jobs, he paid royal wages. Never did he stint. Pridefully, they pointed toward the Palace Hotel. The raising of those white walls was giving work to 4000 laborers. They indicated woollen mills, sugar refineries, foundries, furniture factories, watch-works, lead-towers, carriage factories. All of them were inspired by Ralston. All of them built with his money. That was what he was accomplishing with his millions. What would they be doing were it not for Ralston? In every humble home the name of Ralston was revered. It had become a household word, spoken in bated breath. In scores of them were children who answered to the name: Ralston. In a niche along with Lares and Penates his likeness was venerated.

The charges in the *Call* and *Bulletin* were audacious falsehoods. The editors were downright liars. They would not have him abused. They would wreck the *Call* and *Bulletin*. Their threats reached the owners. Pickering and Fitch asked for police protection. Nothing but strong confidence in their leaders could have saved those papers from ruin, so fierce had grown the animosity. Many wrote the editors:

"Let up on Ralston, or stop our subscriptions."

As a result the circulation of both papers fell off tremendously. As advertising media their columns were already ruined. Hardly a business man would advertise in them.

While the *Call* and *Bulletin* were sowing the wind, and the people were rising in Ralston's defense, stocks began crashing again: "Consolidated Virginia" fell off 55 points, "California" 13, "Ophir" 18. Cash, like lifeblood, was being drained out of Ralston's bank. Confidence in high places had been impaired. Distrust as contagious as measles was spreading east and west. Some of his Ring haunted Ralston's office. They wanted to get rid of their bank stock. They demanded that he exchange their stock for real estate or other securities. Every one of them, Ralston was glad to accommodate. Out of his own hands went one parcel of property after another. Great masses of stock, traceable to Ralston's followers, were being thrown upon a constantly falling market. The deluge was being made greater by those who could not get money to keep their margin good. During the last week of August, the shrinkage of stock values alone amounted to $42,600,000—equivalent to the loss of just as much available security.

But who could have told from the expression of his face that Ralston was in the unsuspected throes of agony? To the outside world, Ralston bore these attacks with the stoicism of an Indian warrior at the stake. To most, he seemed as light-hearted as ever. A few knew how deeply he was wounded. Still he was determined not to yield. There were many more cards to play before election day would decide the fate of Spring Valley water. Everything looked favorable. The supervisors were with him to a man. At the eleventh hour, word reached Ralston that Mayor Otis had decided to veto the scheme.

Then, for the first time, Ralston began to realize the desperate condition of his affairs.

Now some of his friends noted an ominous expression about Ralston's face. At times, it had a haunted look. "Like that of a noble animal at bay." Sometimes there was a tremor of the finely cut lip, combined with a determined look in the eye as if to repress it. He was not so composed. Constantly he jiggled the emblems on his watch-chain. Oft while talking to associates he would be reducing reams of paper to shreds.

One day, shortly after, Ralston sent for Sharon to come to his office. It was hardly more than ten years since Sharon had sat in front of Ralston and had appealed for help—to save himself from bankruptcy. Now Sharon was rated as the second wealthiest man on the Pacific Coast; but conditions were reversed. Ralston was in need of help. As he confided in Sharon, he nervously stroked his finely cropped chin-beard. He needed a million dollars immediately, $900,000 he must have at once.

Sharon had lately loaned Ralston $2,000,000 with which to finish the Palace. He could not raise any more.

Shortly after, Sharon appealed to Mills. Just how much the latter surmised of Ralston's troubles he did not divulge. "Ralston needs help to save himself from failure in personal speculations," Sharon confided, "nine hundred thousand dollars would carry him through."

Even for the wealthiest man in California $900,000 was a large amount.

Mills could not forget the years of close association with his old cashier, nor the constant consideration and courtesy which he had continued to receive from Ralston long after his own retirement from the Bank of California. There were only two things that he could not forgive: the matter of the directorship of the bank and the fact that Ralston had retained his name on the list of stockholders after he had sold his stock. Mills resented those breaches. But he would overlook both of them, he promised. Too, he would ignore a certain lack of frankness on Ralston's part in regard to internal affairs of the bank. He had never felt, he confided to Sharon, that he had had Ralston's complete confidence.

But out of the great fondness which he had always felt towards him, he would agree to help.

Within an hour he went to Ralston's office with a check for some $400,000 in his hand. Ralston was overjoyed at this mark of confidence.

"In the next day or two," Mills went on, "I will arrange to let you have $350,000 more, making a total of $750,000. No doubt you will be able to raise the balance elsewhere."

Then Mills inquired into the security for this loan. And Ralston arranged to turn over the stock of the Virginia and Truckee Railroad, a third interest in the whole company.

Some months, at that very time, it was paying him in dividends as much as $100,000.

With Mills' help, Ralston gave up all idea of yielding to his enemies. Now he would fight them to a finish.

On the evening of August 25, 1875, Ralston felt the toils of his enemies closing more tightly about him. That night his needs for cash were imperative. He must have a million dollars in his vaults before the bank opened next morning.

At once he sent for the superintendent of the Louis and Garnett refinery: "a depository and refinery for gold and silver belonging to various companies." Over it Ralston had complete control.

When the manager arrived Ralston autocratically demanded the amount of bullion in the refinery.

"There is just about two million dollars' worth," the surprised man replied.

"Load every ounce into hacks," Ralston ordered, "take it to the United States Mint and have it struck into twenty-dollar pieces."

CHAPTER XXXIV

SAN FRANCISCO STOCK EXCHANGE: THE 11 O'CLOCK BOARD

August 26, 1875

The next morning when the doors of the Bank of California opened for business, the counters were piled high with gold pieces.

California Street wore its customary appearance. The usual crowd came and went. There was no cause for worry. The clients could see that. Ralston was as rich as Monte Cristo! Look at the gold on his counters.

At the San Francisco Stock Exchange, there were a few who knew what would happen there that morning, but only a few. Not at any price would one of those have given out an inkling. It would have been dishonorable. It might precipitate a calamity that might yet be staved off.

Stocks were like roulette. Give the wheel a turn, who could tell what the next whirl would bring to winner or loser?

Each countenance bore its usual expression as the members, laughing, jostling, joking, filed into the board room and settled themselves into "anxious seats." But behind some of those careless expressions lurked feelings of intense excitement. Like men wearing masks they waited with bated breath for the signal to be given. They had not long to wait. The gong sounded, the caller began with "Ophir."

On the instant there was a commotion. Nearly every broker was on his feet rushing toward the pit with offers of "Ophir" stock for sale. From then on every operator realized that desperation was in the saddle. Evidently orders had been given to place the "last straw" on the camel's back and break the market down still farther. Who had thrown all that "Ophir" stock on the market? Sharon or Flood and O'Brien? On events at that morning's session, careers would depend. Fortunes, prestige, honor, hung in the balance. Who would come through such flames unscathed, the Bonanza Kings or Ralston's Ring?

"Ophir" opened at 55 and was forced steadily downward. "California" opened at 56½ and was forced lower. "Consolidated Virginia" opened at 290 and went gradually but inevitably downward. It was devastating.

For days the market had been weakening. Now it gave way completely. Like a reservoir, that has broken away its embankment, the flood swept down in a resistless torrent carrying everything before it. It seemed like a repetition of the ancient deluge. Off and on, ever since January, the market had acted unsteady; but this break was unprecedented in the suddenness of its appearance and the rapidity of its destructive progression.

Flood and O'Brien, since the "Ophir" débâcle, had become

the leaders on the San Francisco Stock Market. Their bonanzas in "Consolidated Virginia" and "California" had made them a formidable influence in the city's money world.

They had realized that if their ascendancy was to continue, Ralston's Ring must be annihilated. More than once they had sent tremendous stock orders through their broker-in-chief, Colonel E. R. Eyre, into the market, which were designed to cripple the Ralston regime. More than once they had engineered terrific raids while Ralston had been trying to corner "Ophir." So far, the Ring had been able to pass through the financial flames which the Irishmen had lighted for their destruction, unsinged. But only Ralston and his crowd knew at what cost.

Now Ralston realized that if he did not want to perish in the conflagration raging about him he must douse the flames. If his supremacy was to continue, the market must be deluged with Flood and O'Brien stock. The Bonanza Kings must perish.

Any order sent into the Board by Flood and O'Brien or any other operator, in fact any order ever executed in regular or informal session, was dwarfed by the great selling order sent by Sharon into the 11 o'clock session on that August morning of the 26th.

The order was executed by B. B. Rorke, board broker for Woods and Freeborn.

Rorke merely looked at his book as each stock was called, and closing it with a finger at the proper page, sold as long as there was a bid on the floor, keeping as near as possible to the closing price of each stock at the preceding Board.

After the first two or three stocks were called, the nature of Sharon's order became apparent. The brokers were horrified. Sharon had given Rorke an unlimited order to sell "Consolidated Virginia" and "California" and "Ophir" as long as there was a bid. He would break the market. Whatever he accomplished, he intended to sell, sell, sell, and force the bonanza stock into the discard. It was a question of Bonanza Kings or Ralston's Ring.

Not a broker failed to realize the gravity of the situation.

Buyers became shy and wary. Selling became difficult. Only a part of the colossal order could be executed on call. Swiftly many rumors were afloat: Ralston's bank was in trouble. He needed money to tide him over a tight place. Everybody had suspected it, and Sharon had engineered this deal to save him.

Others shrugged their shoulders. Sharon was playing a lone hand. He was aiming at higher stakes than helping Ralston or destroying Flood and O'Brien. He had Sharon alone in mind —Sharon's apotheosis. He intended to become the financial dictator of San Francisco. Not only would he overwhelm Flood and O'Brien, but he would finish Ralston as well.

Down, down went Flood and O'Brien stocks. "Consolidated Virginia" dropped from 290 to 250; "California" from 59½ to 56; and "Ophir" fell from 55 to 43.

Rorke did not record a single transaction, nor enter a sale in his book. Purchasers must take care of their own transactions. As to the extent of his sales, clerks must take care of those; later, copies could be taken from the record. All he had to do was sell—sell—sell. That he intended to do to the best of his ability: sell and ruin—sell and ruin—at any price. What would the brokers have: Bonanza Kings or Ralston's Ring?

All this time prices were falling at a fearful rate. On the Street, "California" dropped off 8½ points; "Consolidated Virginia" fell to 240, a loss of 50 points; "Ophir" sold as low as 36, a loss of 18 points since that memorable morning session began. Catastrophe! Yet not a face among the chief operators had betrayed itself. Although their stocks were being unmercifully pounded, Flood and O'Brien's brokers managed to survive both deluge and flood. Long before it was over, every broker in the board room realized that Ralston had paid the price of his temerity but not Sharon. Hardly singed, he had gone through the ordeal. "Like a cat thrown out of a window," said an old miner of him, "Sharon always lights on his feet."

At two o'clock, before the informal afternoon session began, when some brokers passed the windows of Ralston's bank they observed unusual activity about his counters. Yet not a one, as he entered the Board, mentioned the gathering throng nor the thought that had quickened his pulse as he had gazed. At 2:15 several belated brokers noted that the crowd around Ralston's counters reached the bronze doors; that every individual was pushing and jostling his neighbor in a frantic manner. By 2:30 the brokers saw that the multitude about the counters extended to the street. Just as the army of operators were settling down in the board room, some one raised a cry in the street opposite the Stock Exchange: "There's a run on Ralston's bank!"

The cry fell with the force of an exploding bombshell upon the ears of the listening host. Like a prairie fire, the news ran along the Street, causing the wildest commotion wherever brokers or operators congregated. From all quarters there was a general rush toward the corner of California and Sansome Streets. Some had bankbooks in their hands. Some had papers. Already the handsome gray stone building was besieged by an anxious multitude. Curtains were up. Through the great plate-glass windows those on the outside could see what was going on in the interior of the bank: stacks and stacks of gold coin were piled high upon the counters. Pale clerks with nervous fingers were paying out out gold and silver as fast as checks were presented. Trays gold and silver were being rushed up. Apparently there was no dearth in the vaults. At every pane of every window was a pale face.

As far as the eye could reach, the streets were thronged. In some places the crowd was quiet, in others alive with motion. The steps of all neighboring banks and offices were packed with spectators. Pale faces shone at every window. Wild men were rushing in all directions, papers and bankbooks fluttering in their hands. Distracted women with disordered hair strove to reach the great bronze doors of Ralston's bank, besieged with crowding, struggling, obstreperous white-faced men.

A woman, ghastly with paint and rouge, vainly endeavored to climb into the bank through a closed window, declaring she would have her money, every cent of it. "If her John wasn't in Amador, he'd see that her hard-earned savings weren't stolen, you bet he would." When entrance was entirely out of the question, the frantic woman departed, wringing her hands and protesting amid torrents of tears that never again, no never! would she put her money in strange folks' hands to keep for her. As long as there was a spade with which to dig a hole in the ground, she would bury it.

Each little knot of people had its declaimer who stood with one hand in his trouser pocket and gesticulated wildly with the other.

"I tell you," clamored one speaker energetically, "it's as plain as day. Those papers, the *Call* and *Bulletin*, started the whole thing. Here they've been hammering away at Bill Ralston for the last six months, charging him with speculating heavily on the outside. Now he's a bank president, and if a paper goes to work and slings that kind of charges against him and keeps it up for months, people begin to think over it. Pretty soon there's a run and the bank's gone up."

"The run was started by Flood and O'Brien," countered another, "they locked up all the money in savings banks."

"They've got just as good a right," interjected the first speaker, "to speculate in money as the others have to speculate in wheat or any other article. Why, a few years ago, didn't that same bank there, with Friedlander, send flour up to forty dollars a barrel? They can't blame Flood and O'Brien for speculating in coin."

The scene at the bank became more confused and tumultuous. A detachment of police arrived. They scattered about and kept the crowd about the doors in order. Now there was no more howling or mauling. Suddenly, to their horror, the onlookers saw the great bronze doors of the bank slowly swing together. They heard them clash. But to every one's immediate relief, the public were still being admitted through the small iron-wicket door in the center of the great bronze ones. Where, before, there had been a rushing stream pouring through the entrance, now there was a mere trickle. But at least ingress and egress were still maintained. Even after the bronze doors had been closed, those in the street could see clerks paying out gold and silver from great stacks on the counters, paying out just as fast as checks were presented. There seemed to be no end to the trays of gold continually rushed up. Where there had been one pale face to a pane before, now there were many pale, haggard faces.

"What's the matter on the street?" cried a man with some pretension of being a capitalist. "What in the world is the matter?" And the crowd in front of him, as it surged to and fro, and struggled to obtain favor with the policeman at the wicket and a preferential passage to the bank interior, echoed the interrogation: "What's the matter?"

In answer to that simple question there came a howl of replies, a whirlwind of contradictions. Through the small wicket surged a panic-stricken stream of people with anxious faces. Some were beaming under money-bags, others were groaning because their checks had produced nothing.

Now there were thousands on the street. They rocked to and fro. They assaulted window and door. Men clung to balconies and hung over cornices in their anxiety to get into the bank; on every face dismay was written. Every voice registered utter distrust.

"What right," bawled one, "has a bank manager to dabble in stocks, to 'bull' and 'bear' the market, to give credit to mines that are quoted at ten times their value or that have no value at all?"

"What security is there for depositors if the manager has an iron in the fire for all sorts of schemes?" retorted another.

"How can the president of a bank build hotels, run a real estate office, manufacture furniture, build carriages, make watches, run a theatre, race fast horses and entertain as lavishly as a prince? How can Ralston do all these reckless things and expect his bank to withstand a crash?"

"The *Call* and *Bulletin*," began one, and was choked off.

"Gambling in Comstock stocks has ruined the city," brought out another.

"Flood and O'Brien," retorted a third, "are somehow at the bottom of this trouble. On Wednesday they withdrew a couple of million of dollars from the bank. Besides, they have been recommending several heavy depositors among their friends, to withdraw their deposits."

On went loud protest and bitterer complaint. And all the time Ralston's bank was bleeding, bleeding from every counter and vault, bleeding the silver that had come from "Crown Point" and "Belcher" and the newly minted bullion coins from the refinery.

While the run was at its height, an old depositor, having supreme confidence in the Bank of California, struggled vainly for entrance, declaring that he had $40,000 which he wished to deposit if the crowd would only open its ranks and give him a chance. But the throng drunk with excitement paid no attention to his protests. He struggled and shouted until he was exhausted and speechless. Then away he strode breathing husky anathemas upon the "damned cowards who thought the bank was going to bust!"

A wandering street minstrel, with a long horn, took up the doleful lament from "The Last Rose of Summer." When a sympathetic listener threw him a twenty-dollar gold piece, the musician re-applied his lips to his instrument and entered upon "The Rogue's March." Abruptly he was collared and cuffed into silence. An incipient riot raged about him, which was only quelled when the police hustled him away to the station house.

Enthusiasm for Ralston in that harried mob ran high.

"He's the greatest man San Francisco has ever produced," affirmed one.

"He's a far-seeing, smart fellow," added another.

"He is a friend of stock speculators who have margins to meet," confessed a third.

"His bank's as sound as the credit of San Francisco," affirmed a fourth.

"Bah!" continued a Ralston enthusiast, one eye on the stacks of gold in the bank, the other on the mob vainly trying to scale the wicket door, "it's only a rush! Nobody will lose anything in the end—give the bank a chance——"

CHAPTER XXXV

THE RUN

August 26, 1875

It was about one o'clock that Ralston noticed the run. Quietly all the morning he had watched the storm brewing; but it was not until one o'clock or thereabouts that depositors, in successive waves, began to come up to the counter. From then on he began filling his basket with pieces of torn paper.

As early as ten o'clock Ralston had marked the commotion about the window of Nicholson, the paying teller. Large numbers of checks were being presented. Huge sums, at an unusually rapid rate for that hour of the morning, were being paid out. From the window of his office, Ralston scanned the bank interior to see that everything was in readiness. He was far from worried. Of all days, on this one, his sea training stood him in excellent stead. That life had accustomed him to sudden flurries, squally weather and adverse winds. His bank was a staunch craft. It would weather any ordinary demand. His counters were piled high with gold pieces. Down in his vaults trays were stacked with gold and silver coin to meet this very emergency. He surveyed those preparations with a feeling of quiet satisfaction. He was ready. To prove it he began tearing up a fresh sheet of paper and throwing the pieces on the floor.

Among the early checks presented that morning and paid was one for $250,000 from the large firm of Edward L. Hall & Co. E. J. Baldwin, "Lucky" Baldwin of "Ophir" fame, had a million-dollar credit in Ralston's bank. That morning he indicated a tendency to withdraw it, but on condition that $250,000 of this sum should be paid at once, "Lucky" agreed to allow the balance to remain on deposit until Ralston found it convenient to pay.

The hour of eleven approached. Outside his California Street window Ralston could see a vast crowd assembling, multiplying. At the same time, the number of visitors to the bank rapidly increased. The demands on his recources increased. Among these were $14,000 in checks presented by Maurice Schmitt. Nicholson noted the amount and referred Schmitt to Ralston.

"Wait a short time," Ralston persuaded the perplexed Schmitt, "and re-present them."

Schmitt, in the meanwhile, went to his own banker and complained of the treatment he had just received.

"Do not mention the incident," his bankers begged, "Ralston's bank is as solid as any in the city."

A short time afterward, Schmitt re-presented his checks and received the cash. More heavy checks from substantial, and by no means, timid depositors, continued to arrive. In every case the checks were honored. Still the run remorselessly continued. The noise in the street increased in volume and reached a higher key. But it was not until one o'clock that Ralston saw depositors come up to the counter, wave after wave of them, six and eight deep. Checks had grown to enormous figures. One hundred thousand dollars was nothing. Several calling for $200,000 were presented by depositors not usually disturbed by rumors of financial trouble. All these Ralston paid out without a murmur; but when they kept increasing in number and volume and each moment saw the run become more formidable, Ralston grew uneasy. By two o'clock his bank was densely packed. Space was exhausted. Customers could hardly budge one way or the other. Everywhere excited faces bore an index of the situation.

From his window Ralston could see that California Street was as wild and tumultuous as a wind-tossed sea. Waves of humanity swept up the stairs and swirled about the doors. Like drowning men, people clung to balustrade and window-frame. Inch by inch they fought for right of way, hurling their bodies into any opening breech. Now and then, heavy fists, like great combers, bore down on plate-glass windows as if they would smash a way into the interior by violence. At the doors, wild men, papers fluttering overhead, threw each other ruthlessly aside and tried to trample one another under foot. Among the white faces Ralston noted laborers; pale women with children trailing at their skirts; and policemen trying to keep lines in order. In the crowd he could recognize many friends—friends whose confidence in the bank had never been shaken.

There was Joe King's clerk. He had a bag containing $30,000 in gold; there was one of Schmiedell's attaches, weighted down with three bags containing $60,000; there was Ives with $40,000; there were many more stock dealers and brokers, all laden with bags of coin to deposit. Not for an instant had they lost confidence in Ralston's invincibility. They would prove it by depositing their coin. Vainly they fought toward the wicket. Ralston was shaken when he discovered what they were trying to do. But already he had resolved not to receive any more deposits. On learning that these loyal friends had come to deposit, he gave the order that closed the bronze doors. These men saw outer doors close in their faces. In their ears they heard them clang together. But on they fought for the narrow door in the center. How like the entrance to a prison cell it looked!

From the street window Ralston's gaze could again command the bank interior. Every counter was lined with clients. Nervously, they shoved their checks under the noses of the tellers. Swiftly the tellers glanced at the amounts written upon each one. As their only answer Ralston saw them shove along little heaps of gold or great piles of silver. Every teller had a white, scared look, so had the bookkeepers and the clerks at more distant desks. Their faces appeared as ghastly as white-capped waves seen in the moonlight. Only his old Chinese clerk had preserved his equanimity. He was sitting on a high stool gazing through horn-rimmed spectacles, with glasses as huge as watch-crystals, at the half-crazed crowd pressing forward for money. How contemptuously he stared!

On shelves just beyond the reach of those so vociferously demanding it, Ralston could see pile after pile of gold and silver glistening. He watched fascinated as those stacks dwindled, and full trays were rushed up from below. The clinking coin fairly drowned out the din that arose from the excited throng without. But not even jingling gold nor the raucous street-sounds could drown out the voices of the sea. Supremely they arose: the faint pounding of "Neptune's horses," the hoarse, hollow warning of ferryboats, the sound of outgoing liners moving along under slow bells, the cries of seagulls.

It was after two o'clock—less than an hour before the usual closing time. Could the bank weather such a storm? Would Comstock bullion stretch the hour? By 2:30 the run had intensified into a public demonstration. Men, women, and children were clamoring for coin at counters and door. As fast as possible the tellers kept shoving over money but Ralston saw that it was like pouring water into a knothole. There was not room for another customer at the counters. Suddenly a white-faced clerk stepped across Ralston's paper-littered floor and whispered into his ear: "Only forty thousand dollars in cash left in the vaults." Ralston looked at the clock. It was twenty-five minutes to three. His face flushed purple. Hurriedly he left his cubicle and sought out his telegraph operator. With swift, clipped words he spoke.

"Telegraph New York, Boston, and Chicago to stop payment."

On to paying teller Nicholson's window Ralston strode. His face was pale now but resolute. Like that of a hero conquered but undismayed. Beads of perspiration broke out upon his forehead. Ever so slightly his hand trembled as he stayed Nicholson's swift movements. "Close the door," and Ralston indicated the open wicket. Pens dropped from a dozen nerveless fingers. The paying teller's narrow iron window clanged shut in the face of a clamoring mob.

From without came a vigorous effort to force the door open again. A policeman with strong arms shoved it too. Clang! Heavy iron bolts were shot home. Further ingress was at an end. Without, some one beat a fierce tattoo upon the closed window-door. Teller and clerk stood still in their places and listened. A faint smile of satisfaction swept over their parted lips while a deep-drawn sigh of relief escaped between them.

Within, stillness reigned. Clerks subsided into silence. Only the footfalls of people being ushered out by the police could be heard.

Trustees began to gather. Senator Sharon appeared pale and nervous, D. O. Mills, grave, silent, and uncommunicative. A reporter buttonholed the latter: "Will bills on New York, London, and Oriental correspondents be honored on presentation?"

"Can't tell," retorted the monosyllabic Mills. Michel Reese hurried into the consultation. A meeting of the directors was called. A resolution was introduced and passed.

The meeting was over, funereally the magnates streamed out. At seeing the crowd of newspaper men, Ralston was taken aback. Pencil and notebook in hand, they made a rush at him.

"Walk into the back room," and Ralston ushered them into the board room. They seated themselves about the directors' table, while Ralston remained standing on one side of it.

"In regard to what has taken place," he began when all was still, "it is impossible for us now to make up a statement to present to the public. A resolution has been proposed and adopted by the Board, which will be given you for publication in the morning, which will be all we have to say on the subject. I will add on my own behalf, however, as an officer of the bank, that there is no question whatever as to the ability of the bank to meet all its obligations, with considerable surplus besides, without any reservation." A moment's silence followed.

"Shall you resume business tomorrow at the usual hour?" queried a curious reporter.

"No, we shall not resume business," came the reply.

"How soon do you propose to resume?" persisted the same questioner.

"We don't expect to resume at all."

"Can you tell us somewhere near the amount of money drawn from the Bank of California today?"

"I could not," returned Ralston. "Over $1,400,000 in coin, with considerable other payments besides."

About ten o'clock that night Ralston called his staff about him. He was not content to leave the place where he had ruled for many years, with unquestioned sway, without one last word with his employees. Of one fact he wanted to assure them: the charges which the *Call* and *Bulletin* had made against him were false. After some complimentary remarks to his assistants on their efficiency and fidelity, Ralston continued in a clear manly voice devoid of the slightest nervousness.

"The bank will not resume business! No doubt you will be subjected to some unpleasantness during the disagreeable ordeal that is bound to follow this disaster, but I know you will deport yourselves as men and gentlemen under all circumstances. You know how I have been hounded by certain newspapers in this city; how every act of mine has been willfully misconstrued, and how I have been accused of political intriguing that I have never been guilty of——

"The rumors that have been in circulation about Messrs. Flood and O'Brien crowding the bank are utterly false, and I desire that each and every one of you will flatly contradict them whenever you hear them uttered. On the contrary, the most cordial feeling exists between Messrs. Flood and O'Brien and the bank, and so far from crowding us they have granted us sundry favors. The truth is, the money is not in the State, and unfortunately we had too many depositors; so when the crisis came we could not supply all. As to yourselves, you need have no misgivings about the future, for I this night enter into a contract to provide each and every one of you with a first-class position."

With these words, and kind words had ever been the precursor of a kinder act with Ralston, the fallen chieftain went forth, still grand in his adversity. To the door he was followed by the swelling hearts, subdued sobs and tearful eyes of forty men who had known and loved him well.

CHAPTER XXXVI

MUTINY

August 27, 1875

By five o'clock Ralston was awake. Donning a dark blue immaculate suit, he dressed himself with his usual care. When he had finished, he stretched across his vest a heavy gold chain with several emblems attached. Then he aroused his wife.

"You must take your personal belongings," he told the startled lady, as gently as possible, "and go to your uncle's I'm going to hand over all my property to Sharon."

Mrs. Ralston gave way to tears.

"Fear not," Ralston comforted her cheerfully, "we will commence life anew and rise again even if we live on a hundred dollars a month." Then Ralston ran downstairs. Shortly Jim, the colored butler, with coat and hat in hand, was holding open the door for his master to pass into the street.

That August day had dawned blazing hot. Swiftly the sun had pierced the fog-clouds hovering about the crest of the surrounding hills, and was shining down on the nervous, feverish throng of excited San Franciscans who were making their way toward California Street.

Through this warm, muggy heat and jostling crowd, Ralston strode down Market Street. Before eight o'clock he was at the Palace Hotel. Although he had already surrendered the hotel to Sharon, Ralston's interest in the early completion of the mammoth structure had not slackened. That morning he had some important suggestions to make to King, the contractor, regarding construction.

From the Palace, Ralston rushed over to his bank. Wherever he looked, a sea of swaying, sweltering humanity met his gaze. Montgomery Street became almost impassable. Crowds were so dense that many gasped for breath. Little Ledesdorff Street looked like a huge dish filled with open-mouthed, squirming fish. Here, women in faded finery were milling about. Their rusty black silks flapped about their muddy ankles. Gone were the diamonds from their ears, the sparkle from their eyes, the smile from their lips. Gone was their youth. Torn black veils were stretched taut across their toothless gums. The Comstock, Ralston knew, had robbed these women of everything that womanhood holds dear. Such a sight was humiliating. Nothing was left for them but the bucket shops.

Windows and balconies of the Merchants' Exchange swarmed with spectators. On even the roofs of surrounding buildings, crowds were perched. Wherever he looked were hordes of the curious clinging to gables and chimney-tops. Often, in other days, just such crowds had gathered to watch him draw up in state before the bronze doors of his bank. Then he had been the idol of these very people. Now they were ruined by the havoc he had wrought. Now there would be a run on the banks in which they had their deposits. The hands of the clock in the tower on the Merchants' Exchange pointed to the fatal hour. How many more financial concerns would topple before night?

Before Ralston reached his office he was flushed and covered with perspiration and was mopping his feverish brow with one of his many pocket handkerchiefs.

But the minute he was seated in his wonted place before his great green-baize-covered desk, he became cool and collected, even cheerful. He had made up his mind that the crisis must be met, and meet it he would no matter at what cost to his inner feelings. All morning he busied himself straightening out the intricacies of his involved bank, or giving instructions to his clerks as to the best method of simplifying unpleasant duties. Those who were depressed he buoyed up with a kind word. Often his cheery remarks were followed by an affectionate slap on the shoulder. His whole demeanor said plainer than words: "Buck up! everything will come out all right, we must be of good cheer and meet the catastrophe like men." And he acted so lighthearted that his clerks were surprised.

One of his first acts was to surrender all his property, his villa at Belmont, and his town house on Pine Street, for the benefit of his creditors. As he had told his wife that morning, he was determined to recommence life "without one dollar."

In surrendering his property, Ralston executed a deed of trust, conveying everything, real and personal, to William Sharon, for the benefit of his creditors. He had absolute confidence that Sharon would make the best use of his resources. Their friendship had been one of long standing. They were closer than brothers. That morning the bank's notary legalized the deed.

Sharon in receiving the trust seemed greatly affected. As he pressed Ralston's hand in his, he pledged his honor to stand by his old friend until his last dollar was spent and the last drop of his blood was gone. To the clerks, the Ralston-Sharon bond was one of those magnificent ties that, off and on, had dramatized the lives of the Argonauts.

During the morning Mr. William Burling, a leading broker of the city, dropped into Ralston's office. In the past, Ralston had borrowed huge sums of money from him and Burling wanted a reassuring word regarding the security.

Shocked by Ralston's flushed face and perspiring brow, Burling hesitated to push his inquiry.

"You must go away from the city, Ralston," he urged. "You are threatened with apoplexy."

"Are you a doctor, sir?" retorted Ralston hotly.

"No, I am no doctor, but I can see by your countenance that the blood which ought to be in your body is in your head——"

By Ralston's clock it was 11:30.

Then a *Chronicle* reporter pushed his way into the scene. Ralston, earnestly conversing with several clerks, was leaning on the cashier's counter.

"Mr. Ralston," interrupted the reporter, "we understood last evening that the statement of the directors would be ready to be given to the public this morning. Is it ready?"

Ralston scarcely raised his eyes. More plainly than words his appearance showed the terrific strain under which he was laboring.

"No, it is not ready," he replied very slowly. So great appeared his anguish that the reporter hesitated about pursuing the subject.

Then Ralston straightened up with something of his old-time vigor.

"No, the statement is not ready," he added pleasantly; "we will not be prepared to give you anything new for at least three or four days——"

About noon Ralston called a meeting of the Bank Directors. George H. Howard, D. J. Tallant, John O. Earl, D. O. Mills, Louis Sacks, William Morris, W. E. Sharon, and William Alvord responded and seated themselves about the long table in the directors' room. Every face was pale from shock and fear. As presiding officer, Ralston sat at their head. He had himself well in hand. Hale and debonair as a river captain he appeared. Once in a while he stroked his closely cropped chin-beard or rattled the charms on his watch-chain. Outside, newsboys were shouting: "Big Failure! Bank of California Closes its Doors!"

Of all those present, Ralston seemed the most calm and collected. Never had he appeared to more magnificent advantage. Never had his steamboating-days stood him in better stead. Self-composed, confident, serene, he looked his inquisitors in the eye. Explosion, fire, snags, he was ready for any one of them. For all of them. Besides, these men were his friends—his loyal friends, his crew, as it were. Let come what would. They would stand by him in this emergency. They would see him through.

When all was quiet, Ralston took from his breast pocket the statement he had prepared for the directors. In a firm, low voice he commenced to read.

It was a clean, frank avowal of what had become of the bank's capital funds. Having nothing to conceal, Ralston concealed nothing. Having no excuses to make, he offered none. His friends needed none. Were not these men his best friends? Did not all San Francisco know them as "Ralston's Ring"? There was not one among them whom he had not set well on his way to financial independence. As for Sharon, he was one of his greatest achievements. From a down-and-outer he had turned him into one of the wealthiest men on the Coast. He had made it possible for him to become a United States Senator. He had fed his ambitions. That very day he had exemplified his trust by turning over to him all his wealth for the benefit of his creditors. His confidence in Sharon was absolute and beautiful—the perfect friendship of one man for another.

What more could men want? They had shared in his genius, his wealth, his hospitality and his friendship—and now they would prove what friendship meant. They would help him. Not a one about that table but possessed the financial ability to do so.

They were excited and bewildered, those men whom Ralston had aided and abetted. They could appreciate success, share gains and glory, but could they sympathize with failure?

By his report Ralston showed himself debtor to the bank for over four million dollars, to Sharon two millions, to others about three and a half millions, a total of nine and one-half million dollars. Where had those millions gone? To make San Francisco the greatest city in the West; to aid her industry; to quicken her commerce; to plant, to reap, to weave; to advertise California abroad. Not one selfish thing had he done with them. He stood before them stripped of wealth. His assets amounted to four and one-half millions. He presented a plan for the bank's instant rehabilitation. He asked to be allowed to continue at the helm.

They were amazed, those directors. They were outraged. None more than Sharon. They were bewildered. None more than Sharon.

"I can pay," went on Ralston calmly, "every dollar to every depositor and fifty cents upon the dollar to every stockholder if I am allowed to manage the affairs of the bank—and I am not given to idle boasting.

"I have never lied to you, and, if you will give me your aid and time to sell my Spring Valley Water and other stocks, I am sure I can make good the loss——"

Amazed at the frankness of Ralston's report, the directors appeared completely flabbergasted. Then an exciting discussion broke loose. They disagreed with one another. One director had some harsh things to say. Ralston tried to pacify them: "Gentlemen! Gentlemen!" he began.

"We all knew what Ralston was doing," spoke up another director, "and we have profited by his success. You of all others," and the speaker indicated Sharon, "should stand by him now."

There had been two million in Comstock bullion in the refinery not later than July. The bank examiners had seen it, weighed it. Where was it now? Worse still, there was a lot of bills receivable from irresponsible parties, aggregating in the neighborhood of a million dollars, with no collateral. Where was it? Apparently there was an over-issue of bank stock. Mills had resigned—his name was still on the books. Why? Why? Such were the questions the directors threw at Ralston.

No! The directors would not listen to Ralston's proposition. Since the bank had failed while in his charge and many remarks had been made to his prejudice, such an arrangement was not even tenable. And they proceeded to appoint a committee to examine into the affairs of the bank, with instructions to prosecute their labors throughout the night so that they could report next day.

Human machinery is hardly proof against such a rebuff. Ralston was touched to the quick by Sharon's reticence and the directors' lack of confidence. But his sturdy character never appeared to better advantage. Once he had been ready for snag, explosion, or fire; once he had met and conquered a mutiny with one lone gun and plenty of courage. He did not crack now. His cheeks flushed deeper but he took the blow standing. A harsh return it might be in his hour of distress, but not a sign of humiliation did he show. A whispered conference broke out about him.

When the directors requested him to withdraw from the room while they deliberated, the color on Ralston's cheeks burned a shade deeper. They wished to consult, they said, on matters which would require his absence.

Out of his pocket Ralston drew the bank's keys and laid them on the table. Then the door closed behind him.

Hardly had the catch snapped when Sharon was on his feet.

He offered a resolution: that Ralston be requested to resign the presidency of the Bank of California.

No sooner was the motion seconded than it was unanimously passed. Then Sharon was on his feet again.

He moved that Mr. Ralston's predecessor, Mr. D. O. Mills, be instructed to act as a committee of one from the Board to present the resolution to Mr. Ralston.

Sharon's second motion, too, was unanimously passed.

CHAPTER XXXVII

AT THE GOLDEN GATE

August 27, 1875

Ralston withdrew to his office and threw himself dejectedly down at his desk—his head bent forward. Great beads of perspiration welled up upon his brow. Now and again he brushed a white handkerchief across his flushed face.

It was two o'clock.

Within a few minutes D. O. Mills entered. He held a sheet of paper in his hand. He handed it over to Ralston. He had been instructed by the Board, Mills reported, to give it to him.

While Mills was speaking, Ralston was looking steadily into his eyes. As he finished, Ralston dropped his gaze to the paper in his hand. Quietly he began to read. Where his face had previously only been flushed, now it turned livid. A quiver pervaded his frame and the perspiration burst out afresh upon his forehead.

"Yes," Ralston replied calmly, mopping his brow.

And taking up his pen, rapidly, he began to write:

"San Francisco, Aug. 27, 1875.

"To the Board of Trustees of the Bank of California:

"You will please accept my resignation as president of the bank and *also* as a member of the board of trustees to take effect immediately."

With iron nerve and steady hand he affixed his name:

"Most respectfully yours,

W. C. RALSTON."

With a few pleasant words, Ralston handed back the paper and Mills disappeared behind the Board room door.

Then for the first time Ralston looked down into an abyss of horror. What horrible forms in the guise of friendship floated about that dark abysm: greed, envy, hatred, ambition!

Just then James R. Keene came into the bank. Seeing Ralston with bowed head sitting at his desk he went up to him and put his hands, affectionately, on both of Ralston's shoulders.

"Never mind," Keene encouraged, "I have some money and you shall not want for another bank to manage.

"When we get the affairs of this bank straightened out," he continued, "I am going to get a capital equal to that which it has been swinging and we'll start another."

But Ralston was too dejected to appreciate even this bit of kindhearted facetiousness. With an effort he pulled himself together.

"I shall never be engaged in another banking enterprise," he retorted.

Without the confidence of his fellow men, life to Ralston was nothing. The Comstock had failed. Spring Valley had failed. His bank had failed. His friends had forsaken him—and the people——

As if in answer to that question, up through the open windows along California Street there welled a savage howl—the curses of those who had lost everything in the defunct bank. That was what the people were thinking.

But above the curses of the swindled, above the rattle of traffic, Ralston's ears could catch the welcome throb of the sea—the cool, refreshing boom of breakers, the noise of passing boats, of outgoing liners. Perhaps his bank had failed and friends had forsaken him, but the great kindly sea lay all about, friendly and waiting. At that very moment he longed to throw himself on that wide, heaving bosom and find comfort. A combat with the tide he had so often mastered would give him strength to meet the vexations that now surrounded him. Listlessly Ralston got to his feet.

"Nothing is so bad that it cannot be mended," offered his lawyer, Barnes, who had just entered the bank.

Cheerfully, Ralston nodded to those who were standing near him. As he strode toward the Sansome Street entrance they followed his retreating figure with affection. What a handsome, debonair fellow he was! That his face showed not a trace of the tremendous ordeal through which he had been passing made those men marvel; that he could preserve his characteristic smile and charm of manner under such pressure filled them with admiration. They looked after him with glowing eyes. Ralston was a man in a lifetime.

Pulling his hat well down over his forehead, Ralston sauntered into the street. No longer was a horse and groom waiting at the curb. That morning he had turned the last of them over to Sharon. Unseen, unnoted, he passed into the throng that milled about the doors.

Shortly after Ralston had left his office, Sharon came out of the Board room and called for the envelope marked: "Contract of William Sharon to be delivered to W. C. Ralston only." Slitting open the envelope, he took out the paper within and replaced the envelope. Later, when questioned regarding it, he claimed "there was nothing in it——"

Near the bank doors Ralston ran into his physician, Doctor John Pitman.

Cordially, Ralston grasped him by the hand.

"I feel like a schoolboy off for his holidays," laughed Ralston as he told the doctor that he had just resigned the presidency of the bank. "I'm off for a swim at North Beach. Come on with me." And Ralston mopped his brow as he spoke.

"You're overheated," warned Doctor Pitman, noting Ralston's flushed appearance.

But Ralston laughed off such friendly advice. The thought of those cold waters against his outraged flesh, on that hot August day, was enticing.

And the doctor passed on, promising, if Ralston would wait, to join him at the beach.

Down Sansome Street strode Ralston. He was walking rapidly now, so rapidly that perspiration ran in rivulets off his face. One handkerchief was not enough, a second, a third were pressed into service.

Before he was aware of the fact, Ralston came alongside several boys who were skulking along Sansome Street.

"What are you boys up to?" inquired Ralston with his wonted light-heartedness.

"Nothing, sir," and the boys uncovered in the presence of the smiling banker.

In a moment of abstracted tenderness Ralston patted the head of the lad nearest to him and passed on down the street.

At Clay Street, Ralston turned to the left. When he reached Stockton he turned north, skirted Telegraph Hill and headed toward North Beach. From there came wisps of fog and the racing sounds of a breaking sea. Over the hot, burned August hills diaphanous mists were wreathing. Soon the fog would be blotting them out.

Soon those seven hills would be the scene of all the chaos, riot, and confusion they had known a quarter of a century before. Agitators would declaim from every sand lot. "Down with millionaires," they would shout.

San Francisco would be just where he had found her twenty-four years before, when he had sailed the *New Orleans* through the Golden Gate.

If he paused to listen, Ralston could hear the beginning of those riots; the angry growls of the mob milling about the closed banks on California Street. Above that uproar, the rat-a-tat-tat of the hammers on the Palace Hotel would fill his ears. If he looked back, spire, pinnacle, dome and tower of his beloved city would arrest his eye.

San Francisco had fulfilled his ambitions. The dream had materialized a hundredfold. Out of the black stacks of the Mission Woollen Mills, the West Coast Furniture Company, the Pacific Sugar Refinery, and the Kimball Carriage Factory, and a dozen other establishments which he had fostered, smoke would be pouring. He would hear the whirr of wheels, the roar of machinery that made up the major chords of San Francisco's industrial music. Now it must become a discord. On every side, sight and sound would reward and revile him. But above the racket of excited humanity, of forge and hammer, the murky air was alive with the throb of the surf and the breath of the sea.

Over Leavenworth Hill at a rapid pace strode Ralston, his handkerchief always in requisition. Presently Neptune Beach hove into sight. Through the Golden Gate a strong wind was blowing, driving before it an angry, white-capped sea. On the shore, high rollers, trailing their spume behind them, were racing.

Where a small shelf of hard yellow clay reared itself above the waste of white sand, Ralston sank down. Again and again he mopped his hot face.

Down there on the edge of the breaking water lay the *Fanny Allen*—a wreck of a tug. Ralston must have recalled her. During the winter before, she had been caught in a storm and wrecked on a hidden reef. When the storm had receded, the waves had sucked her back into the bay and then spewed her—a despised derelict—high on the beach.

Out of his pocket Ralston drew some yellow papers. While he listened to the throbbing tide he began to tear them into shreds. Abstractedly, the scraps fell, one by one, through his parted fingers, into the swelling waters below.

For a moment the slips of yellow paper eddied about his feet. A few caught in rocky crevices, but the vast majority, caught by a whirling tide, swirled backward, forward, and then raced toward the murky region beyond the Golden Gate.

Slowly, as the last scraps slipped through his fingers, Ralston got to his feet and continued his way down the hill. Around Selby's Smelting Works he hurried. Great combers with foam-tossed crests were rushing up the shore. Once he had to run back to keep out of their way. Two boys were swimming near the spot where he had to pass.

"What time is it, Mister?" one of them called.

"Half-past three," returned Ralston, looking at his watch.

"Cold?" he shouted.

"No, not very—, not after you get into it."

Along the beach sandpipers scurried. From the siren came deep-noted long-drawn sounds. High overhead seagulls winged the gray sky. Ralston increased his pace until he came to the side door of the Neptune Bath House. Firmly, he knocked upon the panel.

The keeper answered his summons. A look of surprise swept over his face as he spied Ralston. Usually he came at a much later hour.

"Good evening, Richards," Ralston called in a cherry voice as the door opened.

On the table he threw a coin. As was his custom, Richards handed over a Russian towel.

"I need an extra rough one," Ralston added. And the keeper, noting the red, perspiring face before him, handed over his coarsest.

Taking his towels, Ralston disappeared through the door of the nearest dressing room.

Ralston started undressing. His clothes were so damp that they clung to his hot body. But he drew them off and folded them into a neat pile; great beads of perspiration gathered the while upon his face and ran down his chest. The door opened. Richards entered. In his hands were a mat for the floor and more towels. Grateful for the attention, Ralston handed over another coin and disdained the change which the keeper proffered.

"You're pretty warm," remarked Richards, taking in Ralston's perspiring body.

Ralston picked up the coarsest towel. "I'll rub myself well," he smiled, "and take a shower-bath before I go in."

Suiting action to the word, Ralston rubbed himself vigorously, took a cold shower, and donned a pair of trunks.

Then he ran over to Richards' office, his dark blue suit

neatly folded in his arms. Never had he appeared so light-hearted, thought Richards.

"Keep these for me," and Ralston handed over his clothes. "There are valuable papers in my pocket." Richards started with surprise. He could not remember that Ralston had ever left his clothes in his charge before.

Once, as Ralston ran down the steps to the shore, he turned toward the door where Richards was still standing: his face was all aglow. Never, remarked Richards, had Ralston been so intent upon his swim. Brisk as a boy, Ralston cantered down a stretch of beach and out to the end of the last stringer of a temporary wharf. For a moment he paused and looked down at the rollers seething about his feet, then out he gazed through the Golden Gate where a tossing tide was racing toward him.

Soon afterwards he took a header. For a few moments he splashed aimlessly about. Then boldly he struck out in the direction of the stern-wheeler, *Bullion,* lying two or three hundred yards off shore.

Out of the nowhere, a lad appeared. For a while he swam alongside Ralston. Together they rode the breakers. Ralston was swimming with strong, sinewy strokes. So rapidly did his lithe body skim through the water that the lad could hardly keep abreast. Up one wave, down another they went, until the shore lay far behind, and the boy was spent and panting. Cleanly Ralston's body clove the waves. With every stroke he seemed to rejoice in pitting his great strength against that of tide and gale. On either side the water fell back, as a crowd parts to open a passage.

Finally the lad faltered. No longer could he keep up with such powerful strokes. "Oh!" he shouted through the spin-drift, "you're going too far for me." And he turned about.

If Ralston heard, he gave back no sign. Unheeding, onward he swam into the gathering mist. Once in a while up would go his head and off he would toss the spray as all strong swimmers do.

Sometimes he would dive. Once he stayed under water

a long time. When he came to the surface the tide caught him. His strong body thrashed about as if caught in the grip of something he could not master. Gallantly he fought, throwing himself fiercely from side to side. Like a plaything the tide flung him over and over. His head jerked back and forth. His whole body writhed in violent movement. Suddenly up shot one arm, then another, as if to free himself.

Then Ralston lay motionless, face down, in the fast-moving tide.

Swiftly it swept him toward the city he had built, then outward toward the Golden Gate, where the hot August sun, a hazy, round, red disk, was sinking toward a mist-wrapped sea.

CHAPTER XXXVIII

BLACK FRIDAY

August 27, 1875

"How could such a thing be possible?" That was the question in the eye and on the lip of every individual in the room.

There were fifteen men in that apartment. Fifteen dazed men grouped about a long, black, oblong box which rested on a heavily-carved center table. Every one of those fifteen faces recorded utter bewilderment.

Among the fifteen were those who commanded San Francisco financially, politically, and socially. Now they were silent—completely overwhelmed by the swift turn of events. Not a word passed between them. As mute, as immovable as the Vatican Guard they stood about the box-laden table. When a newcomer arrived, those near by ignored him or pressed his hand in silence. Eyes alone formulated the question that lips refused to utter.

"How could such a thing be possible?"

One second, Leese, captain of the San Francisco detective force, the knees of his blue uniform still wet and sandy from those minutes of kneeling on the beach, exhibited the tenderest kind of emotion. The next, his face flushed with indignation, he went stomping about the reception room, upsetting chairs and rattling bronzes on the marble mantel. No longer could he control his feelings. Bitterly his invective burst out against those who had plunged San Francisco into lamentation.

"Just to think," he growled at the gloomy-faced group that hovered over the crude box on the massive table, "just to think that this man, who made every one whom he touched a millionaire, walked out of this house this morning——."

A moment since when Jim, the colored butler, had answered an insistent ring of the doorbell, fifteen men, six of them carrying a damp, crudely-made pine coffin, had filed silently past him and had laid their dripping burden on the center table, in his master's drawing-room. Astonishment had overcome Jim, as he had watched that solemn procession. One after the other, annoyance, surprise, perplexity, and fear had swept across his black face. Suddenly an amazing thought had dawned upon him. "What—, what—," he had stammered as he struck his open palm against his forehead.

"My God! How can that be possible!"

Turning abruptly, he had rushed into the back part of the house and had returned with a cloth to mop up the sandy water which the casket-bearers had tracked across the handsome Axminster carpets.

Unbelievable, yes, it was unbelievable. How had it happened? No one could even guess.

All of the butler's attempts to get any one of those fifteen to tell him what had occurred were failures. Not one seemed capable of uttering two connected sentences. Better satisfied, they appeared, to leave conversation alone and stand in gloomy silence. At last the butler, too, took up the silent vigil about the center table.

Sometimes with mournful, again with indignant expression, those graying men regarded the unsightly box. Now and again tears welled up and were furtively brushed away. Sometimes unashamed, they were allowed to course down furrowed cheeks. James Otis, Mayor of San Francisco, kept clearing his throat; Colonel J. D. Fry blew his nose viciously. While others, like Charles N. Felton and Robert F. Morrow, scowled with anger, clenched their fists and cursed.

Only Sharon spoke. "All I have—" over and over again, during the past twenty-four hours, some of those men had heard that speech. "All I have I owe to him, and to protect his name and memory, I will spend every dollar of it."

But the men about the coffin gave back no reply. Giving Sharon, if anything, a wider berth, they drew more closely about the table as if to ward off some malign influence from what lay thereon.

Suddenly Sharon laid his head upon the mantelpiece and sobbed like a child.

Then followed such a scene as is only possible when strong men lose self-control and give way to overpowering grief.

Completely overcome, Thomas Brown, cashier of the Bank of California, slunk into a shadowy corner of the room. The last twenty-four hours had been more than human endurance could bear. He covered his face with trembling hands as if to blot out the memory of them.

Outside the darkening corridor, Stephen J. Franklin, a venerable associate who had grown gray-headed in bank service, slumped down upon the lower round of the stairs, utterly spent. Never had a more amazed assemblage of men gathered in one room. Not even the last rays of the setting August sun could relieve their dismay.

Then came the Coroner. From among those present he impanelled a jury of eight men and over the coffin administered the oath. As soon as they had agreed to meet him the following day at 11 o'clock, he was gone. Again silence and shadows filled the room.

Outside, twilight came on, cold and cheerless. Corner lamps gave forth a misty light. Fog raced through the streets. Moisture covered the windows and dripped with monotonous plash from the eaves—completely blotting out the crowds assembling along Pine Street.

Silently from sidewalks, and Leavenworth Street's adjacent corners the throng stared at the shuttered windows. Proudly they regarded the great, closed house as if it contained something of import to them.

Swifter than the hoarse warning of the foghorns at the Golden Gate, the news had flown through San Francisco streets, leaving those who heard it utterly amazed. Women wrung their hands, as they listened. Through ashy lips struggled a half-articulated question: Can this be true?

Men with tense white faces collected about street corners, or communed in darkened alleys. Passers-by spoke in whispers. In whispers, too, they asked a question. That dread question to which no man could give a satisfactory reply: How was this possible?

No one thought of sleep. The gathering darkness, the murky street lights, the swirling fog and the hoarse moan of the foghorns, seemed to intensify overwrought feelings. A few desperate men repaired to bar-rooms to drown their thoughts in drink. Cigar-stands did a thriving business. In no time the streets began to reflect the agitation of the people as the gutters filled with half-smoked, half-chewed cigar butts.

That night, a Republican mass meeting had been scheduled at Platt's Hall. Noble Hamilton and Baruck were to speak. But the intense excitement on every hand destroyed any idea of politics. For six months the Spring Valley Water Company had been a burning municipal question. Now, no one cared what the city did with its water supply.

At the California Theatre, the play, "La Tentation" had been advertised, but when doors should have opened, they remained tightly barred. For once the play could not go on. Neither actors nor managers were in any mood for mummery.

By far the greatest crowds surged around newspaper

bulletin boards where every eye was riveted on the dispatches. Every minute saw fresh ones tacked up and old ones torn down. News was all those worried men wanted. Anxiously they devoured every word.

There was great excitement in Virginia City and Gold Hill, ran a Comstock dispatch. Violence was feared. General Batterman with his staff was occupying Sharon's business quarters. A detachment of the National Guard remained under arms all night in their armory, ready for any call from the general. Immense crowds made C Street impassable—especially in front of telegraph and newspaper offices.

A wire from London, England, told a similar tale. On receipt of San Francisco dispatches, financial and commerical circles had been thrown into a state of great excitement. "For a time the utmost confusion existed on the gold exchange—at the opening of the Stock Exchange—the noise and din was great——."

In New York, "the news came upon Wall Street like a thunderclap out of a clear sky." Amidst tremendous confusion, 74,000 shares of stock had rained upon the falling market of the morning board. During the bartering, noise and din had reached panic proportions.

Chicago, Boston, St. Louis, and Lousiville had similar tales to tell. Events of the last few hours in San Francisco had demoralized the whole financial world. Not a Californian betrayed surprise at reading those dispatches. What could be expected after such a major catastrophe?

By 8 o'clock, Montgomery Street was packed so densely that not a carriage could navigate the street. Few went away. More were added every moment. All eager to read the latest bulletins. There was no levity, no display of animosity. There they stood, a hundred deep, stunned into silence. Steadily they gazed at the bulletin board, weighing every word as an emperor might ponder over dispatches upon which the future of his empire depended. As they read, faces grew long and voices more awed. Confusion in London and Paris! A near panic in New York! Militia on the Com-